This Book Comes With Lots of
FREE Online Resources

Nolo's award-winning website has a page dedicated just to this book. Here you can:

KEEP UP TO DATE. When there are important changes to the information in this book, we'll post updates.

GET DISCOUNTS ON NOLO PRODUCTS. Get discounts on hundreds of books, forms, and software.

READ BLOGS. Get the latest info from Nolo authors' blogs.

LISTEN TO PODCASTS. Listen to authors discuss timely issues on topics that interest you.

WATCH VIDEOS. Get a quick introduction to a legal topic with our short videos.

And that's not all.
Nolo.com contains thousands of articles on everyday legal and business issues, plus a plain-English law dictionary, all written by Nolo experts and available for free. You'll also find more useful **books, software, online apps, downloadable forms,** plus a **lawyer directory.**

MAY 2017
FR

⚖ NOLO The Trusted Name
(but don't take our word for it)

"In Nolo you can trust."
THE NEW YORK TIMES

"Nolo is always there in a jam as the nation's premier publisher of do-it-yourself legal books."
NEWSWEEK

"Nolo publications…guide people simply through the how, when, where and why of the law."
THE WASHINGTON POST

"[Nolo's]…material is developed by experienced attorneys who have a knack for making complicated material accessible."
LIBRARY JOURNAL

"When it comes to self-help legal stuff, nobody does a better job than Nolo…"
USA TODAY

"The most prominent U.S. publisher of self-help legal aids."
TIME MAGAZINE

"Nolo is a pioneer in both consumer and business self-help books and software."
LOS ANGELES TIMES

3rd Edition

Nolo's Essential Guide to Child Custody & Support

Attorney Emily Doskow

THIRD EDITION	OCTOBER 2015
Editor	SHAE IRVING
Cover Design	SUSAN PUTNEY
Book Production	COLLEEN CAIN
Proofreading	ROBERT WELLS
Index	UNGER INDEXING
Printing	BANG PRINTING

Doskow, Emily, author.
  Nolo's essential guide to child custody & support / Attorney Emily Doskow. -- Third Edition.
     pages cm
  Includes index.
  ISBN 978-1-4133-2196-8 (pbk.) -- ISBN 978-1-4133-2197-5 (epub ebook)
  1. Custody of children--United States--Popular works. 2. Divorce suits--United States--Popular works. I. Title. II. Title: Essential guide to child custody & support.
  KF547.D67 2015
  346.7301'73--dc23

                             2015013627

This book covers only United States law, unless it specifically states otherwise.

Please note

We believe accurate, plain-English legal information should help you solve many of your own legal problems. But this text is not a substitute for personalized advice from a knowledgeable lawyer. If you want the help of a trained professional—and we'll always point out situations in which we think that's a good idea—consult an attorney licensed to practice in your state.

Acknowledgments

This was a challenging book to write, because the topic of children and divorce is a difficult one to deal with in any context. I want to acknowledge, first, all of the parents who are working hard to do what's right by putting their children's needs first when crafting parenting arrangements in a divorce. It isn't easy, and you have my respect and admiration.

For this third edition, I am grateful to Stephen Stine for his thorough research and help with the charts, and to Nolo's production department for, as always, making my words look good.

I am ever-grateful to my friends and family for cheering me on and providing material assistance while I worked. No one deserves more thanks than my wife, Luan Stauss, whose abiding patience, help, and gentle prodding made it possible for me to actually get this project done.

About the Author

Emily Doskow is a practicing attorney and mediator who has been working with families in the Bay Area for more than 20 years. She specializes in family law, including adoption, surrogacy, parentage issues, prenuptial agreements, and mediated and collaborative divorce. She is a graduate of the Boalt Hall School of Law at the University of California at Berkeley and currently resides in Oakland. As an editor and author for Nolo, she has authored or coauthored numerous titles, including *Nolo's Essential Guide to Divorce*; *The Sharing Solution: How to Save Money, Simplify Your Life & Build Community* (with Janelle Orsi), *The Legal Guide for Lesbian & Gay Couples* (with Frederick Hertz), and many others.

Table of Contents

Introduction: Your Child Custody and Support Companion

If you're considering divorce or have decided to go ahead and separate from your spouse, you're no doubt worried about how this change will affect your children, and also about what the rules are for shared parenting and child support. It's a lot to think about.

Fortunately, there's help. This book will walk you through everything you need to know about child custody, shared parenting, and the rules about supporting your children. Once you've decided to move forward with a divorce, it's hard to know what to do—so we've provided a list of what you need to do right away, in the first month after you make the decision, and some advice about what to do when the dust settles a bit and it's time to assess your options. These tasks include figuring out what kind of process you want to use—uncontested, mediation, collaborative, or an all-out fight—and making interim plans that will allow you some breathing room while you figure out what your long-term arrangements are going to be.

You'll also learn about what it's like to take your divorce to court, and how to deal with custody and support orders if your circumstances change once the orders are in place—or if the other parent isn't complying with the orders.

You may be working with a lawyer, or considering whether you should hire one. Especially when there's a dispute about custody or parenting time, a lawyer can be a big help, and there's more than one way to get that help. You can have a lawyer take over your case and do all of the legal work for you, or you can ask for help with certain parts of the case and then handle the rest yourself. Even if you're representing yourself in your divorce or custody case, you can ask a lawyer for coaching or advice about strategy. This book can help you find the right attorney, no matter how you're intending to use the lawyer's help, and will be your companion as you and the attorney move your case forward.

Just like you are, this book is all about your kids—where they're going to live, how they're going to spend time with both parents (or be protected from a parent who's abusive), and how you're going to provide for them. Stay focused on their needs and on doing what's best for them, and you'll find your way through this challenging time.

Get Updates and More Online

When there are important changes to the information in this book, we'll post updates online, on a page dedicated to this book:

www.nolo.com/back-of-book/NOCS.html

You'll find other useful information there, too, including author blogs, podcasts, and videos.

Basics of Divorce

If you are considering divorce—or are already headed down that path—you have a lot on your mind. Probably the first thing you're thinking about is how divorce will affect your kids: How and when will you spend time with them, what will change about your parenting life, and how will you deal with the finances of raising them when you and your spouse are no longer together? There's no way around the fact that when you have children, the divorce stakes are high, and you want to do everything you can to protect your kids.

The best single thing you can do for your kids is to keep the divorce process as civilized as possible. As you go through your divorce, over and over you'll be required to make a choice between escalating conflict or compromising. Each time you choose to create or continue a dispute with your spouse, you are making it more likely that you'll end up in court in front of a judge, who will then make decisions about your family instead of leaving them to you and your spouse. So when you have a choice—and sometimes you don't, if your spouse won't back down from an unreasonable position—try to take the compromise route. It will make your divorce less expensive, faster, and less painful for everyone.

Before jumping into the details of how custody works and how support is calculated, you need an understanding of the divorce process. This chapter explains how the process generally works and some of your options along the way.

Unmarried couples. If you and the other parent are unmarried, you won't need to get a divorce, but you will need to establish your shared parental rights and get a court order related to parenting time and support payments. See "Parentage Actions for Unmarried Couples," below.

The Big Issues: Child Custody and Support

You and the other parent will either need to work out the issues of custody and support or turn them over to a judge to decide. Working them out yourselves will yield huge benefits, both emotionally and financially.

Here's a brief overview of the questions you'll be looking at. As you review this information, don't forget that all of the issues in your divorce can be resolved without going to court if you and your spouse can reach an agreement.

Custody

There are two kinds of custody: physical and legal. Physical custody is the right to have a child live with you; legal custody is the right to make decisions about the child's welfare and education. It's common for divorced parents to share one or both kinds of custody. For example, a parent can have sole physical custody, with the other parent spending time with the children according to a parenting plan, and both parents can still share legal custody, making decisions together about things like where the kids go to school. It's also possible for one parent to have both sole physical and legal custody, or for the parents to share both.

One of the first things you and the other parent need to do is come up with a temporary agreement about how to share time with your kids while the divorce proceeds. (There's more about this in Chapter 4.) Do it as quickly as you can, to ease your children's insecurity. If you can't agree to a temporary schedule, you'll end up in court right away—an expensive and uncertain way to begin your divorce. Chapter 2 describes custody issues in detail.

Child Support

Chances are that one spouse will pay child support to the other. When the children spend more time with one parent than the other, or if one parent earns more money, the court will award child support to make sure that the kids are taken care of. Every state has its own guidelines for child support, and while you and the other parent can make agreements about child support that differ from the guidelines, you will have to explain your decision to the court and provide assurance that the kids will be adequately supported. Details about support are in Chapters 3 and 4.

Other Divorce Issues: Property and Alimony

Property. If you and your spouse can agree on how to divide your property, the court will simply approve your agreement. If you can't agree, the court will divide things for you. How property is divided depends to some extent on whether you live in a community property state or an equitable distribution state, but the basic rules are these:

Your "marital property" is everything you and your spouse have acquired during your marriage, including money, real estate, investments, pension plans, and so on. Marital debts are obligations you took on together during your married life. You must divide both the property and the debts between you.

Assets or debts that either of you had before your marriage, or that you acquired after the permanent separation, are called separate property or debts. Generally, each of you will keep your separate property and be responsible for your separate debts, but in some states separate property can be divided at divorce.

Alimony. In some divorces, courts award spousal support, also called alimony or maintenance, to one spouse. The longer a couple has been married, the more likely it is that some support will be ordered, especially if one spouse gave up career plans to support the other or care for kids.

For more about property, debts, and alimony, see *Nolo's Essential Guide to Divorce*, by Emily Doskow, and *Divorce & Money*, by Violet Woodhouse with Dale Fetherling, both published by Nolo.

When You Separate

A separation is not a divorce—it's just living apart from your spouse. You're still legally married until you get a judgment of divorce from a court. However, a separation does affect your legal and financial responsibilities toward your spouse. And if you live in a state where courts consider the issue of fault (see "Must You Prove Your Spouse Is at Fault?" below), then initiating a separation might be used against you later.

There are three kinds of separation.

Types of Separation	
Trial	Living apart to decide whether to divorce. May or may not affect property rights, depending on length of separation and activities during separation.
Permanent	Living apart permanently, with or without the intention to divorce. Property and income acquired, and debts incurred, after separation date belong to the spouse who acquires them.
Legal	Legal status different from being married or being divorced; includes distribution of property; spouses are not free to marry again.

Trial Separation

If your relationship is in trouble and you and your spouse aren't sure you're going to stay together, you may choose to live apart while you decide. A trial separation is really any period of time that you're living apart from your spouse without having decided how you're going to move forward.

This kind of separation doesn't change anything in terms of property ownership or the obligation to care for your children. For example, money you earn and things you buy are likely to still be considered jointly owned by you and your spouse, depending on your state's rules about property ownership (in a community property state, everything is jointly owned; in other states, the rules vary). The same is true for debts either of you incur. You can make informal arrangements about caring for your children, or put together a written coparenting schedule and an agreement about support.

Even during a trial separation, it's a good idea to write an informal agreement covering all of these issues. For example, you'll need to decide:

- how and when each of you will spend time with your kids
- whether or not you will continue to share a joint bank account or credit cards
- how you'll budget your spending
- which of you will stay in the family home
- how expenses will be shared, and
- whether you intend to continue to be bound by state laws on property and debt while you are separated—in other words, whether your state's rules about ownership of marital and separate property will apply to you during the separation or whether your separation marks the end of your sharing property and being responsible for each other's debts.

Two sample separation agreements are shown below.

If you're not able to reach temporary agreements about these things pretty quickly, then you may need to make a clear decision one way or the other about whether you're staying together or splitting up, instead of using a trial separation as a time to consider your options.

Sample Separation Agreement
(Continuing to Share Income)

This agreement is between Danica Donaldson and Mark Markham. We have agreed to live separately while we decide whether to divorce or to reconcile. As long as we live separately, these are our agreements:

Mark will move out of our family home at 5500 Normandy Street. Danica will continue to live there with our children. Mark's paycheck will continue to be deposited into our joint checking account at Community One Bank. Danica will continue to deposit any money she earns from part-time work into the joint checking account. Danica will pay the mortgage and other household bills and personal expenses for her and the kids with those funds, and will transfer $2,500 per month into a separate account for Mark to use for his rent and expenses. If there is a shortfall in the joint account, Danica will transfer any additional amounts needed to meet our expenses from our joint savings account at Community One Bank, and will notify Mark of the date and amount of the transfer. Mark won't access this account without talking to Danica first.

Both of us can access information about our joint accounts online, and we agree not to change any passwords on our joint accounts.

During our separation, we'll still be subject to marital property law, and anything we earn or acquire and any debts we take on, will be treated just as if we were still living together. If one of us files a petition for divorce in court, this paragraph will no longer apply.

Mark will come to the house every morning at 8:00 to pick up the children for school. Danica will pick them up from school or aftercare and bring them home every day. Mark will have parenting time with the children every other weekend from Friday after school until Monday dropoff at school, beginning the weekend after we sign this agreement. In addition, he will come over every Wednesday and the family will have dinner together.

Neither parent will pay any child support or alimony because we are still sharing our income and paying all expenses out of joint accounts.

Neither of us is waiving any rights to ask for a different parenting schedule or amount of child support should we decide to divorce. We agree to reconsider the terms of this agreement in three months.

Danica Donaldson
Danica Donaldson

Mark Markham
Mark Markham

Sample Separation Agreement
(Separating Income)

This agreement is between Danica Donaldson and Mark Markham. We have agreed to live separately while we decide whether to divorce or to reconcile. As long as we live separately, these are our agreements:

Mark will move out of our family home at 5500 Normandy Street. Danica will continue to live there with our children. Both of us will open separate checking accounts and deposit our respective paychecks into those accounts. In addition, we will each take half of the funds in our joint savings account at Community One Bank to use for our own expenses, and then close the account. Mark will deposit $2,000 per month into our joint checking account at Community One Bank, and Danica will deposit $1,000 per month into the same account. Danica will pay the mortgage and other household bills with those funds. If there is a shortfall in the joint account, we will contribute additional money in the same two-thirds/one-third proportions to cover the shortfall.

Both of us can continue to access information about our joint accounts online, and we agree not to change any passwords on our joint accounts.

As of the date we sign this agreement, everything that each of us earns will belong entirely to that person, and any debt that either of us incurs will be the sole responsibility of that person. If we reconcile, we must agree in writing to resume sharing property according to marital law.

Mark will come to the house every morning at 8:00 to pick up the children for school. Danica will pick them up from school or aftercare and bring them home every day. Mark will have parenting time with the children every other weekend from Friday after school until Monday dropoff at school, beginning the weekend after we sign this agreement. In addition, he will come over every Wednesday and the family will have dinner together.

Neither parent will pay any child support or alimony as long as we are paying household expenses from the joint account.

Neither of us is waiving any rights to ask for a different parenting schedule or amount of child support should we decide to divorce. We agree to reconsider the terms of this agreement in three months.

Danica Donaldson
_____

Danica Donaldson

Mark Markham
_____

Mark Markham

Permanent Separation

A permanent separation is for people who live apart for an extended period of time without intending to reconcile but also without completing a legal divorce. A permanent separation means that you are no longer responsible for any debts that your spouse incurs. Similarly, you're no longer entitled to any share of property or income that your spouse acquires or earns. If you are very resistant to the idea of a divorce, you can use a permanent separation (or a legal separation, discussed below) to keep your legal life separate from your spouse's without getting a divorce.

If you don't go to court and get an order of legal separation, described below, you'll have to write an agreement that covers your property division and child custody and support questions. You would separate all of your finances and most likely one parent would pay child support to the other. If you're not able to agree on how you want to structure your separation, then you'll need to get an order of legal separation, or move forward with a divorce.

Legal Separation

In most (but not all) states, you can go to family court and get a judgment of legal separation that ends your legal responsibilities to each other, but isn't a final judgment of divorce—you are still married when you are legally separated. Because it's not a divorce, a legal separation doesn't allow you to get married again. The court's order granting the legal separation does include orders about property division, alimony, and child custody and support, just as a divorce would. Why not just get a divorce, then? The reasons include religious beliefs, a desire to keep the family together legally for the sake of children, the need for one spouse to keep the health insurance benefits that would be lost with a divorce, or simple aversion to divorcing despite the desire to live separate lives.

THE LAW IN REAL LIFE

A North Carolina mother filed a petition for child support and custody before separating from her husband. She intended to end the couple's marriage, and argued that it would be in her children's best interests if the court would make a decision on temporary and permanent child custody and support, as well as postseparation support.

The first court to hear the case—called the trial court—dismissed her request because there was no divorce action pending. But when she appealed, the appellate court held that physical separation wasn't necessary to allow a court to make decisions about child custody and support, and that public policy supported allowing the court to make such a decision. However, the court refused to grant alimony, because the alimony laws required "separation" before an award of support could be made.

Annulment

There are two kinds of annulment: civil and religious.

A *civil annulment* ordered by a court not only ends a marriage, it creates a legal fiction that the marriage never existed. A person whose marriage is annulled by a court is legally single, not divorced. In most states, civil annulments are granted for one of these reasons:

- **Fraud or misrepresentation.** One spouse lied about something that was important to the other in getting married, like the ability to have children.
- **No consummation of the marriage.** One spouse is physically unable or unwilling to have sexual intercourse, and the other didn't know it when they got married.
- **Incest, bigamy, or underage party.** Either the spouses are related by blood so that their marriage is illegal under the laws of the state where they married, one of them is married to someone else, or one of them is under the age of consent and didn't receive a parent's approval.

- **Unsound mind.** One spouse (or both) was impaired by alcohol or drugs or didn't have the mental capacity to understand what was happening at the wedding.
- **Force.** One of the parties was forced into getting married.

Although most annulments take place very soon after the wedding, some couples seek an annulment after many years. In that case, the court considers all of the same issues as in a divorce, divides property, and makes decisions about support and custody. Children of a marriage that has been annulled are still "lawful" offspring of the marriage.

A *religious annulment* is usually sought by those who want to be remarried in a religious ceremony, commonly Roman Catholics who can't remarry in the church without an annulment of a previous marriage. A civil annulment is still necessary, but it isn't enough—a Catholic who wants to remarry in the church needs a religious annulment as well. After a religious annulment, the Catholic church still considers children of the marriage legitimate.

The Court Process

Although divorce procedures vary enormously between states and even between counties and courtrooms, there's a general order of things that you can reasonably expect.

The Divorce Process	
Starting the process	One spouse files the document that begins the divorce. In some places it's called a petition; in others it's a complaint or affidavit. It contains basic information about the marriage, children, and property and debts.
Notification of the other spouse	The person who filed the initial document must have it "served" on the other spouse, meaning it must be delivered to that person using a method approved by the court—either personally or by mail.
Temporary agreement or court hearing on temporary support or custody order	If spouses can't agree on temporary agreements about finances and parenting, there is a court hearing on temporary support or child custody.
Exchange of information	Spouses must exchange financial information documenting their property and debts, and additional information that might affect property division, support, or custody.
Negotiation and settlement or trial	Spouses try to negotiate a settlement, either directly or with the help of lawyers or a mediator. The case will either be resolved through a settlement or proceed to a court trial or arbitration.
Judgment of divorce	If spouses come up with an agreement on property, custody, and support, they submit it to the judge for approval. If the judge approves it (which is what usually happens), they get a judgment that ends the marriage. If they can't agree, there is a trial, and the judge decides and issues a judgment.

Residency Requirements— Where Can You File for Divorce?

You don't have to get divorced in the same state where you got married, but you do have to live in a state for a certain length of time before you can get divorced there. A few states have no specified requirement; some require only six weeks; some require a one-year residency, and many more use six months as the required period. Each state's requirement is listed in the "Residency Requirements" chart in the appendix.

$\bigodot$ CAUTION

Special issues for same-sex couples. Same-sex couples who married in states where it's legal can have other residency problems if they don't live in a marriage-equality state when they decide to divorce. See "Divorce for Same-Sex Couples," below.

Waiting Periods

Most states have a waiting period before your divorce can be finalized. The date the nonfiling spouse is served with the initial petition is the date that starts the waiting period running. For example, California, New Hampshire, and many other states have a six-month waiting period, meaning that if you file papers and serve your spouse on May 1, you can get a final judgment entered on November 1. In other states the period is much shorter and in a few states it's as long as a year.

For anyone who has a disputed custody case, the waiting period won't be an issue—your divorce will take longer to complete than any waiting period in the country. You'll probably be busy with hearings and negotiations for more than a year. If your divorce is less contentious, you may get all of your paperwork finished before the waiting period ends; in that case, you generally can submit your paperwork to the court and either get a judgment that shows a later date for the divorce to be finalized, or wait until the time passes and the court sends you the final judgment. If you have some issues to work out but don't expect a major battle, you can expect your divorce to take anywhere from six to 18 months. There's no average amount of time to complete a divorce—some uncontested divorces can be done in a matter of a few months, while very contentious cases drag on for years and years.

Must You Prove Your Spouse Is at Fault?

In the old days, someone who wanted a divorce had to show that the other spouse was the cause of the divorce—in other words, that it was the other person's fault. Even when both people wanted to divorce, they had to decide which of them would take the legal blame, and pick some basis to use for why they were divorcing. Adultery was the most popular choice, but abuse, abandonment, extreme cruelty (inflicting unnecessary emotional or physical suffering on the other spouse), and the physical inability to engage in sexual intercourse that wasn't disclosed before marriage also made the list—even if none of these things had actually happened.

Now, couples can get a "no-fault" divorce in every state. In a no-fault divorce, instead of proving that one spouse is to blame, you merely tell the court that you and your spouse have "irreconcilable differences" or that your relationship has suffered an "irremediable breakdown." In some states, in order to get a no-fault divorce you must have lived apart for a specified period of time.

In many places, no-fault is the only option, but in some states you can choose either fault or no-fault grounds for divorce. You probably won't want to choose a fault divorce if your divorce is uncontested. You might, however, choose a fault divorce if you don't want to wait out the separation period, or if you anticipate a major fight over property or support.

Even if you choose no-fault, some states' courts will still consider fault when dividing property and determining custody and support. So a spouse may accuse the other of misconduct and argue that it should affect support awards or who gets to have custody of the children.

Covenant Marriage and Divorce

If you entered into a "covenant marriage" in Arizona, Arkansas, or Louisiana, you must request a divorce on fault grounds—you may not use no-fault procedures. You're required to get marital counseling before you can file for divorce, and the waiting period before your divorce is final may be longer than that for a noncovenant marriage. You'll definitely need a lawyer's help, especially if you and your spouse disagree about getting a divorce.

A table in the appendix ("Grounds for Divorce") shows whether or not each state offers fault divorce. It also shows how long you must be separated before you can get a no-fault divorce.

Family Court

In every divorce case, a judge has to sign a final judgment—that's the piece of paper that says you're officially divorced. So even if you and your spouse agree about everything, the court still has to be involved in getting your divorce completed.

In most states, divorce cases are handled by a special court, called "family court," "domestic relations court," or "divorce court." This doesn't mean that the court is in a different place from courts that handle other civil (noncriminal) matters (though in some places it is), but just that certain judges deal only with family-related cases such as divorce, child custody and support, and sometimes, adoption.

Having a separate court for family cases means that the judges are knowledgeable and experienced. The court clerks and assistants tend to be knowledgeable as well, which will be especially important if you are representing yourself. Many family courts have self-help centers, where you can get some assistance with filling out your papers and making sure you get things filed and served properly. Many also have very useful websites, where you can find the forms you need as well as some instruction on how to proceed with your divorce. Find your county's court website and you should be able to find the relevant information.

Starting Your Divorce

Your official court divorce begins when one spouse files a form called a "petition" or "complaint." This form tells the court when you were married, when you separated, the names and birth dates of your children, the basics of your property and debts, and that you want a divorce. There will be a filing fee of between $100 and $400 to get the divorce started; when the other spouse files a "response" or "answer," there will be another filing fee in the same amount. There's more about filing and serving (delivering) papers in Chapter 6.

Kinds of Divorces

When it comes to divorce, you have a lot of choices to make. You will decide whether your divorce will be uncontested, contested, or default, and whether you'll use mediation or collaboration, or go all the way to a trial. In addition, there are differences between state laws, like fault or no-fault.

No matter how you choose to make your way through it, divorce is expensive, emotionally challenging, and time-consuming. The most important variable is how well you and your spouse are able to put aside your anger and grief and cooperate on the big issues of money and children. The better you are at working together to make decisions for your changing family structure, the better it is for your financial bottom line—and for your chances of emerging from the divorce with a decent relationship with your ex and a parenting plan you can work with and that will work for your children.

However, some couples are simply not able to come to agreement, especially about parenting issues. This book will help you whether or not you and your spouse can work out a settlement or must turn these decisions over to a judge.

Kinds of Divorce at a Glance		
Kind of Divorce	**How It Works**	**Hassle and Expense**
UNCONTESTED — **Summary or Simplified**	Spouses, who haven't been married long and don't have children or many assets or debts, file together	Relatively simple paperwork; lawyer usually not necessary; often only one filing fee
Default	One spouse files for divorce, the other doesn't respond	Relatively simple paperwork; lawyer may or may not be necessary
Mediated	Trained mediator helps spouses work out settlement agreement without court fight	Less expensive than a contested divorce; can help spouses communicate
Collaborative	Each spouse hires lawyer, but agrees to settle out of court using negotiation and four-way meetings	Can take longer than mediation, but cheaper, nicer, and quicker than contested case
CONTESTED — **Arbitrated**	Spouses hire arbitrator or private judge to hear evidence and decide contested issues outside of court	Faster and slightly less expensive than trial; can be less combative than court trial and provides greater privacy; not allowed everywhere
Contested	Spouses hire lawyers and fight out issues, sometimes all the way to a court trial	Enormously expensive, stressful for everyone (especially children), guaranteed to ruin chances of civil relationship in future

Summary Divorce

In many states, an expedited divorce procedure, often called summary or simplified divorce, is available to couples who haven't been married for very long (usually five years or less), don't own much property, don't have children, and don't have significant joint debts. Both spouses need to agree to the divorce, and they must file court papers jointly. Summary divorces are easy to do yourself, without the help of a lawyer.

Default Divorce

A default divorce is a way to end your marriage when you don't know where your spouse is (after making a serious effort to find out) or when your spouse won't or can't participate in the process. One spouse files divorce papers and then, when the other doesn't respond within a certain period of time, asks the judge to grant the divorce. In some states, you can also agree, at the time you file for divorce, to submit to a default judgment, which usually has the advantage of avoiding a second filing fee.

Uncontested Divorce

An uncontested divorce is the best option from both financial and emotional perspectives. There's no question that it's best from your kids' point of view, because it protects them from having to deal with parents who are in serious conflict. In an uncontested case, you and your spouse work together, possibly with the help of some third parties, like mediators or therapists, to agree on the terms of a divorce and parenting plan. Once you've done that, you file court papers that you both agree on to make the divorce happen.

Uncontested divorces don't involve any kind of formal trial, and in many places you're not even required to go to court. Instead, you file court forms and, possibly, a "marital settlement agreement" that details your agreements about how you want to divide your property and debts, what your custody arrangements for your children will be, and whether support payments will change hands. Your settlement, and your final divorce, will have to be approved by a judge. The judge will usually approve a settlement agreement unless it's clear that the terms are completely unfair to one person or were arranged when one person was under duress.

An uncontested divorce is the least expensive way to go, but it will still take a bite out of your wallet. If you decide to go it alone, without a lawyer, you'll need to gather information, and some of it—like books that will help you—can cost money. There will be court filing fees as well, and those are getting more and more expensive. (In some places they're up to $400 and climbing, though other courts still charge only $100 or so.) And it's entirely possible that you might decide to hire a lawyer for some help or coaching, as well as other professionals like accountants or real estate experts. Many couples use a counselor or a mediator to help them come to agreement on property and custody issues. If you or your spouse has retirement benefits through work, you might need to hire an actuary to value them or a lawyer to prepare the special court order you'll need to divide them.

Even if you do get help from some or all of these professionals, your uncontested divorce should cost less than $5,000. And if you move along efficiently and cooperatively, you should be able to finalize your divorce as soon as your state's waiting period (discussed above) is over.

You can also get help with an uncontested divorce from a legal document preparer, paralegal, or legal typist (different names for the same job), who can help you prepare the court forms for a divorce. A legal document preparer is not a lawyer and isn't allowed to give legal advice, but can direct you to websites, books, and other resources that can help, and then make sure the forms are properly filled out so that your court process goes smoothly. Make sure your legal document preparer is registered with your state's agency that oversees the profession.

You can also complete an uncontested divorce using online services. You submit answers to a questionnaire tailored to your state, and then the online service prepares your paperwork and sends it to you with instructions for service and filing. Some online divorce services are www. legalzoom.com, www.ourdivorceagreement.com, www.completecase.com, www.divorcetoday.com, www.divorcesource.com, and www.onlinedivorce. com. This approach isn't recommended if you have a pension, 403(b), or other retirement plan that requires a special order to divide, or if you have any other complications in your divorce.

Mediated Divorce

In divorce mediation, you and your spouse work with a neutral third party, called a mediator, to try to resolve all of the issues in your divorce. The mediator doesn't make any decisions; that's up to you and your spouse. Instead, the mediator helps you communicate with each other until you can come to an agreement.

Mediation is much less expensive than going to trial. Even more important is the fact that mediation can help to preserve and even improve your relationship with your spouse, which benefits both of you as well as your children. Mediation is discussed in detail in Chapter 5.

Collaborative Divorce

Collaborative divorce involves a lawyer for each spouse, but the divorcing couple and the lawyers, who have special training, agree to try to settle your case cooperatively. The process can be much faster and less expensive than going to trial—and much more conducive to a civil relationship between you and your ex after the divorce. There's a complete discussion of collaborative divorce in Chapter 5.

Contested Divorce

A contested divorce is one in which the spouses can't agree about property, custody, or support, and instead take these issues to a judge (or an arbitrator or private judge) to decide after a trial. The trial might be short, but the entire process is long—and far from pleasant. It can take years, and it will take a huge emotional toll on you, your spouse, and certainly your kids, and also cost you financially. A contested divorce, even one that ends in a settlement rather than a trial, can cost each spouse tens of thousands of dollars.

Parentage Actions for Unmarried Couples

Unmarried parents face the same custody and child support questions as married parents (with the exception of some unmarried same-sex parents; see "Divorce for Same-Sex Couples," below). However, unmarried parents don't use the divorce process to establish orders for custody and support. In fact, because they are not required to use the courts to change their legal status, some unmarried parents who agree on issues of child custody and support don't use the courts at all when they end a relationship. Instead, they make a verbal or written agreement about how they're going to continue parenting together, and follow that agreement (or modifications of it).

As long as things continue to work out between those parents—in other words, as long as they don't have any disagreements about custody, parenting time, or child support—everything will go smoothly. But just as is true with married parents who disagree about custody, parenting time, or support payments, the absence of a court order may come back to haunt them. It's better to submit agreements to the court and get a judge's order confirming them. Unmarried couples do this through a parentage action rather than a divorce. Every state has laws governing parentage that allow a parent to establish parental rights in court. Most of these cases involve fathers and are called paternity actions, because maternity is rarely in question, but sometimes it does come up in surrogacy cases or cases involving same-sex parents.

Many unmarried parents establish a child's paternity at birth using a voluntary declaration form. That form has the force of law, and a parent who has signed it can establish paternity by filing a court petition and attaching the form. A parent without a voluntary declaration will file the same court petition and assert paternity; if the other parent agrees, the court will be able to enter custody, visitation, and support orders. If the other parent disputes paternity, a father seeking parental rights can ask the court to order a paternity test—probably with the help of an attorney.

Once parentage is established, unmarried parents will use the court system the same way married parents do—they can ask the court to enter orders based on agreements they've made, so that that the orders are enforceable, and they can also ask the court to make decisions for them when they're unable to agree on custody or child support.

Divorce for Same-Sex Couples

On June 26, 2015, the United States Supreme Court issued its landmark opinion in *Obergefell v. Hodges*, holding that there is a constitutional right to marry a person of the same sex, and all states must allow such marriages to take place.

Marriage Equality and Divorce

Obergefell changes the legal landscape for same-sex couples everywhere. The right to marry brings with it the right to divorce, and couples who were previously "wedlocked" in states that did not recognize or allow same-sex marriage will now be able to end their legal relationships without having to move to another state and establish residency there. All states must now allow joint tax filing, the right to inherit without a will, and all of the other state and federal rights that come with a legal marriage.

In some states, like California, it's still possible to enter into a domestic partnership. In general these marriage-equivalent relationships provide most of the same rights as marriage on the state level but do not qualify couples for federal benefits such as joint tax filing and Social Security benefits. In some of the states that offer marriage-equivalent relationships, the arrival of marriage equality automatically converts the domestic partnership to a marriage, but in others that is not the case, so if you are unsure of your status, check with a knowledgeable attorney right away.

Whether you have a marriage or a marriage-equivalent domestic partnership or civil union, you must get a legal divorce to end the marriage or equivalent relationship.

Same-Sex Parenting and the Courts

Because married same-sex parents, and those in domestic partnerships and civil unions, have access to the courts to end their relationships, they can also operate just as opposite-sex couples do when it comes to custody and child support decisions. In other words, they can ask the court to affirm their agreements in a court order or make decisions when they're not able to agree.

However, there are two situations in which same-sex parents need to find attorneys with experience in this specialized area. The first is when one partner is challenging the validity of the marriage, domestic partnership, or civil union. The other is when one partner—or someone else—is challenging the other partner's status as a parent. Even with the arrival of full marriage equality, there is still not full parentage equality. Every state presumes that a child born into a marriage is the child of both spouses, but—and this is a big but—in many states the marital presumption can be reversed if it can be proven that the non-birth parent is not genetically related to the child. In other words, a non-biological parent's rights are not secure without completing an adoption or other parentage action—and if not secure, could potentially be challenged by the biological parent in a divorce action. If you find yourself in that situation, hire an experienced, knowledgeable lawyer right away.

 RESOURCE
To find a local attorney with expertise in LGBT matters, contact a legal organization like the National Center for Lesbian Rights (www.nclrights.org) or Lambda Legal (www.lambdalegal.org).

Basics of Child Custody

A custody fight will harm your children more than any other kind of dispute that might come up in the divorce process, and you should do everything you can to avoid it. When it comes to figuring out the details of child custody during and after your divorce, you have two choices: Work it out with your spouse, or have the court decide for you based on the judge's interpretation of what's best for your kids and your family. Years of research, as well as good common sense, tell us that keeping acrimony to a minimum will lead to better outcomes for your kids.

Parents who go ahead with a custody fight often feel that they're doing it for their children and that it is the best way to protect them. If this sounds like you, take the time to explore your real motivations and to consider the real impact on your children. Is it possible that your part in the conflict arises, to some degree, out of a desire to beat the other parent or make sure the other parent isn't happy with the parenting plan? Have you really learned about what the impact will be on your children of being the subjects of a court battle? Take a break and consider these questions before escalating conflict between you and the other parent.

This chapter will give you the basics on custody, and later you'll work through the process of establishing your parenting plan in detail.

Physical and Legal Custody

In a divorce, custody of children is broken down into two elements: legal and physical. It's not unusual for legal and physical custody to be set up differently. For example, parents might have joint legal custody, but not joint physical custody, especially if the parents live some distance apart.

Legal Custody

Having legal custody of your children means that you are responsible for making decisions about the important things in their lives, like where they go to school, what religious instruction they receive, whether they need academic tutoring or psychological counseling, and when they go to the doctor.

During your marriage, you and your spouse probably made these decisions together, and when you divorce, judges want to keep it that way if at all possible. The default preference in the majority of states is for parents to share legal custody and continue to make decisions together for their children. This is called joint legal custody. It can take many forms. Just as in an intact marriage, it's not uncommon for one parent to be the primary caregiver, the same can be true after divorce even if the parents have joint legal custody. For example, a parent who is the primary caregiver might make many decisions that are part of legal custody, like authorizing routine or emergency medical treatment, or choosing a tutor for a child who needs academic help. While the other parent has the legal right to participate in those decisions, it's up to the parents to decide how to make this work as a practical matter. They may agree that it's easier and more efficient for one parent to have greater day-to-day responsibility.

Joint legal custody can become a battleground for parents who aren't able to agree on things that might seem simple, like where the children should get medical care or whether they should take piano lessons. It only takes one parent to create ongoing conflict over this type of question, and it can make life miserable for everyone if every decision becomes a fight.

Judges find that type of decision making miserable, too. If parents fight over every question related to their kids, the judge may appoint a private attorney or mental health professional as a "special master," to move the battles out of the court and provide some structure and control on high-conflict parents. The judge may also give one parent sole custody. That parent then has the sole right to make decisions about the children's health, education, and welfare. A judge might also grant sole legal custody if one parent:

- lives a great distance away
- is abusive or neglectful, or
- isn't involved in the child's day-to-day life and doesn't spend time with the child.

It's also possible for a judge to order joint legal custody, but designate one parent as the tiebreaker in the event the parents can't agree. This isn't that different from the parent having sole legal custody, but it does encourage both parents to be involved, at least in attempting to come to a resolution.

Physical Custody

Physical custody refers to where the children live on a regular basis. It can be shared by both parents or granted to just one.

How custody is ordered at the time of your divorce can affect you later. For example, in some states, a parent with sole physical custody has a presumed right to move away with the kids. To prevent a move, the noncustodial parent must go to court and show that the move would be harmful to the kids. So if the other parent's attorney tries to tell you that it doesn't matter whether you let the other parent have sole physical custody even though you spend significant time with the kids, don't buy it. Check with a lawyer about whether the decision could come back to haunt you later. (And see Chapter 8 for more about relocating with the kids.)

Joint Custody

There's a strong preference among judges to order joint physical custody, where the kids spend significant amounts of time with both parents, in order to guarantee that children have regular contact with both parents. Some states direct judges to assume that joint physical custody is better, and ask any parent who disagrees to provide evidence about why it's not a good idea in that particular case. Shared physical custody means that the kids get to have two engaged and involved parents and two real homes—not one place that is home and one place they go to visit their other parent.

Joint physical custody doesn't always involve an exact 50-50 time split, but it's usually close. This only works, however, if the parents live near enough to each other that the kids can move easily back and forth between houses and can maintain their regular activities no matter which house they're in. Shared physical custody isn't always best when the parents really don't get along—the many transitions between parents create too many opportunities for conflict.

Sole Custody and Visitation

If one parent has the kids most of the time, that parent is usually granted sole physical custody, while the other parent gets the right to regularly schedule time with the kids, called either "visitation" or "parenting time." A very common arrangement is for one parent to stay in the family home with the kids. The children spend most of their time there and see the other parent at regularly set times. In legal terms, the parent with sole physical custody is the custodial parent and the other is the noncustodial parent who has visitation rights.

For a long time, lots of folks had a fairly standard "Wednesday night dinner and every other weekend" arrangement. Commonly, the mother had sole physical custody, and the father had visitation rights for one dinner a week and every other weekend. (Legal custody was often shared, but it wasn't unusual for the mother to have sole legal custody as well.) That schedule is still used regularly, but so are a lot of other schedules.

Creating a Parenting Plan: Out of Court

When you and your spouse no longer live together, you can't assume anything about who will take care of the kids at any given time. You'll need an agreement and a plan about sharing time with your kids, and about what your responsibilities are now. If you and your spouse work together on planning your parenting schedule, you will save yourselves endless time, trouble, and money. There are many ways to share custody and divide parenting time, and figuring it out yourselves (or with the help of a mediator or child custody expert) means you can craft a plan that works for your own unique family. You don't have to start out agreeing on everything or even getting along that well—you just need to have a commitment to keeping your parenting issues out of court and a willingness to compromise.

Your kids may have strong opinions about where they want to live and how much they want to see the noncustodial parent. Very young children won't have much say about custody and visitation, but older kids have their own activities, commitments, and attachments, and these deserve consideration.

If you talk to your kids about custody or visitation, make sure you don't pressure them—and also make sure they know that they're not the ones who are ultimately going to make the final decisions. Just listen to what they have to say and tell them you'll take their views into account. Never tell them that you'll be sad or lonely if they want to spend time with your ex or live in the other parent's home instead of yours.

If you simply can't reach an agreement after giving it your best effort, turn to "When Parents Can't Agree: Going to Court," below.

Sample Parenting Plans

When you're just beginning to figure out what life's going to look like once you separate, it can be hard to imagine what kind of time-sharing arrangement would be best for your family. There are lots of ways to work on this. You can:

- sit down with your spouse and discuss what you each think your kids need
- ask a mediator or child custody evaluator to help you make decisions
- use one of the websites or other resources described below, or
- use some combination of the above.

It can also be helpful to see some examples of what other families have done. Here is a series of parenting plans developed by Joan B. Kelly, Ph.D., an expert in the field of child custody. Each option shows the time share, the number of nights per 28-day period that the child spends with the nonresidential (noncustodial) parent, and some of the factors that affect whether the particular arrangement being described is a good one for your family. Options 6 and 7 are the closest to 50-50 custody, but even in those scenarios the parent with just slightly more time is referred to as the residential parent.

Option 1: Four Overnights

Every other weekend: Friday afternoon to Sunday evening

Factors to consider:

- 12 days' separation from nonresidential parent is too long for many children
- Nonresidential parent's relationship with child is diminished; minimal involvement in school, homework, special projects
- Little time off for residential parent
- Can benefit children when nonresidential parent is very angry or rigid
- Can add a midweek evening visit to reduce separation time, but that creates more transitions and can be rushed or too hectic.

Option 2: Six Overnights

Every other extended weekend: Friday afternoon to Monday morning

Factors to consider:

- Nonresidential parent connects with school experience
- Dropoff and pickup at school or day care means reduced opportunity for conflict at transition
- Three-night period means fewer transitions for child
- Won't work if nonresidential parent lives too far away to drop off child at school or day care.

Option 3: Eight Overnights

Every other weekend and weekly midweek overnight: Friday afternoon to Sunday evening and every Wednesday afternoon to Thursday morning

Factors to consider:

- No separation from either parent greater than six days
- Nonresidential parent engaged with school and homework
- Residential parent gets an evening off during the week
- No transition on Wednesday evening after visitation.

Option 4: Ten Overnights

Every other extended weekend (Friday afternoon to Monday morning) and every Wednesday afternoon to Thursday morning.

Factors to consider:

- Same as in Option 3, plus nonresidential parent more engaged in school and homework
- No separation from either parent greater than seven days.

Option 5: Twelve Overnights

Parent A: Sunday to Thursday; Parent B: Thursday to Sunday

Factors to consider:

- Only one transition per week
- Parent A has mostly school time; Parent B mostly weekend time, so there's an imbalance in activities they're each involved in.

Option 6: Fourteen Overnights

Split time between parents and alternate schedule each week as follows:

Parent A/Week One: Sunday evening to Wednesday morning

Parent B/Week One: Wednesday afternoon to Sunday evening

Parent A/Week Two: Saturday evening to Wednesday morning

Parent B/Week Two: Wednesday morning to Saturday evening

Factors to Consider:

- Both parents have weekday and weekend time
- Only one face-to-face transition per week
- No separation from either parent longer than four days
- Completely equal time share.

Option 7: Fourteen Overnights

Split midweeks and every other weekend:

Parent A: Monday evening to Wednesday evening each week, and every other weekend

Parent B: Wednesday evening to Friday morning each week, and every other weekend

Factors to consider:
- All transitions occur at school or day care
- No separation from either parent greater than five days
- Completely equal time-share
- Both parents have weekday and weekend time
- Can be a challenging schedule for children with physical or learning disabilities or difficult temperament.

These are merely some examples of possible schedules, which you and the other parent can use as a good starting point for discussions. Not all of them will be appropriate for your children. For example, some kids do better with transitions than others, and kids with learning disabilities or other school-related issues might not do well with transitions in the middle of the week. See "Transitions," below, for more about those issues.

For additional examples, as well as tools that can help you sketch out your own parenting plans, check out these websites:
- www.afccnet.org: the website of the Association of Family and Conciliation Courts has lots of resources for parents, including sample parenting plans. Click the link for "Resource Center" and then "Resources for Families."
- http://www.courtrecords.alaska.gov/webdocs/forms/dr-475.pdf. This link takes you to the Alaska state court Model Parenting Agreement.
- www.sharedparentingworks.org/free-parenting-plans: has parenting plans from nearly a dozen states, along with other tools and resources.

RESOURCE
If you're interested in research on child development and divorce, other articles by Dr. Kelly include "Children's Living Arrangements Following Separation and Divorce: Insights from Empirical and Clinical Research," *Family Process Journal,* Volume 46, pages 35–52 (2007), and "Developing Beneficial Parenting Plan Models for Children Following Separation and Divorce," *Journal of American Academy of Matrimonial Lawyers,* Volume 19 (2005), Number 2.

Splitting Up the Kids

Although it's not common, some parents do opt to separate their kids, each taking primary custody of one or more children. Separating siblings during a stressful time like a divorce isn't generally a great idea, but there may be situations where it makes sense—for example, if a large age gap between the kids means they don't have much of a relationship, if one kid has drug or behavioral problems that you think you could deal with better in isolation from siblings, or if one child is simply having problems with one parent and both could use a break.

If you're considering a split custody arrangement, talk to a custody evaluator or a counselor who has experience dealing with children of divorce, and get an evaluation of your family's situation and an opinion on how the kids will handle it. A custody evaluator is a therapist with special training in helping children of divorce by assessing the family situation and offering suggestions (or, in a contested situation, recommendations to the court) about the best parenting arrangement.

Negotiating With the Other Parent

Your goal is to come up with a document that will be comprehensive but flexible, and will serve your children well. There are different ways to negotiate your parenting agreement, each one requiring a different level of involvement and ability to communicate.

Face-to-face discussions. Logistically, the easiest way to make these decisions is to sit down with the other parent, make a list of the issues, and discuss them all like rational adults who both have your kids' best interests as your first priority. Your emotions, of course, may make this difficult or even impossible.

Help from a friend or family member. Some parents are able to set aside feelings about their separation long enough to work out a parenting agreement, but for others, a little help can go a long way. You can ask for that help from a friend or family member, if there's someone on whom you both can agree and who has the temperament to help the two of you work toward an agreement. Make sure it's someone you both trust to stick with the process, to be neutral about what you decide, and to keep your confidences. It's a rare friend who has the ability to act as an amateur mediator—but there are other ways a friend can help you, such as being a sounding board who will vet ideas and give you an honest reality check. Whatever you do, don't pressure anyone into helping you in this way. Only someone who really wants this kind of involvement will be able to be truly helpful.

Help from a mediator or custody evaluator. Mediation is a great way to work out your parenting plan. A mediator is trained to work with difficult issues and help you reach practical solutions that will work for both of you and your kids. (There's a lot more about mediation in Chapter 5.) Even if you and your spouse are able to work out all of the other questions that need to be decided in your divorce, you might want to consider hiring a mediator to help you with just this issue. In fact, even if you're fighting everything else out in court, you should still consider using mediation to address your parenting disputes—after all, your parenting relationship is going to continue long after the divorce is over, and it's worth investing some time and effort to see whether you can reach an agreement and maybe even improve your relationship with the other parent.

Identifying the Issues

You may be surprised at the level of detail required for a useful parenting agreement. There's a lot more to deal with than just the amount of time the kids will spend with each parent—including some issues that you probably haven't thought about yet, and some that won't come up for a while if your kids are young. But the more you can anticipate possibilities and deal with them in advance, the less conflict you will have in the heat of the moment. Here's a list of issues you'll need to cover in your parenting agreement. There may be others, too—the specifics will, naturally, depend on your family situation.

Basic time sharing

- Where the kids will stay
- How the kids will get from one place to another
- Who, besides you and the other parent, is allowed to pick the kids up and transport them
- Whether the parent with custody must ask the other parent first to care for the children if the custodial parent can't

Contact outside of visitation

- Phone schedule for the kids to be in touch with the parent they're not staying with
- Agreement about using email for contact
- Whether the kids are old enough for cell phones, or whether the custodial parent will be responsible for making the contact happen

Family birthdays

- Where the kids will spend their birthdays
- Who is responsible for the birthday party, and whether it's okay to have two parties
- Whether you'll make special arrangements for your birthday or your spouse's, as well as the kids' birthdays

Holidays

- Alternating holidays each year or splitting the day between parents every year
- Definition of a holiday (when the kids don't have school for Presidents' Day, for example, is the person who's responsible for them on Mondays still on duty, or is that Monday treated differently?)
- Special holidays for one parent, like Mother's or Father's Day, or holidays with special significance to one parent
- Sharing time during long school vacations, like spring and winter breaks

Religion

- If each household has a different religion, whether there's a middle ground, or whether the kids will practice the religion of each household when they're there (this may not be an issue if you've agreed on your kids' religious training so far, but if you and your spouse don't see eye to eye on religion, it may take some serious negotiation)

School

- Where the kids will go to school (if you want them to go to private school and your spouse is willing but can't afford it, will you put your money where your mouth is?)
- College planning
- Staying united on making sure your kids are motivated and successful in school

Activities

- How you'll decide on activities, especially if you disagree about the relative importance of such things as sports and music lessons
- Whether there's some limit on how many activities the kids can be involved in

Travel

- Who will keep the children's passports?
- Whether there are any restrictions on where either parent can go with the children, like out of the state or out of the country
- Whether there's a particular age that the kids must reach before they travel by themselves (this is a surprisingly contentious issue)
- Whether there is a limit on the number of consecutive nights the kids can be away from one parent

Going out

- Agreeing on whether your kids are old enough to be going out with groups of friends or dating, and what the ground rules are (while writing it in the agreement may not be necessary, make sure you discuss it and see whether you can agree on what's appropriate)

Privileges and discipline

- Whether TV and computer time is to be limited in both homes
- Nutrition and junk food consumption
- What they're allowed to see at the movies
- Whether teens can go out with friends who are already driving
- Appropriate consequences for breaking rules or failing to do chores (remember, kids engage in divide-and-conquer strategies whenever possible, so try to come to some agreement if you can)

Medical care and insurance

- Who the kids see for medical and dental appointments
- Whether you're required to notify the other parent every time you get medical attention for the kids, even if it's routine
- How you will make medical decisions
- How quickly each parent must notify the other in an emergency
- Who will maintain the kids on their insurance, and who will pay for it if it's not included as a job benefit
- How uninsured expenses will be divided
- What you'll do if the kids need mental health care

Ongoing Communication

- How will you schedule time to discuss your children's needs?
- What will you do if you don't agree about something?

RESOURCE

For a comprehensive list of issues and step-by-step instructions for making a comprehensive parenting plan, see *Building a Parenting Agreement That Works: Child Custody Agreements Step by Step*, by Mimi L. Zemmelman (Nolo), and check some of the resources listed in "Sample Parenting Plans," above.

Transitions

One important element of your parenting plan is how often your kids must transition from one home to the other—this is also called a "changeover." Too many changeovers every week can cause stress for both children and parents, especially in the early days after you separate. Some states consider transitions inherently stressful, too—for example, Arizona has a rule that transitions between divorced parents can't take place within a certain distance of a school.

If your kids seem to be experiencing wear and tear from the transitions, or if you're really having a hard time being in the same place as your spouse, even for a few minutes, try not to make a plan that calls for a changeover every day or two. Instead, opt for a weekly visitation schedule, or schedule the changeovers to occur after school, so that one parent drops the kids off and the other picks them up. That way you won't have to be in the same place at the same time, and the kids won't have to worry about that either.

On the other hand, if you get along okay and the changeovers aren't too stressful, it can be good for kids to feel that they really have two homes. (See tips on making this work in "If You Share Physical Custody," below.)

It's rare, but some parents are willing to do the coming and going themselves, letting the children stay in one family home. Called "bird nesting," this arrangement has the parents taking turns living in the family home with the children, usually with each parent having equal time in the house. It's disruptive for parents, and expensive, given that each parent needs a separate place to live when they're not with the kids. It's a rare set of parents who can share the out-of-house space, but that does happen, too. Either way, what nesting amounts to is parents choosing to handle the complications of transitioning from one place to another instead of that responsibility being on the children.

Creating a Parenting Plan

Once you know how you want to handle your parenting schedule and the issues listed in "Identifying the Issues," above, you can create a written parenting plan that will become part of the final judgment in your divorce. It's not that difficult to create your own parenting plan—you can follow the list of issues above, include the specifics of your parenting time schedule, and add any other provisions you think are necessary. If you've agreed on a parenting plan before resolving the financial part of your divorce, you can have the parenting plan entered as a stipulation (agreement) with the court. See "How to Get Your Agreements Made Into Orders," in Chapter 4.

When Parents Can't Agree: Going to Court

Ideally, you and your spouse will create a parenting plan together, possibly with the help of a third party like a mediator or custody evaluator appointed by the court or chosen by you and the other parent. But if you are not able to create your own parenting plan, ultimately you'll have to submit the question to a judge. In most places, you are required to attend a certain number of mediation sessions before a judge will rule in your case.

The Best Interests Standard

The judge will base the custody decision on a standard that's called "the best interests of the child." This means that the judge will gather information from you, from any third parties (like court-appointed mediators) who have helped you try to work out a parenting plan, and from any witnesses you might present, and will synthesize that information into a conclusion about what parenting schedule will serve the children's best interests.

Be Reasonable

When you're deciding what to ask for in a custody case, consider your children's interests. Don't ask for certain parenting arrangements just because your spouse won't like them, and be sure what you're asking for will work for both you and your children. For example, if you travel frequently, don't request a parenting schedule that would leave your children with other caregivers during a significant portion of the time that's "yours." The judge won't appreciate your apparent indifference to what your kids might want. Likewise, don't insist on something that isn't consistent with your children's activities, interests, and routines.

It's important to understand that your interests come after those of your children. Many parents have spent enormous sums of money arguing for the custody arrangement that suits them best, only to discover that custody decisions aren't based on the best interests of the parents. If you are fighting just because the plan you want works better for you, without taking the kids' needs into consideration, you're going to lose the argument. The judge will factor in the realities of your life—things like where you work, your schedule, and the like—but those will not be the deciding factors. Instead, the court will focus on the children's needs.

How does a court measure a child's best interests? It may seem subjective, but courts have identified a number of ways to do it. In general, judges like to maintain the status quo as much as possible, in the belief that children whose parents are divorcing are best served by having consistency in their schedules and living situations. So if you're insisting that the kids need to be pulled out of school in the middle of a school year so that you can move to a different neighborhood, you're going to have a tough time getting the judge to agree. Of course, if you truly need to move because of work requirements or other unavoidable changes, that's a different story—but you can expect to be questioned closely about your reasons for wanting to make a major change in your kids' situation.

Many states also note factors that judges are not supposed to consider in evaluating a child's best interests. For example, there's not supposed to be any preference for mothers over fathers or vice versa, and the parents' respective financial situations are generally considered irrelevant. In some states, sexual orientation is on the list of factors that are not to be factored in, and race is never to be considered.

Chapter 7, which discusses trials, includes more about the best interests standard. Chapters 7 and 8 address ways the kids' opinions may become a factor in a custody proceeding.

THE LAW IN REAL LIFE

Courts considering best interests do so on the basis of the current situation, not what might happen in the future. The Vermont Supreme Court held that a court order that includes an automatic change of custody at a particular time in the future, or when a certain event occurs, is invalid. The trial court awarded custody to the mother until just before the child was to start kindergarten, and ordered a transfer of custody from the mother to the father from that point through the child's minority. The Supreme Court said that such an order assumed what the child's best interests would be in the future, and was based on speculation. Instead, changes of custody must be based on "real-time determinations" of a child's best interests.

Going to Court

If you aren't able to reach agreement with your spouse, the next step will be for one of you to file papers with the court, asking for a hearing in front of a judge and for the judge to settle the dispute—where the kids should live, how much time they should spend with each parent, or whatever else you can't agree on.

Before you ever get to a hearing, however, the family court will almost certainly require that you attend mandatory mediation sessions—often, even if you've tried mediation before without success. Most courts now employ court-appointed mediators who meet with parents before a court hearing can take place, to make a last-ditch effort to reach an agreement. There's more about court-ordered mediation in Chapter 5. Hearings and trials are covered in Chapters 6 and 8.

Judges often order parents to attend child-rearing classes and require them to draw up parenting plans. In Texas, for example, all divorcing parents are required to set up and follow a parenting plan—the court even appoints a parenting coordinator to assist divorcing parents in figuring out the plan, which must include a process to resolve future conflicts. Other states' laws are similar and include detailed provisions for creating a parenting plan.

If you still can't negotiate an agreement, you'll have a hearing before the family court judge. A hearing, which generally addresses only one issue, is different than a trial, which is most often the final court appearance and the one that will resolve all outstanding issues. This type of hearing is called different things in different places. Sometimes it's called a "show cause" hearing, because the person making the request is required to show good cause for what's requested. Other courts call it a custody hearing or a motion hearing. Some make a distinction between "short cause" and "long cause" hearings, depending on how long the hearing is expected to take. Chapter 6 describes these hearings in detail.

Contentious Issues

While there's a depressingly long list of things that parents can find to disagree about, a few issues tend to come up repeatedly. Even when parents are still married and living together, these are the issues that can cause household and relationship strife; they are sometimes part of the reason for the divorce. This can make it especially difficult to resolve them once the parents are no longer living together.

Religion

When parents don't share the same religion, they may struggle with whether children will be raised in one faith or the other, or allowed to choose for themselves. In general, a parent with sole legal custody has the right to determine what type of religious upbringing the children have, but courts are also reluctant to prohibit a noncustodial parent from, for example, taking a child to church during parenting time. Some judges have ruled that learning two religions is not harmful to children, while others have reached the opposite conclusion and ordered one parent to stop teaching the child a certain religion or taking a child to services. The rules depend on where you live and what the facts are in your situation, and also on how custody is set. As noted above, if you have sole legal custody—meaning you're the decision maker about the children's health and welfare—you do have control over the kids' religious upbringing, but that control isn't unlimited. If you share joint legal custody, you will have to work with the other parent to decide questions of religion, or ask a judge to decide. There aren't a lot of hard and fast rules about religious disputes; courts use the best interests standard to decide these cases as they do with most other things involving custody and care of children.

THE LAW IN REAL LIFE

A New Hampshire court found that it wasn't in a child's best interests to be home-schooled through her mother's church after the father objected. The parents had joint legal custody, and therefore an equal right to make decisions about their daughter. The mother argued that because the home school was a part of her church, the court should make the decision based on constitutional principles, not under the best interests rule, but the court rejected that argument.

A father who had parenting time on alternate Sundays didn't have to take his kids to church during that time, said an Indiana appellate court. The mother asked the court to order the father to attend church with the children or to adjust the parenting time so that she could attend Sunday mass with them. The court held that the children received adequate religious training during the time they were with their mother and that the father, who shared joint custody with her, had the right to do other things with the children during his parenting time.

Medical Care

Parents often argue about appropriate medical treatment for their children, and there are times when the medical care issue and the question of religion are intertwined. For example, a parent might object to certain types of medical treatment—or any treatment at all—because of religious convictions.

> **THE LAW IN REAL LIFE**
>
> A Florida court gave responsibility for health care decisions to a father after the mother objected to having their child vaccinated; the mother's religious beliefs forbade vaccinations. While acknowledging that a parent's religious beliefs should be respected in most cases, the fact that experts had testified that the failure to vaccinate could cause serious harm to the child was enough to give decision-making authority to the father.
>
> In a Kansas case, however, the court refused to change custody from the mother to the father simply because the mother was a Jehovah's Witness who might, at some point the future, refuse medical care for the child. The court held there was no evidence that she had refused medical care so far, that the child was well-adjusted to his home environment, and that religious considerations alone weren't enough to deprive a parent of custodial rights unless there is evidence of real harm to the child.

Contact With Certain Adults

A "paramour provision" is a court's ruling that a divorced parent can't have a new partner or love interest spend the night while the children are with that parent—sometimes they even prohibit the new partner from having any contact with the children. Sometimes the other parent doesn't even need to object. While it used to be much more common for judges to restrain contact between children and their parents' intimates, it does still happen, especially in more conservative locations, and there are even some localities that require all parenting plans to contain a paramour provision. Most of the time, however, any parent seeking a restriction on access will have to show clear evidence that contact with the person at issue is harmful to the children.

THE LAW IN REAL LIFE

In a Tennessee case, a judge ordered that the mother's boyfriend couldn't spend the night at her house while her daughter was there, even though the girl's father hadn't requested any such restriction. The appellate court reversed the case and held that the judge's own views of morality couldn't be the basis for a restriction, especially in the absence of any showing of harm to the child—and especially where the judge applied the rule only to the mother, without a similar restriction on the father's activities. (Another Tennessee case reached the same result—allowing contact between the partner and the kids—where the mother's same-sex partner lived with her.)

In a very unusual case in New York, a family court judge awarded joint custody of a teenage girl to a father and the mother's boyfriend, with whom the girl had lived for 12 years of her life, after the mother died. The court's reasoning was that although the girl had regular contact with her father, the contact was limited, and it would add to the trauma of losing her mother if she also had to move hundreds of miles away to live with him.

It's also not unusual for a divorced parent to object to specific adults spending time with the kids while the kids are with the other parent. For example, one parent might object if a particular friend of the other parent abused drugs or alcohol. A court will consider requests like these, but you'll have to present concrete evidence that the person poses a danger to the child to succeed.

Sexual Orientation

What a gay, lesbian, bisexual, or transgendered parent can expect in terms of custody all depends on where the parent lives. Some states have laws that prohibit judges from using sexual orientation alone to deny custody or limit visitation. In states with large LGBT populations and courts that are used to nontraditional families, sexual orientation shouldn't be a factor in custody or visitation decisions. However, it's always possible that an individual judge could have biases, no matter where you live. And in some states, courts are allowed to consider sexual orientation as a major factor in custody and visitation decisions. It's quite common in those states for judges to rule that a parent's same-sex partner can't be around when children visit, or that the parent can't expose the kids to a "gay lifestyle." In the worst-case scenario, parents can be denied all contact with their children on the basis of their sexual orientation.

Transgender parents are even more likely to find themselves on the losing end of a custody fight—or find that they have to do a lot of education to be treated equally as a parent.

If you're in a legal same-sex marriage or domestic partnership, and you and your partner are both legal parents of your kids, your sexual orientation will have no impact on the court's consideration of custody and visitation matters. The same standards that apply to all divorcing couples will apply to you.

If you think you've suffered illegal discrimination in family court because of your sexual orientation, contact the National Center for Lesbian Rights at www.nclrights.org or the Lambda Legal Defense and Education Fund at www.lambdalegal.org for information. If you're a transgender parent, contact the Transgender Law Center at http://transgenderlawcenter.org.

Making Shared Parenting Work

Marriages end, but children are forever. Shared parenting presents some of the greatest challenges of divorce—and unlike property issues, they're not necessarily permanently resolved when the divorce is final. You will continue to have a relationship with the other parent for many years to come, probably for the rest of your life. In fact, that is a result devoutly to be hoped for, because it would mean that the two of you were able to cooperate enough to share in your kids' lives even as they become adults. But that's the hoped-for future. In the here and now, you need to work out shared parenting, and you need to do it with the focus on what is best for your kids.

If You Share Physical Custody

Parenting time doesn't need to be split exactly 50–50 to create two homes—any parent who is actively parenting should create an environment where the kids feel comfortable and completely at home. Consider these tips:

Make both houses home. Ideally, each home will have everything the kids need: toys, school supplies, clothes, and foods they like. They should also be able to see the same friends when they're with either parent, and not have one set of friends with one parent and another when they're with the other. And if you and your spouse are able to cooperate enough to generate consistent rules about things like bedtimes and video game usage, it'll make your lives much easier.

Consider getting support from others. Even if you think you and your spouse will do okay with a shared physical custody arrangement, it can't hurt to get some tips and support from people who have been through it or have helped other families. Talk to friends who you can see are successfully coparenting after a divorce. You may want to locate a class for divorcing parents or, if you think you need more support, a therapist or custody evaluator who can work with you to improve your shared parenting skills. This can be particularly helpful in a high-conflict situation; the intervention of a third person can defuse tension and facilitate productive negotiations.

Stay in touch. It's important that you keep in touch with your spouse about what's going on with your kids. If it's hard to talk, you can make sure that the school sends progress reports and information to each of you separately, but you'll still have to share information about extracurricular activities as well as moment-to-moment concerns like a child's cold or an upcoming recital. Some parents use a notebook that goes back and forth with the kids, but if you go this route, be sure that whatever you write is absolutely neutral and factual, because the kids are likely to read it.

Email is a common and often very useful way to communicate, and there are also websites where you can set up message boards and calendars for communicating about day-to-day scheduling and parenting issues. The cost is reasonable. For example, check out www.ourfamilywizard.com, www.jointparents.com, www.cofamilies.com, www.custodyxchange.com, www.sharekids.com, or www.parentingtime.net. All of these sites allow you to keep an expense log and to negotiate schedule changes like trading days, for between $100 and $200 per year.

In many relationships, one parent is the primary caretaker for the children. That parent knows where the information about the kids' doctor and dentist is kept, who drives the carpool on what days, and when picture day at school is happening. If you haven't been that parent, get ready for a crash course in management as you start to take care of the kids on your own. You may be surprised to find just how much your spouse has been doing to keep the kids functioning in their busy lives—and a bit overwhelmed at your new responsibilities. If you're the parent who has been doing most of the caretaking, don't keep information from your spouse out of spite or because you want some kind of advantage if you end up in court. Do what's best for your kids and share all the important lists, phone numbers, schedules, and other relevant data.

RESOURCE

Family planning. Free Spirit Publishing offers quite a few resources for families going through divorce, including a kit titled *Juggling Act: Handling Divorce Without Dropping the Ball: A Survival Kit for Parents and Kids,* by Roberta Beyer and Kent Winchester. The kit includes both of Beyer and Winchester's books (*Speaking of Divorce* and *What in the World Do You Do When Your Parents Divorce?*), along with a calendar and communication system for parents. The calendar comes with stickers that make it user-friendly for kids and helps them to get involved in dealing with the schedule in a positive way. And parents find the communication tools helpful.

Another communication tool for parents sharing custody is the *Ekman Co-Parenting Journal,* by Joseph A. Ekman and Bruce Bess, distributed through the About the Kids Foundation at www.aboutthekids.org. This tool allows each parent to record important events.

(Extended) Family Matters

Just as you will continue to have the other parent in your life at least until your children are adults, you'll also keep your in-laws. You may be painfully aware that you and your spouse aren't the only family members concerned about their ongoing relationship with your kids after the divorce. Grandparents and other relatives often have a lot invested in the decisions you make during your divorce. Dealing with them can be a real challenge, especially if you're in a high-conflict situation and family members have taken sides or blamed one spouse for the divorce.

Your Spouse's Family

If you're the parent with primary custody (sometimes called the residential parent), you may have a great deal of control over your children's relationship with their relatives on your spouse's side. If you've had a decent relationship with your in-laws during your marriage, reassure both the kids and the grandparents that you intend to support their relationship in whatever ways are appropriate. If they don't have much of a relationship to start with, you don't have to go out and cultivate one. But if they live nearby and are involved in your kids' everyday lives, let them know that doesn't have to change. The same goes for aunts, uncles, and cousins your children are close to.

On the other hand, if your relationship with your spouse's relatives deteriorated with the divorce or was never good, you may want to let your spouse deal with keeping the kids in contact with that side of the family. Especially if the relatives blame you for the divorce and are hostile, you're within your rights to stay away from them.

If you're in a high-conflict divorce and you are considering trying to object to your kids seeing your spouse's relatives, make sure you understand your state's laws on nonparent visitation. It's not a simple area. In general, nonparents don't have a legal right to ask for visitation with your kids if you don't want to allow it. However, some states use a "best interests of the child" standard in reviewing nonparent visitation cases, and some have specific laws covering grandparent visitation, so if you really don't want your child's grandparents to have any visitation, you may need to show why the contact would be bad for the kids. And unless you have hard evidence that the grandparents or other relatives are abusive or otherwise dangerous to your kids, you don't have any control over who the kids see when your spouse has the kids.

Stepparents

You're a stepparent if your spouse has children from a previous marriage whom you've been parenting during your marriage but haven't adopted. Courts are split on whether, after divorce, you should get visitation after separation with your spouse's children, who aren't legally related to you. But most states at least allow you to go to court and ask for visitation, and some states look to the best interests of the child—rather than the rights of the parents—in making decisions on stepparent visitation.

The length of your marriage and the degree to which you acted as a parent will be the major factors in the court's decision. The judge may also consider the level of conflict in your relationship with your spouse and with the child's other legal parent. If you have a high-conflict divorce, it's less likely that you'll end up spending any meaningful time with your ex's children.

If you're the legal parent and your spouse is the stepparent, try not to abuse the power you likely have to keep your spouse from continuing to spend time with your children. If the kids think of your spouse as a parent, ending that relationship suddenly will be traumatic for them. Try to act in a way that's consistent with the actual relationship between the children and your spouse, even if you don't legally have to.

Major Life Events

Especially if your kids are young, you'll be dealing for many years with big events like school graduations, bar and bat mitzvahs, confirmations and quinceañeras, birthday parties, important sports events, and even your children's weddings and the births of their own children. Other relatives have milestones, too, and want their whole family around to mark them. In other words, your family will be gathering for many years to come, and your family still includes your ex-spouse, as the other parent of your children.

If you tend to be the person who organizes family events, try to be as inclusive as you can with your spouse and your spouse's family— again, whom you invite should be based on whom your child feels close to and would want to have at an event that's special to the child. When you do invite members of your spouse's family, make it clear that they are genuinely welcome, and be gracious when they show up. You may have to take some deep breaths—especially if the list of people your child wants there includes your former spouse's new love interest. Keep your focus on your children's welfare and you'll benefit; they will be more likely to feel that they belong to a family and that they matter to the people who are important to them.

If One Parent Has Primary Physical Custody

If you are the primary custodial parent, having your kids with you the majority of the time may feel like a victory to you, but it comes with an important responsibility: to support your child's relationship with the other parent. You should do this because it's best for your child, but know that if you don't facilitate visitation or if you denigrate your spouse in front of your kids, you may pay for it later in court in the form of a change in the custody or visitation plan. Courts favor parents who coparent cooperatively, and if the other parent can show you're not doing that, there will be consequences.

If you're the noncustodial parent, don't overcompensate for not being with your kids all the time. Your challenge is to establish a second home where your kids feel comfortable, safe, and loved—not to make every minute fun. If you live far away and can't visit weekly, or maybe even monthly, regular phone calls are a must. Current technologies are good news for faraway parents. Email and texting can be good ways to stay in close contact on a daily basis, as can phone calls that include video.

Your parenting plan might include what's called "virtual" visitation, meaning the use of webcams for kids and parents to (literally) see each other. You can schedule regular visitation times just as you would in-person visits. It makes a big difference to a child to actually see a distant parent's face, as opposed to just talking on the phone—especially when kids are younger and often don't enjoy phone conversations.

> ## Ten Rules of Sharing Custody
>
> 1. Never bad-mouth your spouse to your kids.
> 2. Never ask your kids to take messages to the other parent.
> 3. Don't ask your kids to tell you about the other parent's activities or companions.
> 4. Never ask your kids to take sides.
> 5. Let your kids call their other parent anytime they want to.
> 6. Always have an upbeat, positive attitude at transitions.
> 7. Never threaten to restrict visitation if you don't get support payments.
> 8. If your kids want to spend more time with the other parent, consider their requests with an open mind.
> 9. Cut the other parent some slack about a bit of tardiness or other failures to comply to the letter with the schedule (this applies in particular to the parent with primary custody).
> 10. Share information with the other parent about what's going on with your kids when they're with you.

Virtual Visitation at www.internetvisitation.org is a clearinghouse with news, information, and resources for parents trying to bridge distance between themselves and their kids. And there is a plethora of programs like Skype, Facetime, and Google that support virtual visitation

When You Just Can't Get Along With Your Ex

Even if your divorce is very contentious and you and your spouse can't agree on anything, you're still going to have to figure out how to coparent with the least damage to your kids. After all, no matter how difficult you find their other parent, the kids are still entitled to have meaningful relationships with both of their parents. Here are some ideas that might help.

- Ask neutral friends—or a court-sponsored transfer system—to help you with changeovers. Minimize your contact.
- When you do have contact, always be civil. You don't have to pretend you're thrilled to be there, but don't be outright hostile— stay polite and courteous.
- Use email to communicate, and say only the minimum that's needed to deal with the issue at hand. Websites like www.ourfamilywizard.com, www.parentingtime.net, www. jointparents.com, or www.sharekids.com can help by providing a structure for communicating.
- Try not to make changes in the parenting plan after it's in place. Life is unpredictable, and sometimes you may need to ask your spouse to be flexible, but make sure it's really crucial before rocking the boat, even in ways you think should be no big deal. If you need a change, don't demand—ask whether you can be accommodated. ●

Basics of Child Support

All parents, whether or not they're divorced and whether or not they live with their children, are required to support their children financially. That means that both you and your children's other parent are responsible for giving your kids all the necessities of life until they become legal adults—and sometimes longer—regardless of your family's living situation or your marital status.

That part is clear. But there are always questions about how support is calculated, how long it lasts, how it affects your taxes, and where to get the information you need. Let's start with the most fundamental question: who pays?

Who Pays Support?

Which parent makes support payments to the other depends mostly on two factors:

- where the kids spend their time, and
- how much each parent earns.

The general rule is that if the kids spend more than half their time with one parent, then the other parent is required to pay child support. The reasoning is that when kids live most of the time with one parent, that parent will be spending more than the other on housing, food, clothing, and everything else the kids need—in fact, many states presume that the primary residential parent spends all of his or her income on supporting the kids. So the other parent, who is also responsible for support, should be required to contribute to those expenses.

Income also plays a role. Even when spouses share custody 50–50, a parent who earns a lot more than the other usually pays child support to the lower-earning spouse. In unusual cases, if the custodial parent's income is significantly higher than the other parent's income, the noncustodial parent may receive support—in general, based on the amount of time spent with the children.

How Child Support Is Calculated

The basic rule is pretty simple: The higher the paying parent's income, the higher the support payment will be. But every state has its own formula for calculating child support, designed to provide children with the basic support needed to feed, clothe, and care for them, including things like making sure they have medical insurance. Most of the formulas are quite complicated mathematically, running to a few pages in the law books. Fortunately, almost all states offer simple online calculators or worksheets that let regular people easily get an idea of what child support should be. (More on this below.)

If child support is calculated by a formula, why would parents ever be arguing about the amount? The answer is that the state formulas are only guidelines. Judges are allowed to deviate from the formula amount if there is a good reason to. So there is still room for negotiation—or if that fails, court fights—about:

Income. Is one parent not reporting all his or her actual income? Could the paying parent easily get a better-paying job and so afford bigger payments?

Special needs. Does a child have unusual needs that require more support?

Too much money. A paying parent who has a very large income—so large that the standard percentage of that amount would be much more than is necessary for the children—might argue for a lower payment.

Other expenses. A parent with unusual extra expenses might not be able to afford the guideline amount.

All these issues are discussed below in "Deviating From the Guidelines."

The fact remains that unless your family does have unusual circumstances, you're going to end up with a child support amount that is very close to the guideline amount. So don't waste your time, money, and energy fighting about child support; instead, figure out about what the guideline amount will be and try to settle at an amount that's close to it. If you and the other parent can accept the guideline amount or use it as a baseline to decide on an amount of support that seems fair to you, a judge will almost certainly approve it.

How to Estimate Child Support Obligations

Whether you're trying to figure out temporary support or come to a final resolution of your child support amounts, you can use your state's child support guidelines to get a general idea of what a court would order as support.

> **TIP**
> **Especially when you're negotiating temporary support, put your best effort into resolving the issue without involving lawyers or judges.** Temporary support is intended to keep your household running and your kids clothed and fed until you and the other parent can evaluate the financial situation thoroughly and work out an appropriate amount. Escalating things at that early stage just earns you the right to pay twice for the same battle, because it's very likely someone's not going to be happy with the temporary support order and will litigate the issue again.

Getting Access to Child Support Calculators

If you have a lawyer representing you or available to answer questions, the lawyer probably has software that will calculate support for your state. That will get you the most accurate numbers.

If you're not working with a lawyer, you can get an estimate of the guideline amount by using a free online calculator for your state. An online calculator won't give you the exact amount of support that a judge might order, especially if you don't have all the required information, like your spouse's exact income or deductions or how much the kids' health insurance costs. But by entering basic information, including your income and your best guess at the other parent's, basic information about your children, and what child care and medical expenses are, you'll get a decent estimate.

Most state guidelines are available through online calculators (or downloadable worksheets) offered by the court system, the child support enforcement agency for your state, or a commercial website. You can find a website for your state listed in "State Child Support Calculators," in the appendix.

If your state doesn't have any resources to help you, or if they're hard to use, try the simple calculators at www.alllaw.com. (Click "Child Support Calculators" on the left of the screen. It's also possible that your state's website will redirect you to alllaw.com.) Alllaw.com and other free sites will give you a ballpark figure, but it won't be as accurate as either an official government website or the commercial software that lawyers use.

Defining "Income"

All guideline calculations begin with the parents' income. Some states consider both parents' income; others consider only what the noncustodial parent earns.

It might seem that what a person earns is a simple question, but in fact, states define "income" differently, and significant disputes can arise about what constitutes income for child support purposes. Some states use gross income (your entire salary or self-employment earnings); some use net (what you take home). Some include gifts, bonuses, and overtime while others do not. Investment income or passive income from a trust also may or may not be counted as income. An unusual rule in New York says that the court looks at local taxes and also alimony that one parent is paying in the current marriage, not just previous marriages. It's unusual because most courts believe that child support is more important than alimony and calculate child support first, and then evaluate what's left in setting alimony.

THE LAW IN REAL LIFE

A Tennessee appellate court ruled that payments for a leased apartment and car that were made directly to the landlord and the leasing company on behalf of a divorced father should be included in his income for purposes of calculating child support. The court said these perks were "fringe benefits" of the father's employment (which, by the way, was in a company owned by him and his parents) and should count as income.

The Colorado Court of Appeals ruled that Social Security benefits that a divorcing mother received on behalf of her minor child from a prior marriage weren't part of her income for child support purposes. The Social Security benefits belonged to the child alone, the court said, because they were death benefits payable as a result of the death of that child's father.

A tuition credit that a mother received for her two children because she worked in the private school they attended shouldn't be included in her gross income for purposes of calculating support, said the Vermont Supreme Court. The tuition credit did not reduce the mother's living expenses, so it did not count as income.

A father in Tennessee had income not only from a regular job, but also from gambling—his winnings in the relevant year were over $1 million. A trial judge ruled that the winnings should be counted as income even though the father's tax returns showed losses offsetting 100% of his winnings. A state appeals court reversed the decision, on the grounds that the important thing in calculating support is to figure out what a person's true income is.

Other Factors

Income and time spent with the children are the most important factors affecting child support, but state support guidelines commonly also consider other factors, including:

- Child support or alimony either parent receives—or child support or alimony that one parent is paying—from a previous marriage
- Whether either parent is responsible for children from another marriage

- Which parent is paying for health insurance, and the cost
- Which parent is paying for day care, and the cost
- Whether either parent is required to pay union dues or has other amounts deducted from paychecks
- How many children the parent is supporting (many of the expenses of raising children, like providing housing and many other necessities, aren't twice as much for two children as for one; guideline support takes into account the number of children and calculates added support for each)
- Ages of the children (kids get more expensive as they get older, so some states' guidelines provide for automatic changes when a child reaches a certain age—in other words, the guidelines are at one amount for kids under six, and another for kids six to 12, and so on)
- Whether either parent receives irregular income such as bonuses or incentive pay, has stock options, or expects severance pay or other lump-sum payments, and
- Whether either parent lives with a new partner or spouse who contributes to household expenses.

Deviating From the Guidelines

You and the other parent are free, within limits, to make whatever child support decisions you want, including one of you voluntarily parting ways with the guidelines and paying a higher amount or accepting a lower amount because it fits with your plan for your restructured family. For example, you could decide that one of you is going to stay home with the kids until they get to high school and, to facilitate that, the other parent is going to pay more support than the guidelines would require. Even though you agree, the judge will review your joint decision and decide whether the amount is appropriate. In most states, you can't agree to an amount that's different from the guidelines if either parent receives or has applied for public assistance (like food stamps).

If you can't agree, and one parent wants the court to order a support amount that is different from guideline support, that parent will have to persuade the judge to approve it. Whatever your reason for wanting to set an amount different from the guidelines, be prepared to show the judge clear documentation of the reasons for what you're asking for. Bring proof of any fact you're claiming, as well as a budget or spreadsheet showing the relevant financial information.

Arguments for Raising Support Payments

If you and the other parent can't agree on a child support amount, the judge might be persuaded to order an amount higher than state guidelines call for if there are good reasons to do so. Here are some common scenarios.

The noncustodial parent can afford more. The paying parent earns a great deal of money, has significant assets or income from separate property, or receives in-kind compensation like employer-provided housing or vehicle.

The paying parent is shirking. A parent has chosen a career that results in lower earnings than the parent's training or experience could command. For example, say a parent with a lucrative medical practice quit to become a cruise ship physician, for much less money. A court might calculate support based on what the parent could be earning (that's called "imputing" income to the parent), especially if the judge believes the parent took the lower-paying gig to avoid paying support. (In the example stated, the court might also include housing and food expenses, because the parent wouldn't have to pay those while on the ship.). This comes up more often after divorce, when people make life changes, but it can also be a factor in setting initial support.

A child has special needs or interests. A child with unusual medical, psychological, or educational needs may require more support. Also, a judge might order the paying parent to pay an additional amount so that the child can continue a favorite activity such as music or sports.

THE LAW IN REAL LIFE

The Texas Supreme Court held that a parent doesn't have to prove that the other parent is trying to avoid paying child support—the court can still apply state guidelines to the paying parent's earning potential rather than actual earnings. However, the judge should give the parent the chance to state the reasons for the lower earnings, and should factor in reasons such as changing jobs in order to live closer to the children or spend more time with them.

A father who lost his job had to pay support based on what he was earning when he was fired. The Iowa Court of Appeals said the judge should consider whether the parent's failure to reach his earning potential was self-inflicted, as opposed to being a result of circumstances beyond the parent's control. In this case, the court said the father's reduced income was due to his own actions and inactions.

The North Carolina Court of Appeals also held that a father who lost his job after being jailed and registered as a sex offender for sexually abusing his daughter should pay support based on his previous salary. The court ruled that the father's problems finding work were "clearly foreseeable results" of his abuse of his daughter.

Arguments for Lowering Support

Judges also have the power to order a child support amount that's lower than the state guidelines suggest, if circumstances warrant. Here are some examples of arguments that parents make; which may or may not convince a judge to lower support.

The guideline amount is significantly more than what's needed. The noncustodial parent makes so much money that the guideline support amount would be much more than is needed to pay for the children's regular expenses, the judge might reduce the amount. But both parents will always be required to contribute to supporting the kids, and the judge won't mind ordering a payment that allows the children to maintain a lifestyle that's consistent with the parent's wealth, especially if that's how they live when they're with that parent.

One parent is paying for extras. If the paying parent is also paying 100% of expenses for private school, uninsured medical expenses, or other significant expenses that might otherwise be split between the parents, that might be taken into account.

The noncustodial parent truly can't pay. The noncustodial parent earns very little money, has other expenses that make it impossible to meet the guideline amount, or has recently lost a job. The court might reduce payments but would probably order the parents to return to court at a set time for a review of their circumstances.

The paying parent has other family expenses. A parent who has custody of a disabled child or is taking care of an aging parent who requires extensive care and has unusual medical expenses may not be able to afford the guideline amount.

THE LAW IN REAL LIFE

Parents in Michigan split custody of their children, with the daughter living with the mother and the son with the father. The trial court found that the father had alienated the son from the mother and interfered with their relationship, and that the son rarely visited with his mother. The trial court deviated from guideline support and calculated support obligations as though the son spent overnight time with his mother, which reduced her support obligation and increased the father's. The appeals court reversed the decision, saying that deviating from guideline support wasn't an appropriate way to punish the father for his interference or to enforce the existing custody order.

The parent is paying other expenses that benefit the child. Parents who are providing other benefits to the child may argue that those benefits should be considered "in-kind" (nonmonetary) support and offset against support obligations.

THE LAW IN REAL LIFE

A father argued that his payments for mortgage and house-related expenses should count against his child support obligation. The court said no, in a decision that was upheld by the Maine Supreme Judicial Council. The support obligation had to be paid in money unless the expenditure met three criteria, including being directly related to "an essential purpose" of the support obligation. Because the father had an ownership interest in the house that he would protect even if he had no children living there, the payments were for his benefit and not directly related to the support order.

The child is receiving income from another source. It's not unusual for a paying parent to argue that if the child is getting some kind of income—whether it's in the form of cash or benefits—from another source, the parent's support obligation should be reduced by that amount. For the most part, guideline calculators don't take into account in-kind support, with the exception of items like health insurance and child care, both of which are factored into guideline support. Income that is attributed to a child is *not* usually accepted as a reason to decrease a parent's support obligation.

THE LAW IN REAL LIFE

The New Hampshire Supreme Court held that a trial judge correctly refused to reduce a father's child support obligation by the amount his disabled son received every month in the form of Social Security Disability benefits.

Similarly, an Illinois court of appeals supported a trial judge's decision to deny a disabled father's request to reduce his required payments for his son's uncovered medical expenses because the boy received dependent benefits on the basis of his father's disability. The dependent benefits already covered the father's child support obligation, and the amount of the benefit was greater than the amount of support required, but the court said that the balance was "a gratuity" belonging to the child, and couldn't be applied for the benefit of the father, who still had to pay a separate amount for the uncovered medical expenses.

Creating Your Own Written Agreement

If you and your spouse want to try to negotiate support outside of court, it's a good idea for each of you to start by calculating support yourselves. Depending on what resources you use, you may come up with amounts that are pretty close, and that may be enough for you if you're both willing to accept what the guidelines show. If they're really far apart, check your assumptions and make sure you're both using the same numbers. If you want to write your own support agreement and present it to the court, you'll need to cover more than the basic monthly support amount. Here's what to think about.

Issues to Cover

Baseline child support doesn't take into account things like tutoring, summer camp, music lessons, or snowboarding trips. But your agreement can. You can also anticipate future needs and the potential for things to change, and include those items in your agreement—for example, you can ask a court to make orders about possible future events that would result in temporary reductions or increases in support. Remember, too, that you can always ask for a change in the amount of support based on a change of circumstances. See Chapter 9 for more about modifying a support order.

When the Kids Are Away

You might include a provision that if the kids live away from their usual home for more than a month—maybe at a lengthy summer camp— child support is reduced for that month. The custodial parent should still get some support, as there will still be household expenses, so it doesn't make sense to eliminate support entirely or to call for a reduction for less than a month. And this assumes that the parents share the expenses of the camp equally or that the noncustodial parent paid—otherwise the custodial parent would be losing support and paying the camp expenses, which isn't fair.

Financial Changes for Either Parent

Some agreements or court orders provide for an automatic increase in support to keep pace with inflation, or an adjustment—either up or down—if either party's income changes by a certain percentage. The order may incorporate regular increases, for example in connection with a cost of living index, according to your relative incomes, or by some percentage per year (you can predict that kids will get more expensive as they grow).

Every state's rules say that you can ask for a change if there's a meaningful change in circumstances, so make sure your support order includes a provision that you and the other parent keep each other informed of any changes in employment, incomes, or benefits. Your state law may require that, but there's no harm in including it in the agreement or order.

Income Withholding Orders or Direct Payment

All states issue an automatic income withholding order (IWO), also called a wage garnishment, as part of a child support order. This means that the support payments come out of the paying parent's salary and are paid directly by the employer. (Wage garnishments aren't available if the paying parent is self-employed or unemployed.) But you and the other parent can agree to direct payment if you consider it easier that way. If you do decide on direct payment, be sure that the support order says that the recipient parent can garnish the paying parent's wages without going back to court, once there's no payment for a certain number of months. There's more about direct payments and enforcement in Chapter 9.

> **CAUTION**
>
> **See a lawyer if you want to pay child support in a lump sum.** A few states allow the paying parent to pay child support in advance in a lump sum, but most don't. And it's not necessarily a good idea—calculating a fair lump sum amount is a lot harder than figuring out what is an appropriate monthly amount; there's no opportunity to modify support later if the children's needs change; and it relies on the custodial parent to ration the funds appropriately. Think carefully, and ask a lawyer, before making any agreement with your spouse about it.

Securing Payment

If the paying parent is self-employed or has sporadic income and support payments will be made directly, you might want to include something in your agreement about making sure payment happens. Two options are for the paying parent to fund a savings account that the recipient parent is authorized to access only when payments are late by an agreed amount of time, or having the paying parent post a bond—a sort of insurance policy, guaranteeing payment. The latter might be challenging, as bond companies don't usually work with individuals, but you can see whether it's an option where you live. Some states require you to deposit funds with the court, or provide for bonds, which means there will be bonding companies in those states that will work with the paying parent to issue a bond.

You can also address the issue of what would happen if the paying parent becomes disabled and unable to earn income, or dies, while still obligated to pay support. Disability and life insurance can protect children and families from loss of significant income—but an insurance policy purchased for this purpose needs to be owned by the recipient parent, so that the paying parent doesn't have the ability to change the beneficiary.

College Expenses

Although many states allow parents to stop paying support when a child reaches age 18, lots of parents consider a college degree important enough that they agree to continue paying child support as long as the child is in school or reaches age 22 or so. However, one study found that divorce has a severe negative effect on how much support college students receive from parents: only 29% of children with divorced parents get parental support for college expenses, compared with 88% of children from intact families.

If you expect your children to attend college, consider seeking a separate college support order in addition to your divorce order and parenting plan. A few states simply end a court's authority to make orders after a child reaches adulthood, regardless of the parents' agreement, but in most states you can prepare a college plan that the court can enforce later. A college support plan may specify:

- how long support will last (usually expressed in a number of semesters or quarters of college or the age of the child)
- which parent will be responsible for what percentage of expenses each year
- what "expenses" includes—just tuition, or books and living expenses as well
- whether or not the child must be enrolled full time
- whether expenses are to be paid directly to the school, to the student, or to the custodial parent
- which school(s) the parents will pay for
- conditions such as maintaining a certain grade point average or proving regular attendance, and
- whether payments are limited to a certain amount, such as the cost of tuition at a certain state school.

The college support plan has to deal with the uncertainty of how school will be financed—through private payments from the parents, student loans, grants, or, as is most common, a combination of those sources. It's not unusual for parents to agree that college expenses not covered by financial aid will be shared in proportion to the parents' income at the time the student begins attending college. This way the parents don't have to try to predict, especially when the child is young, which parent will be more able to pay these expenses by the time the child is actually ready to attend college. If you want to agree to something like this, it's probably a good idea to have a lawyer's help drawing up the agreement.

Consider Your Own Future

If you find yourself negotiating about how long child support will last, think about how paying your child's college expenses might affect your own retirement planning. In some cases, instead of paying out cash you can make use of student loans, grants, scholarships, and work-study awards.

Financial aid rules can be confusing. The Free Application for Federal Student Aid (FAFSA, available at www.fafsa.ed.gov) is an application for federal college aid that you fill out once every year and use for any schools you're interested in.

The custodial parent is responsible for completing the FAFSA. This means either the parent with primary physical custody or the parent with whom the child physically lived for the majority of the time in the year preceding the application. If the time was split exactly equally, then the parent who provided the most financial support should complete the form (probably the same parent who claimed the child as a dependent on the most recent tax return).

Eligibility for federal aid is based on the household income of only the custodial parent. If the custodial parent has remarried, the stepparent's income will be considered as well. The noncustodial parent's income isn't considered, which is usually to the applicant's advantage. However, child support received from the noncustodial parent must be included as income in the form. That's only the federal aid—private colleges and universities may well require a supplemental application that seeks information about the noncustodial parent's income and resources.

How to Prepare an Agreement

It's absolutely crucial that whatever you agree about child support, you put the agreement in writing and submit it to the court. When you first agree to a support amount and payment schedule, you can just write a short agreement (similar to the separation agreements shown in Chapter 1) and sign it. But it's not binding in court. Without a judge's signature turning your agreement into an order, it's not enforceable and if the paying parent stops paying, you will have to go through the two-step process of first establishing the order and then trying to force the parent to pay.

Every state has its own forms for establishing a child support order, and you'll need to find your state's forms and use them. If you've already filed your initial divorce paperwork, the process should look something like this:

Step 1. Complete a form that sets out your agreements about support. It will probably have the word "agreement" or "stipulation" in the title. Both parents will need to sign the form showing that they agree to the support arrangement. To complete the form, you'll probably have to state the amount of support to be paid, when it will be paid each month, whether the paying parent chooses to exercise the right to have an income withholding order issued, who will be providing and paying for health insurance for the children, and whether the arrangement is intended to be temporary or permanent.

Step 2. Complete a proposed order for the judge to sign, with the same information about your support arrangement.

Step 3. Submit all the paperwork to the court. You may have to pay a filing fee.

If you haven't begun your divorce process, you'll have to do that before you can submit the paperwork for your support agreement. See Chapter 4 for more about that.

Many counties now have self-help centers for family law matters, so if you are working without an attorney, that's probably your best resource for locating the forms and getting them filled out properly. If you do have a lawyer, the lawyer will prepare the appropriate forms for you. You can also check out some of the do-it-yourself resources listed in "How to Get Your Agreements Made Into Orders," in Chapter 4.

Going to Court for a Support Decision

If you don't manage to work out your own support agreement and write it down, then you'll have to ask a court to make a decision for you. The only time it makes sense to spend your time and money doing this is when you have a really significant argument about some important element of the calculation. For example, you might disagree on what constitutes "income" for purposes of calculating support, or feel strongly that your spouse could be earning significantly more than the amount that is being used to arrive at guideline support. For more about what a court hearing is like and how to prepare, see Chapter 6.

Temporary Support While the Divorce Is Pending

If you need child support right now—after all, your divorce might take a year or longer to complete—try to get a temporary agreement in place without resorting to court. Even if you know you and your spouse won't agree on the final child support amount, do your best to agree on a temporary amount of support. Then write up a short agreement that covers these points:

- what the support amount is
- when it is to begin
- when in each month it will be paid, and
- that you agree the amount is temporary.

To figure out the amount, see "How to Estimate Child Support Obligations," above. Or simply look at your income and expenses and ballpark the amount that needs to change hands right away. You're not required to use state child support guidelines to agree about temporary support, though you will be when you create an order to submit to the judge for signature.

Even if you've written down your agreement, you won't be able to get any help enforcing the other parent's agreement to pay support until you go to court and get an order from a judge making it official. So if the other parent has stopped paying for necessary expenses, you'll have to go into court right away for a temporary order. See Chapter 6 for more about what that's like.

If you're in a mediation process, you should immediately report to the mediator—and your consulting lawyer, if you have one—that the other parent isn't paying child support as you agreed. The mediator may schedule a session to discuss support, at which time you can find out whether there's a reason for the nonpayment and discuss how to protect your children's right to support. Your own lawyer, if you have one, may need to get involved if you're not getting anywhere—again, most likely to go into court and get a court order that can be enforced.

If you're not able to agree on an amount, you can take the issue either to mediation or to court. If you're the custodial parent and you can't get the other parent to provide enough money to support you and the children, it may be that your best option is to go to court for a temporary order. This type of court order is sometimes called "pendente lite" (pen-den-tay lee-tay) meaning it applies while the divorce case is pending. Chapter 6 discusses temporary court orders.

Taxes and Your Children

You're probably used to taking your kids into account when you do your taxes each year. With a divorce, there's more to think about, including how you'll share exemptions, credits, and deductions and how you and your former spouse will file your taxes.

Basic Rule for Child Support

You can't take a deduction for money you pay for child support, and you don't declare it as income if you receive it. In other words, child support payments are tax-neutral. As you review the rules below, you might notice that many tax issues are determined by custody choices; it's also true that support transactions are intertwined with taxes.

Dependent Exemptions

When you file your personal income tax return, you are allowed one exemption for each person you claim as a dependent. The dependent exemption amount changes periodically; for 2015, it's $4,000. Most children who live at home qualify as dependents because they meet these three requirements:

- the child is under 19 at the end of the year, or is under 24 and a full-time student, or is disabled
- the child lived with you for more than half the year, and
- the child didn't provide more than half of his or her own support during the tax year.

In general, the parent with primary custody is entitled to the dependent exemptions, because the child lives with that parent for more than half the year. However, you can agree that the noncustodial parent may take the dependent exemptions for one or all of your children. If you're the noncustodial parent, you can take the exemption if all of the following are true:

- your divorce order or separation agreement says that you can take the exemption, or your spouse signs an IRS Form 8332 giving up the exemption
- you and your spouse are legally divorced, are separated under a written separation agreement, or lived apart for the last six months of the tax year
- your child lived with you or your spouse, or both, for at least half the year, and
- you and your spouse paid more than half of your child's support during the year (the rest can be paid by other relatives or public benefits).

If your marital settlement agreement says that the custodial spouse is releasing an exemption to the other spouse, the first requirement will be met when the agreement becomes part of the final divorce order. The custodial parent can give up the exemption for one year, all future years, or specified future years (for example, the next five years, or alternating years until the child is an adult).

Divorcing parents with more than one child sometimes consider splitting exemptions, with each parent taking the exemption for one child. There's nothing improper about this, but you should calculate whether it really provides any tax benefits. Depending on the particular combination of your incomes and your other tax issues, it might not end up being to your advantage. If you're not sure what to do about your exemptions, have a tax professional calculate what your taxes would look like if one parent takes all the exemptions and if the exemptions are split. Then do whatever is most advantageous for both of you.

If you agree to transfer exemptions, include the agreement in the settlement agreement or order. You can always change the decision later and shift the exemptions by using IRS Form 8332. Agreements about dependent exemptions must be in writing, so be sure to use the form—don't just make the change yourselves, or you may receive a visit from the IRS.

Head of Household Status

If you have physical custody of at least one child, you may be able to file as head of household—it's a filing status, like "married" or "single." The head of household tax rate is usually lower than single or married filing separately, and you will receive a higher standard deduction. You can file as a head of household if you:

- are unmarried or "considered unmarried" (see below) on the last day of the tax year
- paid more than half the expenses of keeping up your household during the year, and
- had a qualifying person living with you for more than half the year (a dependent child is a qualifying person).

In order to be "considered unmarried" by the IRS, you have to meet five requirements:

- You must file separately from your spouse.
- You must have paid more than half the expenses of your household during the tax year.
- Your spouse must not have lived with you for the last six months of the tax year.
- You must have had custody of your child for more than half the time during the tax year.
- You can claim the dependent exemption for your child. You meet this test even if you've voluntarily agreed to allow your spouse to claim the exemption.

Tax Credits

In addition to the dependent exemption, a number of tax credits may be available to you, depending on circumstances.

The child tax credit provides a credit for a child who's under 17, didn't provide more than half of his or her own support during the tax year, and lived with you for more than half of the tax year. But if you are a noncustodial parent taking the dependent exemption for that child by agreement with your spouse, you can also take the child tax credit even though your child didn't live with you for more than half of the tax year.

The child care tax credit can be taken only by the custodial parent. It reimburses you for child care expenses up to a certain amount.

The education tax credit is a tax credit for post-high-school education expenses. It can be taken by either a custodial or noncustodial parent and follows the dependent exemption (meaning the same parent takes both).

The earned income tax credit is available only to a custodial parent with earned income below a certain amount. For the 2015 tax year, the income ceiling was $39,131 for one qualifying child, $44,454 for two, and $47,747 for three or more.

RESOURCE

Check out the IRS website. There's a great deal of information about divorce and taxes in these IRS publications:

- Publication 501, *Exemptions, Standard Deduction, and Filing Information*
- Publication 504, *Divorced or Separated Individuals*
- Publication 972, *Child Tax Credit*, and
- Publication 503, *Child and Dependent Care Expenses*.

Health Insurance and Medical Child Support Orders

Payments for medical insurance can be an important part of child support. Often, one parent's employer provides medical insurance for the entire family through a group insurance plan. After separation or divorce, the kids can stay on the same plan they've been on—in fact, under the federal health insurance reform laws passed in 2010, employers are required to allow adult children to remain on a parent's insurance, up to age 26. (In addition, insurers can't refuse to provide insurance for children under 19 on the basis of the child's preexisting medical condition.)

A child support agreement or order might require the parent who isn't providing the insurance to pay part of the premium if it's not fully covered by the employer—or the cost of the insurance will be factored into the calculation of support under the state guidelines. Any settlement agreement or order should also address the issue of who will pay for uninsured medical expenses. If it doesn't, the parent who's providing the insurance, or the parent who takes the kids to their appointments, may end up getting stuck with those expenses.

Most parents are perfectly willing to maintain kids on their health insurance plans after a divorce, and generally the employer has no objection—after all, divorce doesn't change the parent-child relationship between the employee and the kids. But occasionally, an employer argues about covering kids who aren't living with the employee-parent, and of course it's always possible your spouse could fail to pay insurance premiums or refuse to give you the insurance information you need (like the explanation of benefits or coverage information). So if you're the custodial parent and the kids are covered by your spouse's insurance, you should ask the court to enter a Qualified Medical Child Support Order (QMCSO) along with your child support order.

The QMCSO will secure the employer's obligation to continue coverage and your right to get information from the employer and the insurer. Most employment and insurance information is confidential, so you need an order like this to be able to learn the ins and outs of the other parent's coverage, especially if the other parent isn't cooperative about passing information along to you. If for some reason you don't get an order, make sure your settlement agreement says you have the right to do so later if you choose to.

If you have a lawyer, the lawyer will prepare the order. It's also possible that the employer or the insurer has a form that you can use. If not, you should be able to prepare it yourself using the summary plan description from your spouse's group health care plan. You can get the summary plan description by writing to the plan administrator, whose contact information is included in whatever documents you have related to the group health insurance. As a plan beneficiary, you're entitled to the information you'll need to prepare the order (like the identification numbers for the employer and the insurance plan), so if you can't find any helpful paperwork at home and your spouse won't give it to you, contact the human resources department at your spouse's employer and ask for it. Even if you have separate insurance and you're not technically a plan beneficiary, you should be able to get the information on behalf of your children. If you have a problem with that, though, you'll probably have to ask a lawyer to intervene.

The summary plan description should state the requirements for preparing a QMCSO. The order must state, at a minimum:

- the name and last known mailing address of the participant (the employee spouse) and the name and mailing address of each child with a right to receive coverage
- a description of the type of coverage to be provided by the plan (for example, "group health and dental insurance")
- the period of time that coverage is to be provided, and
- the name of each plan to which the order applies (the plan administrator or a human resources employee at your spouse's company can give you this information if you don't already have it).

To see what a QMCSO looks like, check out the sample in *Divorce & Money: How to Make the Best Financial Decisions During Divorce,* by Violet Woodhouse with Dale Fetherling (Nolo). Be sure you prepare the order in time to have it signed along with the rest of the paperwork for your divorce—if the judge doesn't sign it, you won't be able to enforce it. If you're preparing the order yourself, be extra safe and ask the human resources people or the plan administrator at the employer to review it before you submit it to the court, and to give you a letter saying it meets with their approval. That way neither your spouse nor the employer can argue later that there's something wrong with the order.

TIP

You can keep your health insurance, too. If you have been covered under your spouse's insurance and you don't have other coverage of your own, you are entitled to continue your coverage for up to three years under a federal law called COBRA. Learn more about COBRA at www.dol.gov/dol/topic/health-plans/cobra.htm and in *Nolo's Essential Guide to Divorce,* by Emily Doskow (Nolo). ●

When You Decide to Divorce: The First Month

The period just after you decide to divorce—or learn that your spouse has made the decision for you—can be overwhelming and confusing. There is a great deal to think about and a great deal to do. This chapter will help keep you moving forward through the challenges, getting things done bit by bit, until you come out on the other side.

You may need to make some decisions quickly. At the same time, it's important not to make rash decisions in the early days of separation. Even if you just want things to be over with, don't take any big steps, like selling assets, transferring large amounts of money, or agreeing to a custody arrangement, without first talking to someone about the legal and financial consequences. In fact, once either you or your spouse have filed for divorce, you won't be able to do anything like that. Almost all states have laws that once a divorce petition is filed, neither spouse can get rid of property, change beneficiaries, or otherwise compromise any jointly owned property without the other spouse's consent.

If You're the Decider: Breaking the News

If you're the one who's decided to end your marriage, you may think that the problems are obvious to both of you and that the news won't come as a complete shock to your spouse. Don't count on that. Many spouses are surprised, either by the timing of an announcement or because they felt the relationship was under repair—or because they really didn't know that things were that bad.

If you're in counseling, a session can be a good time to break the news, especially if you anticipate receiving a lot of anger in return. Plan what you want to say. Don't expect your spouse to be able to make decisions about things like who will stay in the house and who will move out, or how you will spend time with your kids. You've had time to think about it; your spouse hasn't.

Before you commit to anything, get advice from a lawyer, accountant, or child custody counselor. If you feel pressured for a decision and you don't know what to say, stick to your position and try one of these clear statements: "I'd prefer to deal with that later," or "I'm not prepared to talk about that now," or "I think we should bring that issue to mediation."

Talking to the Kids

The challenges of parenting during divorce begin when it's time to tell your children that the divorce is happening. Chances are they already know something's wrong, so don't delay—you'll be doing them a favor by telling them what's going on. It's best to do it before making any major changes, like having one parent move out.

If possible, you and your spouse should talk to the kids together. This can reassure them that you both love them and will always be their parents, even though you won't be living together anymore. But if time won't allow it or if your relationship has deteriorated so badly that you don't think you can do it without arguing, at least try to make sure that you both give them the same message.

If your kids are close in age, you can talk to them at the same time, but if they are years apart and in different developmental stages, you might need to have more than one conversation. If that's the case, make sure the conversations happen close together in time, so the kids have the same information at pretty much the same time.

When you do talk, try to stay as calm as you can. This will help them understand that even though it's hard and painful, you are making a decision you can live with and everyone will be okay. Don't sob uncontrollably or rage at your spouse—that's really disturbing to kids, especially if they're young. At the same time, make sure the kids know that they can say anything to you and that it's okay for them to express their own anger, disappointment, and sadness.

It's very, very common for kids to blame themselves for a divorce. Your kids need to know that the divorce isn't their fault, that you thought about it for a long time before making a decision, and that your decision has nothing to do with them or their behavior.

It can reassure kids that they aren't at fault if you tell them the real reason for the divorce: "We aren't happy living together anymore." Don't offer anything more detailed, especially if infidelity, substance abuse, or some other adult problem has precipitated the divorce. If they press you for reasons, explain (as many times as necessary) that the reasons are grown-up issues.

The adult concerns that are behind your decision to divorce are probably not actually what your children are concerned about, even if they ask. What they really want to know is where they will sleep at night and who will tuck them in—or if they're older, whether they'll have to switch schools and how their friends will react. Make sure you reassure the kids that they will still see the parent who's moving out or who will be the noncustodial parent.

Keep repeating the important messages:

- The divorce is not their fault.
- They will always have both parents, and they have your permission and encouragement to continue to love their other parent.
- Their lives will return to being more predictable and routine after they get through the initial transition.
- You will tell them the truth about what's going on and listen to their feelings.
- You will always love them, and so will their other parent.

If you're in a high-conflict situation, and you think your spouse might try to keep you from seeing the kids—or if your spouse is abusive or neglectful and you're going to seek limited or supervised visitation—then plan carefully for this part of the conversation. In most cases, even with parents who are far from perfect, children want to see and spend time with both of their parents. Unless your plan is to keep them from seeing your former spouse at all, it is important to let the kids know that they'll still get to see their other parent, and that you won't abandon them either and will always be there for them.

If there was ever a time to get some professional advice, this is it, so look for guidance from a therapist on how to talk to your kids about the custody fight. You can't protect them entirely from unpleasantness, but there are ways to be honest with them that will have a less negative effect.

There's much more about helping your kids adjust, and taking care of yourself and of them, in "Take Care of Yourself and Your Kids," below.

Telling Others About the Divorce

It's a good idea to let the people who'll be around your kids know about the divorce—their teachers, caregivers, and even their friends' parents. That way, if they notice behavioral changes signaling that your child is having trouble coping, they'll understand why and will know they should alert you to what's going on.

Figure Out Immediate Housing and Custody Issues

It's important to make some immediate agreements about who is going to live where. It's also important to remember that agreements you make now don't have to be permanent. You can't know right now how things are going to end up, so focus on making the agreement that works for everyone now, and keep your options open for the future. Put your temporary agreement in writing, being sure to include a date that you'll return to address the issue again. At that time you can make a long-term decision, agree to continue as you are with an understanding that it's still temporary, or make a new temporary agreement if you're going to change the living arrangements.

It may be very obvious, to both you and your spouse, which one of you should leave your family home. Perhaps one of you travels a great deal and doesn't need much in the way of a place to stay—a small, inexpensive apartment would be enough. Maybe one of you has such a strong attachment to the house that it's clear that person will end up living there and might as well stay. Or, as is very common, one spouse does more of the parenting and wants to stay in the house and continue caring for the kids.

It's also not unusual for both spouses to stay in the family home for a short time after they decide to divorce. It might make it easier on the children not to make any big changes quickly. On the other hand, often having one parent move out is the thing that will help them understand the reality of the divorce, so don't put it off too long.

The Kids and Your Home

If it's at all possible, try to keep the kids where they are, at least for a while, as they adjust to the news of the divorce and the change in their family. Kids tend to be very attached to their rooms, their stuff, and their routines. They're already experiencing a big change, so allowing them to stay in the same physical place can be helpful.

Usually, one parent stays in the family house with the kids for a while, and the other parent rents a nearby house or apartment—in an ideal world, close enough for the kids to walk to, if they're old enough, or at least near enough for the transportation to be relatively easy. If you and your spouse are able to cooperate, you can work together to find the best housing for the one who is moving out. If you're the one staying, it's in your interest to help because it may get your spouse out of the house more quickly. It also benefits your kids by ensuring that both homes are appropriate for them.

If you're anticipating conflict because you are going to seek sole custody over your spouse's objections, then from a strategic perspective the worst thing you can do is to move out without the kids. If you leave the kids in the house with your spouse, then you've admitted that you think it's a safe and healthy environment for them. Also, judges don't like to disturb the status quo—so wherever your kids go when you separate is going to be the starting point for a discussion of where they'll live permanently. That doesn't mean there's no way you could get a change, but it will be harder.

If you're expecting to share physical custody, moving out is less risky. But if you are worried that moving out might lessen your chances of getting shared custody, ask your spouse to sign an agreement that says that the move won't affect later decisions about custody and visitation.

If You Rent

If you're renting your place, you and your spouse are probably both listed as tenants on the lease or rental agreement. That means that the person who moves out will still be legally responsible for paying the rent until the lease ends or you terminate the rental agreement. If you want to make sure that the spouse who moves out will not be responsible to the landlord for rent, you'll need to take the steps explained below.

If You Have a Lease

A lease obligates both of you to pay rent until the date the lease ends. (Residential leases commonly last for a year.) That obligation will continue after you split up, even if you and your spouse sign an agreement stating otherwise. Unless you get the landlord to agree otherwise, if the staying spouse fails to pay the rent, the landlord can come after the other spouse for the rent, even if that person hasn't lived there for months.

To end the moving spouse's responsibility for future rent, the staying spouse should ask the landlord for a new lease and sign it alone. The new lease will end the original landlord–tenant relationship, and the landlord can ask for current credit information for the new solo tenant—and can even seek to change the terms of the lease, which will be brand new. (If the staying spouse doesn't qualify, or the new terms aren't acceptable, it's time to look for a new place.)

The landlord does not have to agree to terminate the lease and write a new one for one spouse only. Some landlords, fearful that the remaining spouse won't be able to make the rent, will want to keep the absent spouse in the wings as a potential source of payment. The departing spouse may end up on the hook for part of the rent in any event, if it's considered a necessity for the spouse who stays. One can sometimes be held responsible for expenses incurred by the other after separation if the expense is necessary, especially for the kids.

Domestic Violence and Rental Property

There's an exception to the rule that the landlord doesn't have to redo the lease for one spouse as part of the divorce: when there's violence in the home. Many states offer protection to a victim who can provide documentation of the violence, such as a police report or protective order from a court. Some states allow a victim of domestic violence to terminate a lease early, on short notice or without any notice at all, and to leave without responsibility for future rent. A handful of states allow the landlord to terminate the lease as to the abuser only, and force a move-out while allowing the victim to stay. There may also be a right for the victim to stay under a month-to-month rental agreement. There's more about domestic violence generally in Chapter 10, and you can contact the National Domestic Violence Hotline at 800-799-SAFE or www.thehotline.org.

If You Rent Month-to-Month

Instead of a lease, you may have a month-to-month rental agreement, which renews every month unless you or the landlord terminates it with proper notice (30 days, in most states). You may have had a rental agreement from the outset, or perhaps your original tenancy turned into a month-to-month arrangement when your lease ended but you stayed on with the consent of the landlord, a very common scenario.

With a rental agreement, it's much easier to end the landlord–tenant relationship and establish a solo tenancy. You don't need the landlord's consent. You or your spouse can give your landlord a termination notice, being careful to abide by your state's rules for how many days' notice you must give the landlord and how you should deliver the notice. After the notice period ends, so does the tenancy, which means neither of you has any further responsibility to pay rent.

If one spouse wants to stay on, that person will have to reapply for the rental, as a new, solo tenant. The landlord may take this opportunity to change the terms of the rental agreement or insist on a lease.

If You Own

If you own your home, you and your spouse probably share joint responsibility for the mortgage. The spouse who moves out is still responsible for paying the mortgage and property taxes, as well as dealing with repairs and everything else that comes with home ownership. Both of you should also continue to receive the benefits of owning property, including the mortgage interest deduction and any appreciation in the home's value.

When you own your house jointly and have been living in it together, generally neither spouse is more entitled to stay in the family home than the other. You'll have to decide who leaves and who stays—or have a judge decide. Getting a decision from a court will take time, so if you're both really stubborn, you may end up living in the same house while you wait for a decision. If your relationship is so high-conflict that you can't work out even a temporary arrangement, you will likely need a lawyer to help you argue your side of that dispute. (See Chapter 6 to learn more about what a court hearing on this issue might be like.)

If the house is only in one spouse's name, however, the owner spouse might be able to make the other one move out, but it would depend on factors like how long you've lived in the house together, which one of you pays the mortgage and property taxes, who's likely to be taking care of the kids, and other factors that your state might consider relevant. In a community property state in particular, even if only one spouse is on the title, it's entirely possible that the house is marital property, at least in part. If any joint income was used to pay the mortgage, then the community (meaning both spouses) probably has an interest in it.

To get an order forcing one spouse to leave the house (often called a "kickout" order), in most circumstances you'll have to already have a divorce case filed, or go ahead and file one. The question of who lives where is part of the divorce process. Unless there's an urgent need, as in a case of domestic violence (see below), you won't be able to get an immediate decision. If your spouse is the only one on the title and tries to get the police or sheriff to evict you based on that fact, make sure you let the authorities know that you're in the midst of a divorce (even if you haven't filed). They may not understand the ins and outs of marital property, but they'll know not to take one person's word for anything, and they're unlikely to force you out.

Domestic Violence and Your House

When domestic abuse is proven, a judge will order the abusive spouse to leave the family home. If you or your children are in physical danger from your spouse, get out of the house quickly, taking the children with you. See a lawyer and file for custody right away, to make sure a charge of kidnapping won't stick. Then go to court and get a restraining order, ordering your spouse to move out and stay away from the house and from you and the kids. Change the locks after you get the court order. Chapter 10 has more about domestic violence and other forms of abuse.

Make a Temporary Parenting Plan

As soon as both parents aren't living under the same roof, you should create a temporary parenting plan. You may be able to get by for a while on an ad hoc basis, but having a written plan, even if it's temporary, will make everyone's life a lot easier—especially the kids.

Chapter 2 gives examples of different parenting schedules and explains the different ways parents can negotiate a parenting plan. If you're not able to work with the other parent through negotiation or mediation to come up with a plan, and especially if you're already in conflict about where the kids should live, you probably should request a temporary custody order right away. There are so many decisions you need to make each day about your kids—Who will drive them to soccer practice? Do they need help with homework? What's for dinner?—that dealing with uncertainty about what's going to happen the next day or the one after that will quickly become exhausting for both parents and children. The court isn't going to make those decisions for you, but a predictable parenting schedule will go a long way to resolve the smaller challenges. Chapter 6 explains what happens when you go to court for a temporary order.

If you're able to reach a temporary resolution on your own, it's a good idea to write it down and, especially if you're worried that the other parent won't comply with it, then submit it to the court and ask a judge to confirm it as an order. That way the court can enforce it—in other words, make the other parent do what's been agreed to.

Here's a sample agreement. The last paragraph says that you can change the agreement later even if there's no change of circumstances— it's important to put that in because in general, courts won't change custody arrangements unless the parent seeking the change can show that there's been a meaningful change in circumstances that will justify the adjustment. (You'll learn more about that in Chapter 8.) This agreement differs from the separation agreements in Chapter 1— those agreements are useful before there's a divorce action, and they cover primarily how finances will be treated. You generally won't file a separation agreement with the court. A parenting plan like the sample here is something you can file with the court and turn into an order if you want the court to be able to enforce it.

Sample Temporary Parenting Plan

Temporary Parenting Plan

This agreement is between Roland Chambers and Sarah Chambers. We are married and intend to divorce. Sarah will move out of our apartment at 4545 Oak Street, and Roland and the children will continue living there for now. We'll spend time with the kids according to the following schedule:

Sarah will come to the apartment every Tuesday and Thursday at 5 p.m. and spend the evening with the kids there, while Roland leaves the house until 9 p.m. Sarah will feed them dinner and make sure their homework is done and they have baths. Every other Friday, starting the Friday after this agreement is signed, Sarah will pick both children up from school and keep them for the weekend, bringing them to school on Monday morning. During Roland's parenting time, if there are times that he is not able to care for the children, he will give Sarah the opportunity to have parenting time with them before he asks someone else to provide child care.

We will alternate major holidays as long as this agreement is in effect. The first holiday coming up is the Fourth of July, and Sarah will have the kids on July 4th. The next holiday is Labor Day and Roland will have the children then. If the children have a day off school that isn't a holiday, Sarah will have first choice of caring for them; otherwise Roland will arrange for child care.

We both agree not to denigrate the other parent in front of the children, and we will not discuss anything about our divorce or child custody or support arrangements during transitions with the children. If either of us needs a change in the parenting schedule, we'll use email to communicate about arrangements. We both agree to respond to any email from the other parent within 24 hours.

This is a temporary agreement and neither of us is giving up our right to ask for a different arrangement later, even if there is no change of

Sample Temporary Parenting Plan (cont'd)

circumstances for either of us. We agree that a court can enter this agreement as an order. This agreement will remain in effect until we enter a new agreement, make a permanent parenting plan, or get a court order with a different parenting schedule.

Roland Chambers   6/15/20xx
Roland Chambers   Date

Sarah Chambers   6/15/20xx
Sarah Chambers   Date

Start Addressing Money Issues

As you encounter the reality of supporting two households on the same money that has been supporting one, you'll likely find yourself in a stressful financial situation. Added to the stress of deciding to separate, this can seem overwhelming; it can help if you remember that you don't need to make permanent decisions now.

Start by determining who needs how much to get through the month, which bills are due and how they'll get paid, and whether you need to do anything differently right away, like getting rid of your cable TV, gym membership, or other discretionary expenses, using a home equity line of credit to free up cash during the transition, or otherwise adjusting how you deal with money. If one of you has already filed a divorce action in court, you're under a restraining order not to make any big decisions unilaterally, so if you decide to make any significant financial moves, make sure you document the fact that both of you are agreeing to it.

Next, start working with your spouse to come up with an interim support agreement; you'll want it in place by the end of the month. If you can't agree, you'll need to start preparing to go to court to get what you and the children need.

It's a big change for some people, but remember that your life is now your own, and you can keep your personal information, including your financial information, private. If you and your spouse are still living together and you don't feel secure that your mail will come to you unopened or you don't necessarily want your spouse seeing where your mail is coming from, get a post office box where you can receive mail. If you have a shared family computer, don't use it for divorce-related email correspondence or document preparation. Even after you delete something, a skilled computer user can retrieve it.

Gather Financial Information

To settle on a child support amount (as well as to divide your property fairly and determine alimony if one spouse seeks it), you'll need extensive financial information. Current pay stubs for both you and your spouse are the starting point for any child support calculation. (Chapter 3 explains how to estimate child support payments using your state's guidelines.) Also put together information about the kids' health insurance: how the premiums are paid, what the uninsured expenses tend to be, and the like.

In addition, you'll need a complete assessment of your assets and debts. Most every state requires that spouses exchange financial information as part of the divorce process, and you'll be ahead of the game in terms of filling out forms if you have already put that information together. If you're working with a lawyer, the lawyer will be grateful that you've done some of the work in advance, as well. Start by collecting:

- deeds
- recent mortgage statements
- life and disability insurance policies
- retirement plan statements and plan documents
- business interests
- tax returns for the past five years
- wills and trusts, and
- bank, brokerage, and retirement account statements.

If your spouse has been taking care of family finances and you're in the dark, do not under any circumstances stay there—you need to shine a light on the situation right away. Go through all the papers you can find and make copies of everything you think you might need. If the paperwork isn't in the house, ask your spouse to bring it so that you can review and copy it.

If your spouse refuses, or if you don't think you're getting everything you're entitled to, you can use procedures called "discovery" to get records after you file for divorce. Chapters 6 and 12 will help you decide whether you're able to do this yourself or should hire a lawyer. If your spouse won't agree to pay an amount that you think is fair and you're at a big disadvantage in the near term from not having the records, consider getting a lawyer right away for help with this. Not knowing anything about the finances can hurt you when it comes to negotiating about temporary support.

Another good way to start making sure you have the financial information you need is to find your state's divorce forms online, and locate the forms you would need to file for child support. Look at the forms to see what financial information you'll need.

Decide How to Handle Immediate Expenses

It's time to assess your living expenses and determine how to keep the household running in the short term. You need to do this quickly— ideally, before one spouse moves out. A spouse who moves out of the family home sometimes forgets that the family's expenses are still his or her responsibility. So before anyone leaves, try to make decisions about who will be responsible for what bills, and how they'll get paid.

Couples who both work and both deposit all their earnings into a joint account can continue doing that for a while, and simply pay all expenses out of that account, including the rent and other expenses for a spouse who's moved out of the house. It won't work in the long run, because you need to start being clear about whose money is whose, but for the first month or so, it's fine. Some people do it for much longer.

Another option is for both of you to open separate accounts, if you don't already have them. You'll need to decide how much money one spouse may need to transfer to the other for expenses. For example, the higher-earning spouse may agree to deposit $2,000 per month in the other's account, or just write a check for that amount, for the first few months.

If you don't come to an agreement about expenses, and your spouse stops contributing to household expenses and supporting the children, or closes out joint accounts, don't delay: Hire a lawyer and go to court. Chapter 6 explains how.

Settle on Temporary Child Support

As soon as parents separate and the kids divide their time between two households, the question of child support arises.

Chapter 3 explains how to calculate child support for your family. The easiest way to deal with this issue is to arrive at an estimate of guideline support (discussed in Chapter 3) and agree to it in writing, with a provision that says the support amount isn't permanent and doesn't necessarily represent the final guideline calculations. That way you'll be able to pay your expenses while still buying yourselves some time to negotiate further. You'll probably be making a parenting plan as well, so you can use the same agreement as shown above in "Make a Temporary Parenting Plan." If you want to include a support provision, change the title to "Temporary Parenting Plan and Support Agreement," and add the following language:

Sample Child Support Terms

Sarah will pay Roland $450 each month as child support for both children, payable on the first of each month. We determined this amount based on the children's needs and both parents' income. We know the amount might not be in line with our state's child support guidelines, but we believe it meets our children's needs. We agree that it's a temporary amount and neither of us gives up our right to ask for a different arrangement later.

Roland will keep the children on his health insurance through work, and will continue to pay for the insurance.

If you can't reach an agreement, you need child support, and your spouse isn't paying, don't delay in setting a court hearing. You can ask a court to order your spouse to make child and spousal support payments immediately, called temporary or "pendente lite" (during the pending action) support. The court can issue a permanent support order later.

If you think you're in for a fight over money, you may want a lawyer's help to get this request done quickly and get some money coming in. You'll have to pay the lawyer, but it's possible the court will order your spouse to pay part of your lawyer's fees right away. Chapter 6 has more about support hearings, and also about working with lawyers versus going it alone.

Create a Spending Plan

Some people call it a budget, but "spending plan" sounds so much more positive. Whatever term you use, you need a record of your current spending habits and a plan for dealing with all of your expenses going forward. For one thing, in almost every court you'll have to provide that information to the judge before child support can be established. But even if you don't intend to end up in court arguing over child support (smart), knowing what your financial needs are is the first step in figuring out how to meet them—either by negotiating with your spouse over the amount of child support, figuring out how you're going to bring in some more money, or learning how to cut your expenses.

RESOURCE

Help with financial questions. For detailed worksheets that will help you figure out your spending situation, see *Divorce & Money: How to Make the Best Financial Decisions During Divorce,* by Violet Woodhouse with Dale Fetherling (Nolo).

Close Joint Bank Accounts

It's a good idea to close many of your joint accounts, including bank checking and savings accounts and credit cards, as soon as possible. If you and your spouse decide to keep one joint checking account open for household expenses, that's fine, but you should begin to deposit your own paycheck into a separate account of your own and then transfer money into the household account. This makes it clear that money you're earning is now your separate income, rather than marital property. When you close an account, you can divide the money equally or, if you agree, have one person keep more—either because that person's going to be paying more of the expenses, or in order to balance out some other decision you've made, like having the other person keep the car that's worth more.

If you don't split the money equally, write down how you've divided it and why, and put both of your signatures on the agreement. For example, "We have closed our joint savings account at Bank of America, ending in 1234, and each of us has kept half of the balance of $12,400," or "We have closed our joint savings account at Union Bank, ending in 5678. Of the balance of $12,400, Jack has kept $8,000 and Jill has kept $4,400. The $3,600 difference is to compensate Jack for Jill keeping all of the video equipment that we own. Jill won't owe Jack any more money for that equipment. We haven't made any decisions about the rest of our property." The last sentence is to make clear that you've dealt with only one issue and will need to decide about the rest of your assets when you settle the rest of your divorce.

If you and your spouse aren't on speaking terms or can't agree about money, you do have the right to take half of the money out of your joint accounts. If you're doing that without your spouse's agreement, take these steps:

- Get documentation of how much was in the account before you took out your half. A receipt from the ATM or the bank teller, a computer screen shot, or a printout of the account on that date, would all be fine.
- Take only half and no more, and don't close the account.
- Let your spouse know that you've taken the money afterwards.

If you decide not to take the money out because you think it might escalate conflict, at the very least you do need to document how much is in the accounts as of the time you separate. Make sure you get that information and keep it.

You may have other types of financial accounts, like 401(k)s, 529 college savings accounts, brokerage accounts, or other investment or retirement accounts. In most cases it's best to leave these alone until you're ready to resolve the financial issues involved in your divorce. However, as with your bank accounts, make sure you know exactly how much is in these accounts as of the date you and your spouse separated, and keep evidence of what the amounts were.

Close Joint Credit Card Accounts

If you don't have credit in your own name, you may need to leave at least one of your credit card accounts open until you can establish it. Otherwise, or after you've gotten a card in your own name, close your joint credit accounts. Even if you think you trust your spouse to continue to be responsible with your joint credit cards, close them anyway. An account that is current, with no outstanding balance, can be closed any time by calling the card company and then sending a follow-up letter explaining that you and the other card owner are divorcing and you want the account closed. Some card companies may balk at closing the account just on one person's say-so. If your spouse won't sign a letter requesting that the account be closed, add to your own letter a statement saying "I forfeit my ability to make any more charges on this account, and will not be responsible for any charges made after our date of separation." Give the date that you separated, and send the cut-up card back to the card company. Send a copy of the letter to your spouse.

If there's a balance on the card, then your letter should say that you want the account closed as to any further charges, and confirm that you and your spouse will be responsible for the existing charges.

If you don't take care of this, your good credit could be at risk from your spouse's actions. If your spouse runs up debts on a joint credit card after you separate and doesn't pay, the bank will come after you because you are the other owner of the account, regardless of when you separated. You might eventually get your spouse to reimburse you for whatever you have to pay, but you'll go through a lot of hassle getting there, not to mention the potential for damage to your credit rating.

Getting Back to Work Outside the Home

If you've been staying at home with your kids, the financial realities of divorce may force you back to work. This can be a frightening prospect, especially if you've been out of the workforce for a while and are facing a challenging economy.

Go about it methodically, starting with your résumé. There's nothing unusual about having stayed home to care for your children, so don't try to hide it. But consider what's called a "functional résumé," organized around your job skills and training instead of chronology. Address your time away from paid work in a cover letter.

If your job skills are seriously out of date, look into getting some retraining. Community colleges, adult schools, and private training programs all offer programs that may help.

Your next step is to mine your contact list for people who might be helpful in your search, whether you're just looking for something to bring in some cash until the postseparation chaos subsides or you're ready for your next career. Don't forget about schools you went to, even if you graduated many years ago—often alumnae are entitled to job placement services at no cost and with no time limit. You can also look for general information about job searching and preparing a résumé through your state employment development department, job websites, or a career counselor. Some sites that might be helpful include www.careerplanner. com, www.careerbuilder.com, and www.jobhuntersbible.com, the official site of the classic career counseling book *What Color Is Your Parachute?* by Richard Bolles (Ten Speed Press).

RESOURCE

Taking control of your financial situation. *Divorce & Money: How to Make the Best Financial Decisions During Divorce*, by Violet Woodhouse with Dale Fetherling (Nolo), has more about debt and credit issues in divorce, as well as general financial advice.

Solve Your Money Troubles: Debt, Credit & Bankruptcy, and *Credit Repair,* both by Margaret Reiter and Robin Leonard and both published by Nolo, offer very useful credit and debt advice.

Get Organized

As the days march on, you may feel like you're in a fog. It can really help to get organized as soon as possible, by setting up a filing system. Whether you represent yourself or work with a lawyer, there's a lot of information you'll need to gather and a lot of paperwork to deal with, and being systematic about it from the beginning will make the process easier.

Set Up a Filing System

Are you the kind of person who loves office supplies and already has lots of color-coded, well-considered organizational systems in place? Great. Use your skills to create a special system that will work for this new project: your divorce. If you're not hyperorganized by nature, it's probably even more important to arrange things so it will be simple to keep track of all the papers that will come flooding in soon. You don't want to waste time and energy searching for misplaced documents all the time.

You don't have to make anything fancy. Just get folders or three-ring binders and designate one for each of the financial documents described in "Gather Financial Information," above. You'll also need folders to organize your court paperwork. One good way to go is to make separate folders for:

- papers that you don't need now but are keeping for your records
- papers related to any upcoming hearings or other events, and
- documents that you're in the process of completing for your lawyer or the court.

Finally, make a folder for anything related to your kids that might be useful when you're negotiating (or, if that fails, arguing in court) about custody arrangements. It might include, for example, report cards or notes from school, medical records, and even notes you've made about behavioral changes you've seen that you think are related to their relationship with the other parent or to something about your parenting schedule that you don't think is good for the kids. You may never need these documents if you and your spouse are able to reach an agreement about parenting time. But if you anticipate a battle, these records will support your position. There's more about gathering this type of evidence in later chapters.

Gather Information About the Kids

In many families, one parent is much more involved in the children's day-to-day activities than the other. Sometimes it's because the parent is a stay-at-home caretaker or works part time, and other times it's simply what works best.

If you're that person, do what's best for your kids by gathering all of the information the other parent will need to be an effective caretaker. That means a list of all the kids' medical providers and their contact information (as well as medical information about the kids if they have allergies or take any medication regularly), a calendar of regularly scheduled events like music lessons, tutoring, or soccer practice, and a list of friends and their parents, again with contact information.

If it annoys you to do this work for your spouse, keep in mind that it could make life easier for your kids—and isn't that your number one goal? In addition, one of the criteria that most courts use in deciding custody cases is who will do a better job of supporting the children's relationship with the other parent. (So, make a note of what you did to show that support.) If you take steps that are obviously intended to sabotage that relationship rather than support it, you're likely to pay for it later if you end up in front of a judge.

File Court Papers

When you're ready, you or your spouse must file the papers that will start the legal process of getting divorced. People have very different feelings about the timing. Some couples wait months or years after they separate to get the official court divorce started, not because they think they'll reconcile but because they don't see any reason for filing immediately—or because there are emotions holding one or both people back. In some cases it's to your advantage to wait—for example, if you know your spouse is expecting a big year-end bonus, or if you're close to a milestone like ten or 20 years, which can matter for things like Social Security and military pensions. But in other cases, getting the divorce filed can be important, because it creates a paper trail of when you separated, which can be significant to the division of property. It also ensures that you won't get stuck with the consequences of any bad financial decisions your spouse makes after you begin living apart, like committing to some kind of debt or making a bad investment with joint funds.

If you are in a high-conflict situation, you'll definitely want to get the divorce on file right away. You won't be able to ask for a hearing to get short-term child support or living expenses from your spouse if you don't have a case opened. Often the paperwork to start the divorce and the paperwork asking for support are filed at the same time.

To start the divorce process, you'll need a form that's usually called a "petition" or "complaint." In most places you're also required to complete a "summons" or other form that advises the other parent that you've filed for divorce. You'll have to have the summons, along with the initial document, "served" on the other parent, which means that you must arrange for it to be delivered to your spouse following strict court rules. (See "Serving Papers," in Chapter 6.) If your spouse started the divorce and you were served with the petition or complaint, you won't have to complete a summons. The first document you will file will probably be called a "response" or "answer."

If you are going to represent yourself in your divorce and will need to prepare court forms yourself, see "Preparing Court Documents" in Chapter 6.

How to Get Your Agreements Made Into Orders

You may have agreed on a parenting schedule and an amount of child support that one parent will pay the other, and put your agreements in writing. That's great—you've saved yourself significant time, money, and hassle. But how can you be sure that the other parent will do what the agreement says? There's no way to guarantee that except to get a court to issue an order. Exactly how to do that will depend on your court's processes. Your court probably has forms for telling the court what you want to do about parenting time and support, and you may end up transferring the information from your written agreement onto the court forms, or attaching your agreement to a court form. Your goal is to get a judge to approve your agreement and sign an order saying you both have to abide by it.

Many courts have self-help centers for people representing themselves in family court—if there's a self-help center at your court, that's where you can get the information about how to get your order entered. If not, ask the court clerk where to find the resources you need to help you. If you are having trouble getting to the point of getting an order entered, you might want to ask a lawyer to help you. Some lawyers are willing to do specific tasks for you while you keep control over your case. There's more about filing papers in Chapter 6, and more about working with lawyers in Chapter 12.

Take Care of Yourself and Your Kids

You are probably starting to adjust, at least a little bit, to your new world order. But you are still in the midst of a very significant (and for many people traumatic) life event, and you need to watch out for yourself as well as for your children. Of course that's true not just in the first month of your divorce, but all through the process. Here are some ideas on making a difficult transition as smooth as is possible.

What Not to Do

In addition to all the things you need to do to take care of your kids in these early days, you can make your life, and theirs, easier by not doing a few other things.

Don't pick fights. Try to keep from fighting over every single thing. For one thing, it will make your children miserable—and don't think that you can keep the conflict out of their hearing. For another, the more entrenched you and your spouse get in your positions early on, the worse things are likely to be later.

Don't rise to the bait. Even if your spouse is trying to argue with you at every turn, try to create a mantra that you can repeat—perhaps something about agreeing to disagree. Stay calm and don't let your spouse goad you into a battle.

Don't forget to pay attention to your kids. You may find that after the initial announcement of the divorce, the kids are pretty quiet on the subject. This may be because they know that you're having a hard time and don't want to add to your worries. Make sure you check in with them and give them room to talk about what they're doing and feeling. If they're really struggling, get help for them from a therapist.

Don't neglect your own emotional health. Divorce is a huge life event, right up there with losing a loved one. And your kids need you to be functioning well, to help them. There's no shame in seeking help in dealing with your emotions, whether it's counseling from someone in your religious community or a therapist, or another form of help that works for you. (See below for more resources and help finding a therapist.)

RESOURCE

Books for parents about kids and divorce. *Speaking of Divorce: How to Talk With Your Kids and Help Them Cope*, by Roberta Beyer and Kent Winchester (Free Spirit Publishing), has lots of concrete suggestions for how to have all the different conversations you'll need to have with your children as the divorce progresses.

Mom's House, Dad's House: Making Two Homes for Your Child, by Isolina Ricci, Ph.D. (Simon and Schuster). This book is a perennial bestseller for a reason: its straightforward approach to coping with separating your households and the impact on your kids.

Helping Your Kids Cope with Divorce the Sandcastles Way, by M. Gary Neuman, L.M.H.C., with Patricia Romanowski (Random House). This method of working with children has been praised by professionals and parents.

The Good Divorce: Keeping Your Family Together When Your Marriage Comes Apart, by Constance Ahrons, Ph.D. (HarperCollins). While a "good divorce" might seem like an oxymoron, this book starts with the assumption that your family is still a family—just with a different structure—and that it's possible to have a positive transition to your new structure.

Being a Great Divorced Father: Real-Life Advice From a Dad Who's Been There, by Paul Mandelstein (Nolo), helps fathers deal with the unique challenges of divorce for dads.

Dealing With Conflict

It's well documented that a highly conflicted divorce is much, much harder on kids than a fairly amicable one. In other words, no matter what you think about your spouse or how difficult things are between you, try to shield your kids as much as you can.

If you do have a high-conflict divorce and the conflict is about parenting time or other issues relating to the children, you can take steps to reduce the impact on them, like trying not to argue in their presence, and not giving them lots of detail about the court fight. But there's no way you can fully protect them if you're going all out to fight about custody or a parenting schedule. If you're fighting with your spouse about the kids, they will know it, and they will suffer for it. Look at Chapter 5 for advice on how to use alternatives to court, and try to resolve your disagreements without a court fight that will traumatize your kids.

Getting Help for Yourself

For many people, divorce leads, eventually, to positive changes. This may or may not end up being true for you, but leave the possibility open that you will find your way there. In the meantime, if you are struggling with anger, frustration, anxiety, and other challenging emotions but you haven't yet sought out meaningful help or support, now is the time to consider it. Venting to your friends and family may not be enough to get you through all of the difficult decisions and feelings that arise during a divorce—a process that requires you to restructure your entire life and many of your relationships, including your most important one. Seriously consider getting help from someone outside of your personal circle.

If you belong to a religious community, you may turn to a pastor, rabbi, or other leader for counseling, or to a divorce support group if your community has one. There are therapists who focus their practices on divorce work. A divorce therapist will support you through the divorce process by focusing on helping you accept the end of the marriage, mitigating feelings of guilt and self-blame or anger and blaming directed at your spouse, moving toward a functional relationship with your spouse around parenting issues, and developing new routines that will help you to live a healthier postdivorce life. You can also get help with parenting skills—and especially if you are the primary caretaker, getting help during the tumultuous early months can be a real help.

There are different types of mental health professionals you could consult. A **psychiatrist** is a medical doctor who can prescribe medication as well as provide treatment. A **clinical psychologist** has advanced training and a doctoral degree (Ph.D., Psy.D., Ed.D.). A **licensed clinical social worker (LCSW)** or **Marriage and Family Therapist (MFT)** has a Master's degree in clinical social work; some are trained in psychotherapy like psychiatrists and psychologists, but requirements differ from state to state.

If you decide to see a therapist, choose wisely. Start by asking for referrals from people you know—they will be the most reliable judges. But the therapist that was right for your best friend might not be right for you, so try to get a number of referrals, and meet with a few people before making a decision. (You'll have to pay for these meetings, but it's entirely worth it to make sure you find someone you can work well with.) The most important thing is how you feel when you are in a session with the therapist. You should feel comfortable talking about whatever your concerns are, and confident that the therapist will not judge you. A few things you might want to ask, to get a sense of the therapist's experience and background, how the therapist operates, and how you feel about this particular person, include:

1. Does the therapist have the appropriate licenses for your state? If you don't know what those are, check with your state's professional licensing board. (Also check whether any complaints have been filed against this therapist.) Does the therapist have a degree like MFT, Ph.D., or MSW?

2. What experience does the therapist have working with clients who are going through divorce? Does the therapist know at least the basics of child development, in order to be able to help you assess how your kids are doing?

3. How does the therapist describe his or her approach to the therapy process and the relationship between therapist and client? Can you understand what the therapist is saying about what the process will look like, or does it sound like a lot of double-speak to you? Do you like what you hear?

4. Will the therapist help you develop tools to manage your own anxiety, anger, and fear as you work through the divorce process? In other words, is the therapist willing to see the process as a way for you to learn not to need therapy anymore?

5. Does the therapist emphasize ethical rules? Does the therapist consult with other therapists on challenging issues, and accept feedback and guidance?

This list only scratches the surface of the kinds of questions you might want to ask before making a decision about a therapist. For much more about the therapy process and about how to choose a good therapist for yourself and your children, see www.goodtherapy.org.

Getting Help for the Kids

Just like you, your children are dealing with new and difficult feelings. You have an opportunity to affect their future in a positive way by how you deal with their feelings during this vulnerable and difficult time. Most kids move through a divorce without needing professional help, especially if the adults around them are consistently present, honest, and reassuring. These factors are the most important in determining the outcome for kids, psychologically speaking. If you're going through a high-conflict divorce, there is no question that your children are suffering from it, and you might want to consider looking into some counseling for them as well as for yourself.

Keep in Touch and Watch for Signs of Trouble

No matter how old your kids are or how they took the news, continuing to talk with them and making yourself available to listen to what they have to say will help the most. Don't force them, but do ask them regularly how they are doing, and then make time and space to listen. If you have more than one child, make sure you spend time alone with each one in a way that makes room for conversation. When they do talk, listen carefully and without judgment, and respond gently no matter how difficult it is to hear what they are saying. Don't get angry. Keep your body language neutral and open (that means don't cross your arms or legs).

Most kids go through a hard time when their parents first separate, especially if they have to move, but they all act differently depending on their ages and temperaments. While some acting out is to be expected— and of course, some of these behaviors come with the territory at certain ages—you should also expect to see improvement over time. If things don't improve and the behavior is disrupting your family life, it's probably time to intervene.

For younger kids, you might seek outside help if you see extremes in the following areas:
- regression in learned skills, either physical or cognitive
- regression in toilet training
- change in sleeping habits, night terrors, or desire to sleep with you

- change in eating habits
- physical complaints or frequent illness, or
- tantrums, resistance to discipline, or difficult interactions with peers.

With school-age and teenage kids, pay attention to:
- rebellion against discipline, chores, or family interactions
- secrecy
- problems with schoolwork or peer relationships at school
- change in eating habits
- change in sleeping habits, or
- physical complaints of headaches, stomachaches, or other ailments.

If you're worried about any of these behaviors or others, your first step should be to find out whether the same behavior is going on when your child is with the other parent. Your spouse might have some interesting observations. If you don't communicate well with your spouse, you may have to skip this step. This is especially true if you're in a custody battle and you don't want to give your spouse information that might be used against you. However, don't sacrifice your children's well-being to your legal needs. If it seems important to get information from your spouse (or help for your kids), don't worry that it might affect your case—just do it.

You might also try contacting your child's teacher or school counselor. Child care professionals and teachers often have extensive experience dealing with divorcing families, plus general knowledge about helping kids through divorce—and they might be able to give you a referral to a child psychologist if you want advice or counseling for your child. Moreover, a teacher who sees your child day after day may well have some insight about behavioral changes and patterns.

You already know to let your child's school know that your family structure is changing, but take an extra step and find out whether there's someone at the school whom your child trusts and who can look out for the child's welfare. You may want to try setting up some regular appointments between your child and the counselor, or just asking the school to identify a particular adult who will make contact with your child and be available to talk and provide support. You could also find a therapist to work with your child until things get better.

Finding a Therapist and Talking With Your Child About Therapy

Start your search by asking your pediatrician or your own doctor for a referral. The doctor may know a therapist, social worker, or other mental health professional who could have suggestions. You may need to meet with a number of people before you find the person you think is right for your child, and you may have to pay for those meetings—some therapists don't charge for these investigatory meetings, but others do. Make sure you are clear in advance about whether there will be a charge.

The same types of mental health professionals described in "Getting Help for Yourself," above, also treat children. There are lots of different types of therapy, which you can learn about on websites like www.goodtherapy.org or www.kidshealth.org.

Your child may not want to go to therapy, believing it's a stigmatizing experience or that it will involve shots or other kinds of pain. It's important to be honest with your child about the reasons for the visit, and to provide reassurance that the visit won't involve anything painful and will just help with problem-solving and making the child feel better. Tell your child that the visit will be confidential and the therapist can't share anything outside of the room—unless that's not the case. If the therapist is going to prepare a report for the court, don't mislead your child into thinking that the meetings are confidential when they're not.

While your child's treatment may end up having some strategic benefit for your case if the therapist reports back that the other parent's actions are harming the child, that's not its primary purpose. Make sure you keep the focus on the actual care and the child's well-being, not on the custody dispute. Don't ever coach your child to say something to the therapist in hopes it will go in the record and give you some kind of advantage. Let the child's therapy belong to the child, and keep your adult relationships separate. The same is true if there's an evaluation performed by a therapist appointed by the court—even though you know that this evaluation will be reported back to the court, don't give your child any instructions about what to say or how to behave in the evaluation.

RESOURCE

There are lots of books for kids about divorce, so check your local library or bookstore for age-appropriate ones. A few good ones for each age group:

At Daddy's on Saturdays, by Linda Walvoord Girard (Albert Whitman & Co.), is for young grade-school children and has text and pictures about a young girl learning to adjust to seeing her father on weekends.

Two Homes, by Claire Masurel (Candlewick Press), is a picture book for very young children about going back and forth between Mom's and Dad's houses. Also for the very young set, *Standing on My Own Two Feet*, by Tamara Schmitz (Price Stern Sloan).

Dinosaurs Divorce: A Guide for Changing Families, by Laurene Krasny Brown and Marc Brown (Little, Brown & Co.), is an extremely popular book for good reason—it uses humorous drawings and simple, but straightforward, text to deal with the difficult issues of divorce, including having two homes, birthdays and holidays, stepparents you don't like, and what to do when your parents bad-mouth each other.

How I Survived My Parents' Big Scary Divorce, by Audrey Lavin (BookSurge), is another title for the four-to-eight-year-old set, about a feisty girl coming to terms with her parents' divorce.

Kids' Divorce Workbook: A Practical Guide That Helps Kids Understand Divorce Happens to the Nicest Kids, by Michael S. Prokop (Alegra House), offers space for kids to write and draw about their feelings, alongside the words and drawings of other children dealing with divorce. An excellent resource for kids who might be more comfortable with writing or drawing.

Help Hope & Happiness, by Libby Rees (Aultbea Publishing), is written by a ten-year-old and contains her advice for kids on coping with divorce; the book is only available from www.amazon.co.uk.

Flora & Ulysses, by noted children's author Kate DiCamillo, is a book for kids 8–12, about a squirrel with superpowers who helps a young girl manage her experience of her parents' divorce. Sweet, with wonderful illustrations.

What in the World Do You Do When Your Parents Divorce? A Survival Guide for Kids, by Roberta Beyer and Kent Winchester (Free Spirit Publishing), is aimed at kids seven to 12 years old, and explains divorce, new living situations, and dealing with difficult feelings in ways that should resonate with the preteen set.

The Divorce Helpbook for Teens, by Cynthia MacGregor (Impact Publishers), is a thorough, plain-language book that does not condescend as it offers guidance on navigating the challenges of divorce.

Kids and New Relationships

If you are already involved in a new relationship when you are still dealing with the nitty-gritty of your divorce, you are coping with some complicated issues. This is, of course, even more true if the new relationship was part of what precipitated the divorce. Kids often have a hard time with parents having a new love interest after a separation, and if they perceive that the new person caused the divorce, you're likely to have a struggle establishing a relationship between your kids and your new partner.

In that circumstance, you'll have to be the grown-up and make some sacrifices. Put your kids first and don't try to integrate your new partner into your family right away—try to spend adult time when the kids are with their other parent. Definitely don't bring a new partner into your home unless and until you are sure that the relationship is serious.

If you're not in a new relationship already, then try not to rush into anything—and again, be especially careful about bringing a new partner home to meet your kids until you're sure the relationship is serious. Don't ask your new partner to pick up the kids or otherwise get involved in changeovers, transitions, or the kids' activities until you all are more used to the new status quo.

If your marriage ended because of your spouse's new relationship, you may find it particularly challenging to accept the new partner. It's very likely that you'll consider your spouse's behavior, especially when it comes to having the new person participate in activities and home life with your kids, precipitate and inappropriate. And it may well be. But there is very little you can do about this unless the new person is objectively inappropriate to be around children because of substance abuse issues or a history of child abuse. (If that's the case, take steps to arrange for supervised or limited visitation—see Chapter 6.) Otherwise, you're going to have to grin and bear it.

Whatever you do, don't complain to your kids about your spouse or the new partner. The kids might have their own negative take, especially if they perceive the new relationship as having caused the divorce, but even if they try to engage you in bad-mouthing the happy couple, try to refrain and to model acceptance for your kids. Everyone will be a lot happier in the long run if you help them accept their new reality instead of struggling against it. ●

Avoiding a Custody or Support Trial: Alternatives to Court

The first months after separation are filled with details and decisions: who will pick up the kids from soccer practice next week, who will pay the overdue cable bill, do I need to get a job, where will we live? But it's crucial to step away from the barrage of day-to-day issues to look at some big-picture questions. The biggest: Whether you and your spouse will have a court fight over custody and support or will negotiate and settle these issues yourselves.

Your answer will have a huge impact on your wallet and your sanity. If you work out custody, support, and property, a divorce is still painful—but the legal part is just paperwork and waiting periods. If you don't work out an agreement, you're in for months (or even years) of expensive, unpleasant court proceedings.

This chapter explains alternatives to trial that can make your divorce much less painful for everyone in your family, as well as less expensive. As you consider them, remind yourself to make the decisions in your divorce with your children uppermost in your mind at all times.

Why You Should Avoid a Court Fight

With each little negotiation you have with your spouse, you move in one direction or another: toward an out-of-court resolution of your divorce or toward a court fight over money or custody. In other words, whether you're aware of it or not, you are constantly affecting how your divorce will go. These decisions will determine your quality of life for at least the next year or, if you decide on the court fight, two or three years—or more.

Most uncontested divorces can be completed in less than a year. If you handle it yourselves or with minimal help from an attorney, it won't cost you much more than the court filing fees. Those fees are anywhere from $200 to $1,000 total, depending on where you live. If you do get some very limited help from an attorney, figure on another $1,000 to $2,500. Even if you use mediation, you probably won't spend more than $10,000, probably significantly less. In stark contrast, a custody fight in court will take at least a year—very likely several—and cost each spouse from $15,000 to $50,000 or more if you go all the way to a trial.

There are also options in between, where you can get some expert help and advice but keep the process cooperative. These are covered below, in "Negotiating With Your Spouse."

The emotional cost to you and your children is no less significant. You will spend more time than you can now imagine worrying about your case, communicating with your lawyer, dealing with paperwork, and going to court. Universally, experts conclude that it isn't the divorce itself that creates significant emotional problems for children, but the way that parents deal with the process. Children in families where the divorce is relatively amicable, with no contested court process and parents who make an effort to be civil to each other, have much better outcomes than children whose parents engage in a protracted divorce—especially if the long, drawn-out battle is about the children. They are more likely to succeed in school and in future relationships and less likely to have problems with authority or develop depression, anxiety, or substance abuse problems.

In other words, every decision you make isn't just about the next few years of your own life—it's also about your kids' futures. Imagine your child working hard to learn a part in the school play, only to look out into the audience and see you and your ex sitting at opposite ends of the hall, and anticipate having to divide time between the two of you at the celebration afterwards, because you can't stand to speak to each other. Imagine your child knowing that you and your ex won't sit together, dance together, or offer a toast to each other at a wedding or graduation ceremony. And consider how it will feel to you at every turn to be competing with your ex for your child's attention and to know that every family event will have a cloud of negativity over it because of your toxic relationship. Sound pleasant? For the most part, it is within your power to avoid such scenarios.

It can be really difficult to compromise, especially when you are dealing with a spouse who's unreasonable or who you believe isn't acting in your children's best interest. No matter what you do, though, don't fall into the trap of believing that you can cut your spouse out of your kids' lives completely by winning in court. Unless your spouse is seriously abusive, that's simply not going to happen, and you are wasting your time, money, and energy. Instead, put your energy into figuring out how to arrange a parenting plan that you feel is good enough, even if it's not everything you want. Yes, you want what is best for your children, and there are times that you need to fight to get that. But in most cases, a compromise is going to be better in the long run, for both you and your kids.

Negotiating With Your Spouse

You have quite a few options when it comes to different ways to negotiate with your spouse about child custody or support.

Some people are fortunate enough to be able to sit down and work out a parenting schedule together, focusing on their children's best interests and on what will work out best for the new two-household situation. If you find that you and your spouse can talk things out without any assistance, wonderful! You can use a resource like *Building a Parenting Agreement That Works: Child Custody Agreements Step by Step*, by Mimi L. Zemmelman (Nolo), to create your own parenting plan. (See Chapter 4 for more about what a plan might look like.)

Once you have a plan, you'll submit it to the court for signature along with the rest of the paperwork that you'll need to do to complete your divorce. If you're working with a lawyer, the lawyer will take care of getting all of these papers filed. If you're not, you'll take care of it yourself. Chapter 6 explains more about how to file paperwork in court.

If you and your spouse try to figure it all out yourselves and can't, or if you decide not to try going that route, there are still a lot of ways you can avoid going to court, beginning with mediation.

Mediation

Especially if you've already had some contact with the court about your divorce (or you read Chapter 1), you've heard the term "mediation." In mediation, you and the other parent sit down together with a neutral third party, called a mediator, who helps you discuss and work out your concerns about parenting time and financial responsibilities.

The mediator helps you to communicate, works with you to develop options, and makes sure your plans are realistic and will work for everyone. The decisions stay in your hands—the mediator doesn't decide what happens or tell you what to do.

The mediator's goal is to help you reach a resolution that will work for you, and not to push you in any particular direction. Most of the time, the mediator doesn't even care whether the agreement you make is the same as what a judge might order. As long as it's not patently unfair to one person, and there was no bullying or duress in the process, the mediator will let you create your own definition of what's right for your family. (Of course, if the agreement you reach is clearly unfair, the mediator may refuse to help you turn it into a court order, but that doesn't happen very often.)

In many states, courts are well aware of how damaging custody battles are, and require parents who can't agree about custody to go to mediation. At the end of the process, the mediator may make recommendations to the judge. If your local court does require mediation, in most cases you can decide whether you want to use your court's mediation services or find a private mediator to work with.

Is Mediation for You?

Mediation has a lot going for it. In almost every case, it's less expensive than going to court, it's private, and it allows you to reach a decision that will work for your family. People who reach an agreement in mediation stick with the plan they've made much more often than people who have a judge make a plan for them. Mediation can also help parents learn to communicate better, which in turn can help you have a more peaceful future as you continue parenting together. Establishing a relationship with an effective mediator also gives you somewhere to go if you need to return and work out issues that come up later.

The cost of mediation is usually much lower than other ways of reaching decisions in your divorce. Many couples who are mediating also use "consulting attorneys" to coach them through the process and prepare or review the settlement agreement at the end. And in a mediated divorce, just as in every other divorce, you may need the help of actuaries, appraisers, and other professionals to value your assets. All in all, you might expect to pay between $2,000 and $6,000 for your share of a mediated divorce. This is far less expensive than a contested divorce that settles before trial, and much, much cheaper than a case that goes all the way to trial.

However, not every couple belongs in mediation. For example, if there is violence in your relationship, consider carefully before you agree to participate in mediation. One way to try to overcome the power imbalance that's inherent in an abusive marriage is to agree to mediation only if you bring an attorney with you. If you are hoping to get through your divorce without a lawyer, you could condition your participation on having a support person in the mediation to help you make sure you stand up for yourself. Whatever you decide, be sure that you are confident that you can take care of yourself.

Another potential downside to mediation is that by definition, the mediator can't force either of you to do anything, and a person who wants to delay the proceedings or avoid paying support can abuse the process by agreeing to mediation and then stalling. If you need support or other decisions made early in the process, you may need to go to court. You can still use mediation at a later point to resolve the rest of the issues in your divorce.

Don't reject mediation just because you and your spouse see a particular issue in very different ways—in other words, don't give up before you've begun. Mediation is a powerful process, and many cases that seem impossible to resolve at the beginning end up in a settlement if the spouses are committed to the process.

Advantages of Mediation

Mediation:

- is much less expensive than a trial or a series of court hearings
- usually ends in a settlement of all of the issues in your divorce
- is confidential, with no public record of what goes on in your sessions
- lets you arrive at a resolution based on your own ideas of what is fair, rather than having one imposed upon you based solely on the legal rules
- is controlled by you and your spouse, not the court, and
- can improve communication between you and your spouse, helping you avoid or resolve future conflicts

Kinds of Mediation

Here are the major kinds of mediation.

Court-Connected Mediation

When courts send divorcing parents to mediation, it is usually very low-cost or even free. Court-ordered mediation is almost always limited to issues related to your children. If you want a mediator to help you make decisions about dividing your property as well, you'll probably want to hire a private mediator to mediate your entire divorce, so you don't have to go through two processes at once. Even if you're planning on hiring a private mediator, however, you may be required to attend a minimum number of court-related mediation sessions about issues related to your kids.

Court mediators are skilled and experienced. But many courts limit the number of sessions to which you are entitled, and you don't have much control over scheduling.

Mediation as the Default

Australia and some European countries require mediation for all divorce cases before couples go to court. In contrast, in most U.S. states, only cases involving child custody go to mediation.

Many lawyers and commentators feel that sending all cases to mediation—except where there are allegations of domestic violence or child abuse—would lead to better outcomes and more efficient systems. The practice does appear to be gaining some traction here—North Carolina and Utah have mandatory mediation rules for all cases. Two-thirds of those mediations result in settlements, and half of the rest achieve partial settlement, reducing the court costs of resolving the remaining issues.

Private Mediation

Many divorcing couples who can afford it hire a private mediator; this allows them to choose the mediator and to schedule sessions at their convenience. It also offers somewhat more control over the content of the sessions.

Private divorce mediators charge from about $200 to $500 an hour, depending on where you live and on the mediator's background and experience. How many hours your mediation takes will depend on how complicated the issues are and how well you and your spouse negotiate and compromise. If your concerns aren't too complex and you are motivated to resolve things, you might need only one or two sessions. If your relationship dynamics are difficult or you're really mired in conflict over the kids, the number of sessions could move up, sometimes even toward double digits.

Private mediators have different styles. Some are very directive, controlling the process and staying focused on the goal of getting to agreement. Others are more process-oriented, attending more to the feelings that come up and allowing those to direct the process, at least in the initial stages. Others are a combination of these styles.

The Best of Both Worlds?

A private mediator could be a lawyer or a therapist; both professions offer mediation services for divorcing couples. Some mediators also offer co-mediation—meaning that both an attorney-mediator and a therapist-mediator would work with you at the same time. This could be especially helpful if you have difficult communication issues or if your disputes over your children rest on concerns about best interests that would benefit from a therapist's expertise. Co-mediation can be more expensive, but not necessarily more than seeing both types of professionals separately.

Community Mediation

Nonprofit community mediation agencies sometimes provide a low-cost alternative for divorcing couples. Community mediators are nearly always volunteers, trained to mediate in panels of two or three and to deal with many different kinds of issues. Some of the mediators may be lawyers or therapists who mediate professionally and also donate their time; the rest are from all different walks of life.

Some community mediation services don't do divorce-related cases. And you probably wouldn't want to go to a community mediation service for a really high-conflict custody issue. But if you and your spouse agree on most things but simply can't work out one thorny issue about your time share, you might try community mediation for that single issue. The biggest advantage of community mediation is its very low cost. Community mediation is almost always process-oriented and focused on the ongoing relationship between the people involved.

What Kind of Mediator Do You Need?

Many divorce mediators are lawyers or therapists; some are both. It's up to you what type of mediator you think will work best for your situation.

Lawyer-mediators have the advantage of being able to educate you about the law, as well as having the skills to prepare your court forms and a settlement agreement if you do resolve your differences. Lawyers acting as mediators can't, however, give legal advice to either of you. They can only give legal information—for example, what they think a judge is likely to do. A lawyer-mediator generally charges lawyer rates, so expect to pay between $200 and $500 per hour, depending on a variety of factors.

Therapist-mediators offer some distinct benefits, especially if communication between you and your spouse has broken down badly. A therapist-mediator is often less expensive than a lawyer-mediator—closer to the low end of the lawyer-mediator scale. A combination of the two is a great option as well. The blend of skills when you meet with an attorney and a mediator at the same time can lead to a really effective and efficient process, though it will obviously be more expensive than using only one professional at a time.

Specialists in child custody, child development, or parenting can mediate a custody dispute. Especially when you and your spouse have very different ideas about what's best for your kids, very different parenting styles, or a significant disagreement about what your parenting schedule should be, an expert with experience in these areas can be a great help.

Lay mediators, trained in the basics of family law and skilled in mediation, also offer services to divorcing couples. If your case isn't legally or emotionally complicated, and what you really need is help communicating and making decisions, a lay mediator can probably help you at a lower cost than a mediator who is also a lawyer or therapist.

Finding a Mediator

If you're working with an attorney, your lawyer probably has experience with quite a few mediators and is well-positioned to suggest someone who would work well for your case. However, you should feel free to quiz your attorney about why this mediator is the right one for you, and to research the proposed mediator yourself.

Finding a mediator to help you when you have serious conflicts over child custody can be a little more challenging than when you're dealing primarily with financial issues. Some mediators won't work with parents who are in conflict about their kids, instead referring them to custody mediators or child development experts while the original mediator helps with just the division of property. Other mediators are more comfortable working with couples to resolve custody issues at the same time as property and support questions.

While it might seem cumbersome and expensive to hire separate mediators to deal with property and custody, the advantage is that your custody mediator will be focused on the issues that probably matter to you most, and you can leave the rest of your concerns outside. And of course, if you have already reached an agreement about financial matters and you don't need a mediator for those issues, it makes the most sense to hire a mediator with more expertise in working with parents. Make your decision based on the mediator who feels most comfortable to both of you. If that person doesn't work on custody matters, accept a recommendation for a custody mediator and work with both. And if you find a mediator you both like who does both, you're all set.

If you are representing yourself and need to locate a divorce mediator on your own, try to get recommendations from someone whose judgment you trust. You can ask lawyers, financial advisers, therapists, or spiritual advisers you know for referrals, as well as friends who've been through a divorce. If you can't find direct, personal referrals, here are some other ideas:

- Check www.mediate.com and www.divorcenet.com, which have links to mediator referrals, as do many other divorce websites and lawyer directories, including Nolo's directory at www.nolo.com (click "Find a Lawyer").
- Contact national mediation or family law organizations, including the Association for Conflict Resolution (www.acrnet.org), the Association of Family and Conciliation Courts (www.afccnet.org), and the American Arbitration Association (www.adr.org).
- Call your local community mediation center and ask for a recommendation.
- Call your local bar association or a local organization of therapists or financial professionals.
- Call your local legal aid office.
- Search online or look in the phone book for "mediation," "divorce mediation," or "dispute resolution."

Make sure that you get referrals for divorce and custody mediators, not general or business mediators. Not all mediators are created equal, and you should work only with a mediator who has experience in divorce cases—preferably, cases involving children.

Once you have some names, you'll face the task of choosing the mediator who's right for your case. Depending on how well you and the other parent get along, you might be able to divide up the list and each interview some mediators, then report back to each other and try to make a decision that way. If you don't trust your spouse enough to accept an opinion about the mediators, then you'll each have to talk to each of the prospects.

It's important that both you and your spouse be comfortable with the mediator. Ask whatever questions you need to until you get a sense of the mediator's style and personality and can be fairly confident that both of you can work with this mediator. Ask the mediator for references from former clients—mediation is a confidential process, so the mediator can't give you that information without asking permission, but it's possible some former clients might be willing to talk to you.

Don't try to persuade your spouse to accept someone you like a lot but who your spouse has doubts about—it's too likely to backfire and end up with your spouse walking out of the mediation with the excuse of not liking the mediator. And while it's great to be accommodating and you want to get the process moving forward, accept someone your spouse has suggested only if you feel comfortable with the person. If your spouse proposes a mediator who does feel comfortable to you, even if that mediator's not your first choice, agree without further argument. It's more important to move the divorce forward than to spend a lot of energy arguing about who you work with. Agreeing to the mediator your spouse suggests may even turn out to be a strategic advantage if your spouse later argues that the mediation process wasn't fair or the mediator took your side.

RESOURCE

There's much more about choosing a mediator in *Divorce Without Court: A Guide to Mediation & Collaborative Divorce,* by Katherine E. Stoner (Nolo).

The Mediation Process

Different mediators work differently, and each brings personal touches to the process. But most mediations tend to move along similar lines. The process begins with a brief conversation with the mediator or an assistant before the first session, to collect background information about you and your spouse, your marriage, and what the issues are. Some mediators want a great deal of basic information before the mediation begins, while others prefer to gather all of the information in the first meeting when everyone is present.

Most mediators will meet you in a private office or conference room, and you'll generally all sit together around a table in a way that encourages interaction. It's very common for mediators to use a white board to record options and ideas. The mediator will usually start with introductions and an opening statement, in which you'll hear how the mediator plans to facilitate your process. If you don't know it already, here's where you'll learn whether the mediator intends to work with everyone in the same room for the entire mediation, or expects to have some separate sessions with you and with your spouse. The mediator will also check on whether there are any time limitations or other needs that must be accommodated in this first session. You may also get to have some input on how the process is structured; if you want to offer your ideas, speak up. The mediator should be willing to listen.

The mediator may also take care of some housekeeping business, if that hasn't happened already—for example, asking you to sign an agreement that says that you'll keep what's said in the mediation confidential, and that you understand that the mediator can't disclose any of what goes on there if, later, there's a court proceeding. At the same time, the mediator will be trying to make you feel comfortable and establish rapport with both you and your spouse.

Lawyers in Mediation

If you are represented by an attorney, should your attorney attend the mediation with you? This is something you'll work out with the mediator, your attorney, your spouse, and your spouse's attorney. Very often, lawyers don't attend mediation sessions with divorcing spouses. This keeps costs down and ensures that you and your spouse do the talking and make the decisions—lawyers have a tendency to take over.

Unless your lawyer thinks it's important that you be represented, and even if you're a little bit nervous about it, try the first mediation session without your attorney. (Though if your spouse insists on having an attorney present, you'll want to do the same.) If your lawyer is not representing you but is consulting with you just for purposes of mediation, you'll almost certainly attend the first mediation session on your own. Either way, if you go by yourself and find that you can't state your position clearly or stand up for yourself, consider bringing your lawyer to later sessions.

Your Part in the Mediation

After the mediator has gone over the basics, you will get a chance to make a short statement about your situation, as will your spouse. Some mediators will ask you to answer a few specific questions, like what your goal is for the mediation or what you consider the biggest challenge in communicating with your spouse or in dealing with coparenting. Others will just let you say whatever you want to about your marriage, your divorce, your kids, what's brought you to mediation, and what you would like to get out of it.

It's a good idea to plan ahead to make the most of this first opportunity to express yourself. Think about what you might want to say and how you can set a positive tone and assert your desires and intentions. Try to focus on the present and the future, not on why your marriage is ending. Unless you think the problems in your marriage will affect how the mediation goes or are relevant to your parenting concerns, leave the past in the past. Try to be both clear and positive about what you expect from the mediation—for example, "I'm hoping we can resolve everything quickly and cooperatively," not "I want her to stop being so unreasonable."

Begin with what's most important to you. If you think there are some things that you'll have an easier time compromising about, say that too. For example, "Establishing a workable schedule for getting the kids to school every day is my main priority, and I'm going to need help with it now that they go to different schools. I think once we get that worked out, we'll have an easier time with the rest of the scheduling, and I'm open to whatever solutions might work."

Offer your commitment to doing what's best for your kids and for the family as a whole. Stay focused on those goals.

Assessing the Situation

After you and your spouse have each had a chance to speak, the mediator is likely to ask some questions to clarify or get more information about what you've said. The mediator may also summarize what you've said, to be sure that both the mediator and your spouse have understood all of your points. The same will go for your spouse.

The next step will be to assess where you agree and where you need some work to get to agreement. The mediator will make a list, usually on a white board or easel and pad, of items you already agree on and the ones you'll need to cover in the mediation. Once you have a sense of what needs to be accomplished, you, your spouse, and the mediator will plan how you are going to accomplish it.

By that time, the first session may be over, even though you haven't really begun to negotiate any actual issues. It's very likely that you will need to gather more information, especially if you are dealing with property issues as well as custody questions. For example, if you don't know what child care options exist in your area, then you can't have an intelligent negotiation about your kids' after-school care. The mediator will help you figure out what information you need and ask each of you to commit to bringing certain things for the next session.

Try to get the second session on the calendar before you leave the first one. It's important to keep the momentum going by not letting too much time pass between sessions—a couple of weeks at the most—but you also need to be sure you have enough time to accomplish whatever you've promised to do.

Negotiating an Agreement

When you come back for additional mediation sessions, you'll generally start by checking in about what's been accomplished so far and where things stand. You'll discuss what you expect to accomplish at that day's session and whether you and your spouse have gathered all the information that's required to make decisions.

The mediator may suggest that you deal with simpler issues first. Resolving them builds trust and encourages compromise when it comes to the more difficult issues. Settling a divorce, like almost any other dispute, has an aspect of horse-trading about it, especially when it comes to property. If you let your spouse take the expensive stereo system that she spent so much time assembling, she may be more likely to agree that you can have the computer you have been sharing. That type of bargaining won't apply as much to issues relating to your children, of course.

Negotiating agreements isn't always linear. You may start at what feels like the end, and you may find yourself needing to gather still more information at various points in the process. The mediator will help you to stay on track and will encourage you and your spouse to express your opinions, positions, and what's important to you. He or she should also help you to listen to each other in ways that will make a resolution more likely. (Some of the ways the mediator helps you with communication may be the most valuable aspects of the mediation, because you will be able to take them away with you and use them in your ongoing parenting relationship.) The mediator will encourage you to brainstorm and come up with a wide range of possible solutions.

The two most important things you can do to make your mediation successful are to:

- be open to compromise, and
- really listen and try to understand your spouse's point of view.

Understanding your spouse's position doesn't mean you have to agree with it, and often you won't. But it's difficult to have an effective negotiation if you don't know what your spouse wants or why. It's possible that once you do understand what your spouse's real concerns are, you will have an idea about how to resolve your conflict that hasn't been considered yet. Your efforts at understanding will also encourage your spouse to do the same, and you are more likely to reach a solution that works for you if your spouse really understands what is important to you.

Being open to compromise means that you are not attached to one particular solution. You can't just put your idea on the table and expect your spouse to accept it. A compromise that works is one that takes both of your interests into account. Consider the possibility that your spouse might have valid ideas as well, and take the time to think them through instead of rejecting them out of hand.

Reality Testing

It's an enormous relief to reach an agreement that you think is going to work. When you get to that point, or believe you are getting close, the mediator will help you make sure that your idea will actually work by doing what is often called "reality testing." Taking the information gathered about your family throughout the course of the mediation, the mediator will ask detailed questions about how the proposed settlement might work in real life. For example, you may have decided on a parenting schedule based on a strict 50–50 time share. Some pushback from the mediator could help you realize that the schedule just isn't realistic for your kids, who would have to move back and forth between houses multiple times each week in order to accommodate both parents' work schedules. In other words, the schedule worked for the adults but not for the children. Finding out that your best-laid plans won't work may force you to go back to the brainstorming or negotiating stages, but it will be well worth your time, because you will end up with an agreement that will work and will last.

Your consulting attorneys should also do some reality testing, and you may make some revisions to the agreement after they get through with it. Be patient with this part of the process—it's another piece that's critical to making sure you have an agreement that will stand the test of time.

Completing the Agreement

Once your negotiations are finished and you have found a solution, either the mediator or one of your attorneys will write an agreement and, in many cases, a parenting schedule or parenting plan. (Many courts require that you file a separate parenting plan.) These documents will be incorporated with the rest of your divorce paperwork and will become part of your divorce judgment, which means that a court could enforce them if one of you doesn't do what the agreement says you'll do. There's a wide range of ways to enforce an order, discussed in more detail in Chapters 8 and 9. One of you could go back into court or go to your state child support enforcement agency, depending on whether it's a support or a parenting issue. If it's about support, enforcement could include establishing an income withholding order or a punishment like having the nonpaying parent's professional license or passport suspended or revoked. If it's about parenting, the judge could require that parenting time be supervised, that transitions be made at neutral spots, or could threaten a parent who's really out of line with jail time for being in contempt of court.

Collaborative Divorce

Battling lawyers almost always escalate conflict during a divorce. In response, some lawyers developed a process that can work well even in high-conflict situations and especially where children are involved. It's called "collaborative divorce" and is a process that involves lawyers, but puts them in a role that's different from the usual ways that lawyers operate. Collaborative divorce provides the protection and resources of having a lawyer but also offers a high likelihood of resolution outside of court.

In a collaborative divorce, you and your spouse each hire your own lawyer. But you hire special kinds of lawyers: ones who have undergone collaborative divorce training. They are committed to working cooperatively to try to settle your divorce issues outside of court. You and your spouse both agree to disclose all the information that's necessary for fair negotiations, and to meet with each other and both lawyers to discuss settlement.

You all agree that if your divorce doesn't settle through the collaborative process, your original attorneys will withdraw and you'll hire different ones to take your case to trial. That way your lawyers have no financial incentive to have the case go to trial, because they would lose your business. You also have a strong financial incentive to settle—otherwise, you'd have to pay a second lawyer to get up to speed on your case and do the trial.

Collaborative divorce very often involves other professionals—usually an accountant, actuary, and a therapist. Many parties in a collaborative divorce not only have their own attorney but also work with a therapist who's trained as a "divorce coach." That's a therapist who has special expertise with divorce and can help you make important decisions, manage your emotions, and negotiate confidently. All of the people assisting with your divorce stay in touch with each other and work together to help you come up with an appropriate resolution.

The other professional who can be enormously useful in a collaborative process is a custody evaluator or parenting expert. One of the reasons that collaborative divorce is less expensive than more adversarial methods of divorcing is that you and your spouse will agree on a single expert for each issue. For example, you can work together to hire an expert on custody and parenting and then meet together with that person to talk about what parenting arrangement will be best for your children.

Collaborative divorce can work particularly well when there's a custody dispute, because of the support the lawyers, coaches, and parenting specialist provide. You and the other parent have lawyers and coaches to help you prepare for negotiations, which can help to calm extreme emotions and support compromise.

In most cases, a collaborative process is much faster, and much less painful, than a contested divorce. Having a lawyer can help you feel more confident that you are protecting your own interests while still negotiating in a way that will keep you out of court. Collaborating can make an enormous difference not just to your bottom line, but to your kids' emotional health as you model working together to resolve difficult issues.

The downside is the cost. If the collaborative process doesn't succeed and you are forced to hire a new attorney, you'll have to pay for that lawyer to get up to speed on your case. Before agreeing to a collaborative process, be absolutely sure that you won't give in to something that doesn't work for you just in order to avoid the extra cost of abandoning collaboration and going to court. Think twice, in particular, if your spouse has much greater resources than you do, because it's more likely that your spouse will threaten a court battle if you don't agree to settle.

If you go for a collaborative divorce, expect to pay at least $10,000 to $20,000 for your share, and possibly more if there are a lot of complex issues or challenging dynamics. Between scheduling all the necessary meetings, gathering information, and getting lawyers to prepare paperwork, your divorce may take a year or more. Of course, if you easily reach an agreement and everyone is very efficient, you may be able to finalize things as soon as the waiting period in your state is over, at the lower end of the cost spectrum.

RESOURCE

Get more information. For more information about collaborative divorce, check out *Divorce Without Court: A Guide to Mediation & Collaborative Divorce,* by Katherine E. Stoner (Nolo), or *Collaborative Divorce: The Revolutionary New Way to Restructure Your Family, Resolve Legal Issues, and Move on With Your Life,* by Pauline Tesler and Peggy Thompson (HarperCollins).

Arbitration

If you try mediation or collaboration and it doesn't work out, or if things are so bad that you can't even make an effort at negotiating with the other parent, you'll have to ask someone else to make your decisions for you. Most people think of judges as the ones making those decisions, and in most cases that's true. But if you live in a state that allows it, you also have the option of increasing the speed and privacy of your divorce battle by using arbitration.

An arbitration allows you and your spouse to hire a private individual, called an arbitrator, to make the same decisions that a judge could make. Arbitration is relatively new in divorce cases, although it's been used for years in other kinds of lawsuits. Recently, it's become more popular among divorce lawyers and clients as a good alternative to a court trial, because the timing and the process are more predictable. Before you go too far in thinking about arbitration, however, find out whether it's available in your state—some states don't allow it in divorce cases.

Because arbitrators (and private judges, discussed below) have a much smaller number of cases at one time than a regular judge, you're likely to get much more attention, much sooner, than if you were in court. You're also more likely to be able to use phone conferencing and off-hours meetings that meet your logistical needs better than the requirements of court.

Arbitrators are usually lawyers or retired judges, whom you pay hourly. You and your spouse will agree on the arbitrator, probably from a list of people suggested by your lawyer and your spouse's lawyer. (You don't pick an arbitrator until you've gone through the collection of evidence and you know that you're not going to resolve your case through a settlement.)

Just as if you were going to court, you schedule a hearing and each side prepares arguments and evidence. You're likely to be able to schedule a hearing with an arbitrator much more quickly than you would get a case to trial.

One of the great benefits of arbitration is the ability to be sure the hearing will take place on the date you scheduled it. It's not at all unusual for a court hearing to be rescheduled by the judge on the very day that you were expecting to go to court. It's also not unusual to have a hearing or trial broken up into multiple parts according to the judge's schedule, so that you are in court for two hours one day and then don't return for another three weeks to complete the final two hours of your hearing. This is both stressful and expensive, because your attorney must prepare twice; also, if you have witnesses, particularly expert witnesses, not knowing whether they'll testify on the first day of your court trial means you may have to pay them to come to court twice.

Arbitration isn't cheap, but it won't cost as much as a court trial. That's because it shouldn't take quite as long for your lawyer to prepare for the hearing, and the arbitration itself may be shorter because the arbitrator won't be as strict about evidence as a judge would be. You may have less preparation, too.

The arbitrator isn't required to follow the law, either. This doesn't mean you can't argue your position based on your state's legal rules—it's important to know what those rules are. But if you think the rules aren't fair in your particular case, you can argue for a result that's different than what a court might come to by following established legal precedents. Probably the best thing about the legal rules not applying is that you don't have to follow formal rules of evidence—these are the rules that trip up self-represented people most often, and that cause delays because of lengthy debates over what is and isn't admissible.

An arbitrator's decision generally is binding, which means if you don't like it, you can't ask for a do-over and go to court for a second chance. You also can't appeal the decision to a higher court, so you are stuck with whatever the arbitrator decides. Because of the inherent unpredictability of divorce cases, some people don't like that idea—though others appreciate the certainty that arbitration offers.

Whatever decision you get from the arbitrator must be presented to the court and made part of your final judgment of divorce, which only a state court judge can issue. In general, everything that you do up to the arbitration date—like filing papers, asking for temporary orders, and exchanging information according to the court rules—is also controlled by court rules.

The Arbitrator

The arbitrator is usually a lawyer or a retired judge, whom you pay hourly. If there are lawyers involved in your case, they will help with the selection of the arbitrator—and one of the advantages of arbitration is that you can choose an arbitrator who has experience with the particular issues you're dealing with. Many arbitrators are former family law judges or attorneys with years of experience. If your case is focused on some very specific issue, like custody of a child with special needs or a debate about whether one party can move away, you can even look for an arbitrator with particular expertise in that area. The arbitrator doesn't necessarily have to be an attorney—if your case turns on nonlegal issues, you could hire a custody expert or other professional to decide your case, or go with a panel of arbitrators comprising an attorney and a nonattorney.

The Arbitration Process

In most cases, you choose the arbitrator after you've already gone through the collection of evidence—the process called "discovery." You could schedule your arbitration without sharing a lot of information, but that's not recommended. For one thing, many states require you and your spouse to exchange financial information and to confirm to the court that you've done so, no matter what process you are using. Given that you'll have to do it anyway, you might as well share the information before the arbitration so that everyone can consider it. For another thing, it's difficult to know what you are arguing about if you don't have all the information.

Once you've selected an arbitrator, you'll be able to schedule the hearing at your convenience, rather than being controlled by the court schedule, and you'll undoubtedly have your hearing much earlier than you would if you had to wait for a court date.

An arbitration hearing is private, unlike a trial, which is open to the public. However, although the hearing is private, your court records will still be public if you use arbitration. Most of the papers involved in your divorce, including the petition, the final judgment and settlement agreement, and any briefs on your disputes, are public. Some of your financial information isn't part of the court file, but some of it will be.

At the arbitration, the lawyers present their cases to the arbitrator, and then the arbitrator makes decisions. The process is usually less formal than in a courtroom, because the rules of evidence don't apply (unless you agree that they should) and the arbitrator isn't dressed in a robe and sitting on a high bench.

Cost is another upside to arbitration; although it's still expensive, it won't cost as much as a trial. That's because it shouldn't take quite as long for your lawyer to prepare for the hearing, and the arbitration itself may be shorter because the arbitrator won't be as strict about evidence as a judge would be. However, you also have the advantage of being able to take as long as you need to present your case. You and your spouse may want to agree on some time limits, but you won't have any imposed on you from outside, as you might in a courtroom where the judge can control how long the process takes and you may not get to present all of the evidence you think is important.

Although the arbitrator's decision is binding and not subject to appeal, it's important to remember that child custody and support decisions are never final. Until the child reaches the age of majority, the court continues to have jurisdiction, meaning you can always go to court and seek a change in your parenting arrangement or an increase or decrease in child support if you can prove that there's been a change of circumstances and, in the case of the parenting plan, that the current situation isn't in the child's best interests.

Private Judging

About half of the states now allow private judging in family law cases. Private judging is similar to arbitration, but it is closer to a regular court trial because the private judge, most often a retired judicial officer and sometimes an experienced attorney, is appointed as a temporary judge (called a Judge Pro Tem) by the court that's in charge of your case. The proposed private judge—agreed upon by you and the other parent— must take the same oath of office that a permanent judge does and agree to comply with all the same rules of judicial ethics and court rules. The court follows up to make sure your case is brought to a conclusion. You pay the private judge just as you would an arbitrator.

A private judge has all the same powers as a regular judge, with just a few exceptions—for example, in California and many other states, the judge can't make a file confidential. Unlike arbitration, where only the arbitrator sees the papers you submit in support of your position in the case, all of the documents you submit to a private judge go into your court file, which means they're available to the public. Also, you may have to give the public notice of the time and place of your hearing in front of a private judge—it's not like you're likely to get an audience, but if privacy is a big concern for you, then arbitration is a better choice.

The private judge is required to follow all court rules, including evidence rules, unless you and the other parent agree otherwise. If you are representing yourself, you definitely want to agree to relax the evidence rules. If you have an attorney, you and the lawyer will decide together what is most appropriate for your case and then try to come to an agreement with the other parent and the other parent's lawyer.

Going to Trial

Taking a custody or child support issue all the way to trial is the least desirable result for everyone in the family. Just in case the drawbacks aren't obvious, here's a summary:

Ruinous expense. A divorce trial usually costs each spouse tens of thousands of dollars. Assuming each side's lawyer charges $250 per hour (probably a low estimate), and assuming an ordinary amount of information gathering and pretrial court proceedings, an average divorce might run each of you $30,000—and that figure could easily go higher with a few added complexities.

Ruined family relations. If you think things can't get any worse between you and your spouse, think about what years of expensive and upsetting battles will do.

Huge amounts of your time and energy taken up. The process will almost certainly take more than a year, and the free time you used to be able to devote to your family, friends, or pleasant pastimes will be devoted to trial preparation, gathering financial documents, depositions, meetings with lawyers, meetings with custody evaluators, and more meetings.

An unpredictable outcome. You're putting the most private family decisions in the hands of strangers—judges and custody evaluators, court-appointed experts who may weigh in on your family's future. You don't know what they'll decide.

An unsatisfactory outcome. Whatever the court decides, you're unlikely to be happy with all of it.

Stressed, unhappy, anxious kids. What could be worse, for your children, than a protracted battle between their parents? It will cast a very dark cloud over the family for a very long time.

The trial process is discussed in detail in Chapter 7. ●

Dealing With the Court: Paperwork and Court Hearings

Fighting over custody or support in court is always destructive—it hurts the kids, it hurts your future relationship with their other parent, and it costs a ton. Unfortunately, sometimes it's just not possible to avoid court. For example, it may be that you can't agree on an amount for child support or on who will pay for certain expenses, or perhaps you disagree about the parenting schedule or about where your children should go to school. When you're not able to reach an agreement, even a temporary one, on an issue like this, your option of last resort is to ask a judge to make the decision for you.

Here's how to proceed when circumstances—either an unreasonable spouse or an unresolvable impasse—force you into a courtroom fight over custody or support. (If a lawyer is handling your case, just skip the parts that cover taking care of your own court case.) This chapter concentrates on the basics of dealing with your local family court: learning the rules, meeting the court clerks, finding the right forms, and filing them. It also covers short court hearings at which you're asking for a temporary court order about custody or support. Chapter 7 covers full-blown court trials.

Types of Court Hearings

There are two different kinds of court proceedings if you have a custody or support dispute. You may find yourself in either or both.

Hearings for Temporary Custody or Support Orders

Court proceedings that happen early in the case are often called "pendente lite," (pronounced pen-den-tay lee-tay) meaning "pending the litigation." In other words, the case isn't over, but the court will make temporary decisions that will be in effect until the court issues final orders. Some courts also call these "short-cause," "motion," or "law and motion" hearings. You would schedule a short-cause hearing if, for example, your spouse refused to pay any child support and you didn't have income of your own.

If you are seeking a temporary order on a very complicated issue, you might go to court for a "long cause" hearing, meaning a pendente lite hearing that is longer than the usual 30 minutes to one hour allotted to hearings on temporary orders.

If you're considering whether to go forward with a hearing early on in your case, it's important to know that in many cases, temporary court orders end up being permanent. Either the parents and children get used to the status quo and find that it works just fine, or in the course of the divorce process the parents agree to some slightly revised version of what was ordered and don't ever go to trial.

Trial

It will probably be months before you have a full trial that resolves all of the outstanding issues in your divorce case. Most divorce trials are not long, drawn-out affairs. Many take a day or two, or even just a morning. There are no juries in divorce trials, except in Texas and Georgia, and in Georgia, the jury can't decide custody or visitation, only financial issues. (In just a few other states, you can ask for a jury trial in some circumstances, but this is very unusual.)

Just to confuse things, in some places, a trial is often called a "long cause" hearing. You'll have to learn the terminology of your local court—you can get a lesson from the court clerk, from a local attorney, or by reading a copy of the local rules, discussed below. Chapter 7 takes on the issue of custody and support trials in depth.

Scheduling a Hearing

If you've already filed the paperwork to start your divorce, then you have a case number and a court file already. If you haven't done this, then you'll probably file your initial divorce papers and the paperwork related to your court hearing together. (See "Preparing Court Documents," below.) To schedule a hearing to ask a judge for a temporary support or custody order, call the court clerk or go into the clerk's office (see "The Court Clerk," below). Some courts require that you have all of your paperwork ready for filing before they will schedule your hearing; in other courts you can get the date and then make sure you file the papers far enough ahead of time to comply with the rules about timing. The clerk can tell you which process the court follows. The tricky part of scheduling is making sure you plan the hearing on a date that gives you enough time to deliver the paperwork to the other parent (called "serving" the other parent)—there are always strict requirements about how far in advance you have to deliver the papers to the other parent, so that the other parent has time to respond. (See "Serving Papers," below.)

Even if your need feels immediate, you can't expect to get a hearing date right away. Especially in large urban areas, court calendars can be very crowded, and it could be a month or two, or even longer, before your case can be heard. If something really drastic is going on, like the other parent is preventing you from seeing the kids or you need money urgently and can't raise it through family, friends, or available credit, you may want to hire an attorney to help you get an emergency hearing. (It's not that you couldn't do it yourself, but you are likely to get faster results if you hire someone who's done it before.) Even an emergency hearing probably won't be fast enough for you—unless there's domestic violence, you'll still probably have to wait a week or two.

Where Is My Courthouse?

You can find your local courthouse by searching on the Internet for "[your county] Court." You'll get the general court website, and you can look for links to the family court—the clerk for the family court might be in a different location (a different window, a different floor, or a different courthouse entirely) from the main court clerk. The website may also have links to forms that you can download.

If you live in a large county, there may be more than one courthouse, so be sure you find out where you're supposed to file your papers—that information should also be available on the website, or by calling the court clerk. You can also find the location of your courthouse by looking in the government pages of the telephone book.

Dealing With the Other Parent's Attorney

If both you and the other parent are representing yourselves, you don't have to worry about any of the rules about whom you can contact about what. But if the other parent has an attorney and you're going it alone, you are required to communicate only with the attorney about the divorce. Of course, you'll probably still be talking with the other parent about things like what time to pick up the kids, but you can't discuss something like when to schedule a deposition. For anything that relates to the court case, you must talk to the attorney.

Preparing Court Documents

For many people, the paperwork involved in going to court is the biggest obstacle to representing themselves. It can be daunting, especially if you are intending to present a large amount of evidence—for example, if you and the other parent disagree about your child's education, and you need to prove that your child has special needs that will only be met at a certain school. But if you are able to pay attention to the details, follow instructions, and work methodically through the steps, you can definitely represent yourself in family court.

In most places, there are standard, fill-in-the-blanks forms for almost everything you will need to do in court. The forms may be issued by the state for use in every court in the state, or they may be created by the local court. Sometimes you may need both state and local forms. Where there's not a form, you may have to prepare your own legal documents, called "pleadings." There are books that contain sample pleadings to help you put those together. See Chapter 12 for help with legal research.

The Court Clerk

The court clerks work in the front office of the court—any time you submit paperwork, schedule a hearing, or need a blank form that isn't available on the Internet, the court clerk will be the person helping you.

Each judge also has a courtroom clerk who takes care of the details of running the courtroom. In some courts you may deal with the judge's clerk for scheduling matters.

Court clerks aren't allowed to give you legal advice, so although you can ask them which forms you need, and they will check to be sure everything is properly signed and you've submitted the right fees, they will not help you with what boxes to check or tell you about important deadlines.

How to Find Court Forms

Many court forms are now available online. If they're not, or if you're not a big computer user, you can usually get them from your local court clerk or from your court's self-help center, if there is one. The clerk's office may charge you for a divorce forms packet, but you'll have the advantage of being sure you have all the forms that are required. This is especially helpful if you need a combination of state and local forms; it can be cumbersome to gather them online.

If you prefer going online, check the chart in the appendix called "Court and Court-Related Websites," for a list of Web addresses where you can find local court rules and forms for many states, along with free information about state divorce laws. If your state's court website doesn't offer much, you'll find another online source of information and forms listed.

When you do locate forms online, you'll have a choice about how to go about completing them. You can always print out the blank form and complete it by hand—most courts will accept handwritten forms as long as they're legible and neat. Some sites allow you to complete the form online, but not to save it—in other words, you can complete it and print it, but if you don't do it all in one sitting, or if you find a mistake, you'll have to start over from scratch next time you come back to the website. Other sites allow you to complete the form and then save a draft or final version to your own computer.

How to Complete Forms

Filling out forms of various kinds is something most of us have had to do many times in our lives, but court forms can be intimidating. Fortunately, because family law cases very often involve people who are representing themselves, courts are making an effort to make their forms more user-friendly and easier for nonlawyers to understand. (Unfortunately, not all of them have succeeded.). Here are some tips for dealing with court forms.

Prepare a draft. Whether you're typing the form on a computer, planning to use a typing service, or handwriting it (which is allowed in most places), always print out an extra copy that you can use to practice on. This will help you consider the answers beforehand and avoid making mistakes when you complete the final version of the form. When you're using forms online, some court websites don't allow you to save the form— you can print out whatever you've done, but once you close the document, you lose all of your work. Having a draft will make it easier if you need to go back to the form and start from scratch.

Ask questions before you file. A form may ask for information you don't have or may confuse you. You may be able to find answers to your questions on the same website where you found your forms; court sites often have information and instructions along with the forms. If the question doesn't require legal advice, you can ask the court clerk, but if it does—like asking what you should propose as a parenting time share— the clerk won't be able to help you. If you can't figure out the answer yourself, you might need a lawyer's advice. It's better to get the answers before you turn in your paperwork to the court, than to have to change it later or to lose some of your rights because you didn't find out the necessary information. For example, if you wrongly believe that you have no choice but to agree to a 50–50 sharing of parenting time, and you and the other parent submit an agreement to the court, which becomes a court order once the judge signs it, you won't be able to get the order changed unless there's a change in your circumstances. A lawyer could have told you that an exactly equal parenting schedule isn't required.

Follow instructions. Some of the forms will include instructions, or you might have to find instructions by asking the court clerk or an attorney. (The court clerk won't tell you how to fill out the form, but might point you to some resources.) In addition, it's likely that your state has rules of court and that your court has its own "local rules" about how many copies you should submit or how they should be hole-punched. (See "Rules of Court and Local Rules," below.) However and wherever you find the instructions, make sure you follow them. You might not think it matters whether or not you actually punch two holes in the top of the document, but it surely matters to the clerk. They probably won't refuse to file your papers because they're not hole-punched correctly, but they will if you don't bring the right filing fee. Likewise, if you complete the wrong section of a form, you are going to confuse things in ways that may come back to haunt you. Take the time to pay attention to the details and it will pay off.

Rules of Court and Local Rules

If you are going to represent yourself through your entire case, you'll have to learn about your state's laws—not just about custody and support, but also the rules of evidence, which control how you present your evidence when you get into the courtroom. In addition, whenever you are dealing with paperwork, two types of rules are very important:

State rules of court. These include rules about deadlines, how papers should be completed, the appropriate forms to use, and other procedures. If your state judicial system has a website, your state's rules of court are likely to be there. Otherwise, just search for "[your state] rules of court" or "[your state] laws," and you should find them.

Local rules. The local rules pertain only to your courthouse or to all of the courthouses in your county. They cover things like which courthouse or judge handles which kinds of cases, how and where to file documents and whether you can appear by telephone at a hearing. You can probably find your local rules on the county court website. If they're not online, ask the court clerk for a copy, or go to your local law library and ask the librarian. (Every county has a law library that's open to the public—sometimes it's part of the courthouse and other times it's a separate location. Check online or ask the court clerk where yours is.)

Filing Your Forms

When it comes to custody and support issues, almost all of the forms you prepare will need to be filed with the court clerk, which means they'll become part of your court file. Some courts don't require you to file financial documents—you're just required to exchange them with your spouse.

You can file papers by mail or in person by going into the clerk's office. If you're representing yourself, it's always a good idea to take your papers in person if you have the time, because the clerk will check them over and if there are any problems, you may be able to fix them on the spot. But if you don't have time, it's fine to file by mail. Just be sure you follow these instructions.

Electronic or Fax Filing

Some courts now offer lawyers and self-represented parties the ability to file documents by fax or electronically via email. In some places this service is only available to attorneys whose firms have an account with the company providing e-filing services to the court. In others you will be able to access the services after you've set up an account that includes your contact and billing information. Ask your court clerk or check the court website to find out whether e-filing and fax filing are available in your court.

Make plenty of copies. Before you turn your papers in to the court clerk, make sure you have at least two extra copies for the clerk to stamp and hand back to you. You will need one copy for your records and one copy to serve on (deliver to) the other parent. And it never hurts to have an extra. The clerk will keep the original signed document and at least one copy, possibly two. (Hint: sign the original in blue ink so that you can tell it apart from the photocopies.) If you're mailing the forms, keep one copy in your file in case they go astray. And make sure you send a cover letter that says exactly what you're submitting and asks the clerk to file the papers and return the file-endorsed copies to you. Include a return envelope with adequate postage to have the papers returned once they're filed.

Don't forget the filing fee. Some papers that you file with the court must be accompanied by a fee. If you file your own petition or complaint for divorce, or if you are filing it along with papers seeking support or custody, there will unquestionably be a fee—the amount varies between about $100 and $400 depending on where you live. If you file your petition and pay a fee, you may or may not have to pay an additional fee when you submit the paperwork to schedule a court hearing on custody or support. If you do, it will be much lower, from $20 to $100. You may also have to pay a fee to submit a stipulation (agreement) between you and the other parent that you're asking the judge to sign as an order.

Before you take or send your papers for filing, check your court's website or ask the clerk to find out the fee amount and what types of payment are accepted.

How to Create Pleadings

Most forms that you'll use in your divorce are fill-in-the-blanks forms. However, on occasion there may be no form for exactly what you need, and you'll have to create your own "pleading" documents. (It's called a pleading because you're usually asking for something.)

Pleadings are submitted on pleading paper, which just means paper that's numbered down the left side and, usually, has lines down both sides. Creating pleadings on your own has become much easier in recent years—many computer programs (including Microsoft Word) allow you to create numbered lines on any page. There are also templates available on the Internet, at websites like www.legalpleadingtemplate.com.

Your local court might have special rules for pleadings, like requiring that they include a footer, be hole-punched in a particular way, or include a cover sheet of a particular kind. Ask the court clerk or check the local or state rules.

The content of your pleading will depend on what type of document you need to submit. If you are required to submit a pleading, you may want to ask for a lawyer's help. And look at the resources described in Chapter 12 for help finding books with sample pleadings.

Documents You Might Need

The paperwork you'll need to seek temporary support or custody orders early in your divorce case varies enormously from state to state, but certain types of documents are likely to be required. The word "motion" comes up a lot, because whatever you're asking the court to do is referred to as "moving" the court for an order. The paperwork you're filing is sometimes collectively called a "motion," and the hearing may be called a motion hearing.

The list below should give you a general idea of what documents you'll need for a temporary support or custody hearing. If your state requires a completely different set of documents, don't panic. Go by what your local court says, follow the general instructions here about preparing forms and declarations for court, and your paperwork should be fine.

Here are the kinds of documents you'll probably need:

- A document for the judge to sign that requires the other parent to show up in court. This is sometimes called an "Order to Show Cause" or "Order to Appear." You will prepare and submit the form and the clerk will stamp a judge's signature on it, after which you'll serve it on the other parent.

- A document stating what orders you're asking the judge to make, if the Order to Show Cause or similar document described just above doesn't contain that information. This could be called anything from the very nondescriptive "Application for Order" to the more helpful "Petition for Child Custody."

- A declaration or affidavit (sworn statement) stating the facts on which your request is based. (See "Declarations," below, to learn all about preparing a declaration.)

- A proposed order for the judge to sign, giving you what you're asking for. It will be called an "Order," "Judgment," or "Decree," and whenever you refer to it, you should call it the "proposed" order. When you prepare the proposed order, you'll fill out the form as though the judge agreed with you about everything.

The judge will use your order if the hearing goes 100% your way; if it doesn't, either the other parent will have prepared an alternative order, or the judge will tell either you or the other parent to prepare a different order and submit it to the court soon after the hearing. It's also possible that the judge will prepare an order and print it out right there at the hearing or send it to you later.

Declarations

A declaration is a written statement by a party or a witness, signed under penalty of perjury—which means that if you lie in a declaration, you commit the crime of perjury. A declaration presents information to support one side's argument. If you ask the court for an order on child support or custody, you'll probably submit declarations to support your request. It's very likely that you'll submit a declaration of your own, stating the facts you know from your own personal knowledge. It's also possible that you will arrange to get declarations from other witnesses who have information about the facts that you're trying to prove to support your argument. These witnesses could be family members or friends who witnessed events you want the judge to know about, or experts such as a child custody counselor.

In many short-cause hearings, declarations are the only type of evidence that's allowed. In other words, you can't bring live witnesses to court; instead, you must submit evidence through declarations. In long cause hearings and trials, both written declarations and live testimony are usually allowed.

If you want witnesses to testify in person at a short-cause hearing, talk to the judge's clerk before the hearing. You need to find out whether witnesses are allowed, and if they are, how to arrange for them to come and how to notify the other parent about the witnesses you intend to present.

Outline of a Declaration

There are a few elements that every declaration should include.

Identity of the person making the statement. If you're writing a declaration, the first sentence should state your name and your role in the case, confirm that you are an adult, and state that the declaration is based on your own knowledge. For example, "I, Timothy Lawrence, am an adult resident of Lake County and the petitioner in this action. I make this declaration of my own knowledge and if called to testify to the matters stated here, I could competently testify to those matters."

Why the statement is being offered to the court. Say what you're asking for at the beginning and the end. "This declaration is in support of my request for a change of custody." Or, if it's a witness declaration, it might say, "I am Timothy Lawrence's next-door neighbor, and I make this declaration in support of Timothy's petition for custody of his daughter, Sarah."

An explanation of the status quo and of what's being requested. Explain the current situation and let the court know about any existing orders. For example, in a case relating to parenting time: "Since 2010, my ex-wife has had primary custody, and I have spent time with my daughter every other weekend and every Wednesday evening, including overnight. Our court order dated January 14, 2010, sets out the schedule. I am requesting a change in the parenting schedule to spend two overnights a week with my daughter."

The facts on which you base your request. These are the reasons why you are asking for what you're asking, or the explanation of what has changed. This will be the bulk of your declaration.

A statement that the declaration is made under penalty of perjury, or whatever similar statement your court requires. This will come just before the signature, which is also a necessity.

Your Declaration

A declaration is a great way to provide information that will get the judge on your side. Follow these important rules to make sure that you get the maximum persuasive power out of the declaration and don't make the judge mistrust what you say or feel annoyed at how you're saying it.

Always be honest. Don't include anything that isn't true based on your own knowledge, and don't exaggerate. You may need to admit to facts that don't necessarily make you look good. Go ahead and do it. You'll get points for honesty, and if you think a brief explanation would help, you can include it. For example: "I was late to pick up my son on three different occasions, all of which resulted from my boss keeping me late at work without warning and despite my requests to leave. I now have a different supervisor who is more respectful of my time and my family responsibilities, and I don't anticipate any more problems with pickups."

Keep it brief. Make your points in the fewest possible number of words. Every judge in a family court has a very large caseload and will be reading through a lot of declarations to prepare for an afternoon of hearings. Yours will get more favorable attention if it's crisp, clear, and short.

Stick to the facts. It's critical that you keep declarations limited strictly to facts, and leave out any opinions—your own or those of others that you might feel inclined to report to the judge. (See "Fact Versus Opinion," below.)

Say only what you know personally. Your declaration should contain only things you either know or saw yourself. If you saw your spouse speeding with your kids in the car, you can say it. But you can't say, "My brother-in-law told me he saw my wife talking on her cell phone while she was driving and my kids were in the car." You'll have to get your brother-in-law to sign his own declaration about that fact—otherwise it's something called "hearsay," which isn't admissible in court. (See "Declarations From Others," below.)

That means no speculation. If the kids come home from overnights at the other parent's house with bags under their eyes, just say that—don't speculate that they were allowed to stay up past their bedtime. Anything the children tell you is hearsay just like anything another adult tells you, so you can't include that either. Plus, it's a terrible idea to involve your children in your parenting conflicts in any way.

Clearly say what you want the court to do. Besides the facts, the only other thing you'll include in your declaration is what you're asking the court for—for example, to change your custody schedule. That information is probably in other documents that you're filing with the court, too, but it never hurts to reiterate it. As with everything else, keep it concise. "For these reasons, I am asking the court to allow my daughter to stay overnight with me on Sundays instead of taking her back to the other parent's house according to the current schedule."

Don't vent angry or negative feelings about the other parent. Saying negative things about the other parent will never get a judge on your side. Even if your ex is completely irresponsible and, in your opinion, a bad parent, don't clutter your declaration with accusations that have nothing to do with what you're trying to prove. Of course, if negative facts about your spouse are relevant—for example, he was just arrested for drug possession and you're trying to get full custody of your children—you should state them. But state them as facts ("My husband was arrested for possession of cocaine on February 12 and is currently out on bail awaiting trial") rather than opinion ("My husband is a complete loser with a drug problem").

Fact Versus Opinion

It can be challenging to differentiate fact from opinion sometimes when you are enmeshed in a high-conflict situation. Here are some examples that might help.

Opinion: My ex-husband is a neglectful parent.
Fact: On two recent occasions (May 1 and 15) I arrived at my ex-husband's house to pick up my three-year-old daughter and found her playing unsupervised near the swimming pool.

Opinion: My wife doesn't care about our son's medical needs.
Fact: My son, who is required to take medicine every day for ADHD, came back from a one-week stay at his mother's house with the same amount of medication that he left with. He was fidgety, inattentive, and talked nonstop for the next three days until the medication kicked in again. All of these were symptoms that had abated with regular medication.

Opinion: The kids will be better off moving to Ohio with me than staying here with their dad.
Fact: I am asking to move the children to Ohio with me because I have a job offer that will pay me $15,000 more per year than I am currently making, in a position with more opportunities for advancement. In addition, I will be living within five miles of my parents and my sister and her children, which will allow my children to know this part of the family better. My salary will allow me to pay travel expenses for the children to visit their father regularly. If they stay here, they will be in paid child care after school, as their father has no family nearby or other resources for child care.

Declarations From Others

In addition to your own declaration, you may want to submit declarations from others who have personal knowledge about your family. Just as was true for your own declaration, these people can testify only to things that are their own personal knowledge, including events that they saw or heard themselves—not things they were told about by other people or assume happened.

Just like your declaration, these declarations should:

- be clear and concise
- state only facts and not opinions
- be respectful of the other parent, and
- keep to the point.

Ask anyone who has personal knowledge of important facts to write a declaration. For example, if your child care worker has told you that on the mornings your ex brings the kids to day care they are always hungry and say they haven't had breakfast, ask her whether she'll sign a statement. Try to get declarations from people whom a judge would consider neutral, like a teacher or coach. Better still if you can get someone who would be expected to be on your spouse's side, like a relative or friend of your spouse. You can expect the judge to be just a bit skeptical of declarations from your mother or your best friend.

Ask a friend, neighbor, relative, or other third party to submit a declaration only if they have personal knowledge of something specific that you want to prove to the judge. Don't ask them to submit a declaration that just says what a great parent or great person you are or how much your kids love you. (Unless the other parent is arguing that your daughter is miserable when she has to be with you, in which case it's okay for them to submit a declaration saying that when you come to pick up your daughter after a play date she always runs to you and gives you a big hug and a big smile.)

Make sure you don't put words in the mouth of anyone you ask to write a declaration. You should certainly explain the difference between opinion and facts and ask them to be sure they only state facts, but don't ever suggest what they should say—only the topics to cover. It's okay for you to do the typing for them or to type up something they've handwritten and have them sign it, but it would be better to have someone else do that so there's no question about whether you added or subtracted things.

How to Create a Declaration

It's possible that the court will give you get everything you need, in terms of the format, to create a declaration. Many states have pre-printed declaration forms (and often they include helpful things like the declaration under penalty of perjury that's required). If there's no declaration form available, you can prepare your own using the instructions in "How to Create Pleadings" and "Outline of a Declaration," above. Another good resource for creating your own documents is *Represent Yourself in Court: How to Prepare & Try a Winning Case*, by Paul Bergman and Sara Berman (Nolo).

> **TIP**
> **Make it look good.** This doesn't mean spinning the facts to your advantage, but literally making your paperwork look as professional as possible. You shouldn't handwrite a declaration unless you really, really have no other option—the judge will find it an inconvenience, for one thing, and it may also reflect poorly on your attitude toward the proceedings. If you truly don't have access to a computer or typewriter, you can always write out what you want to say and take it to a typing service or ask a friend to type it up for you.

Serving Papers

Any time you file documents in court, you also have to provide a copy to the other party—in this case, the other parent. This is called "serving" papers. Serving papers simply means having them delivered in a legally approved way, according to your state's law. In most places you cannot serve the papers yourself. You have to have someone else do it, and then sign a document stating that they did so, usually called a "proof" or "declaration" of service. Or you may be able to just mail the papers. These methods of service are discussed below.

Personal Service

Serving someone personally means hand-delivering the documents to that person. You can't do it yourself, because you're a party to the case. You can either hire someone—a process server or, in most places, the local sheriff—or ask a reliable friend, someone who'll be sure to comply with the law (and won't just drop the papers off on the doorstep and call it a day) and who will be available to sign the proof of service.

If you want to hire someone, check with the court clerk about having the sheriff's office serve the papers; that is often the least expensive route. Or look up "process servers" or "private investigators" to find someone who is experienced with serving papers.

The court clerk should be able to give you more information about getting your spouse served with the papers. And make sure you know exactly what needs to be served. In many places, you're required to include forms that the other parent can use to respond to the court. For example, if you file the petition or complaint form to start the divorce, the other parent is required to respond within a certain period of time, and in many places you are required to also serve the blank form for the response.

Service by Mail and Acknowledgment

In most states, you can serve the papers that start the divorce by mail if the other person agrees. If the other person won't cooperate with that, you must have your spouse personally served. To accomplish service by notice and acknowledgment, you must include a form that your spouse signs to acknowledge that the papers were received, and your spouse must send it back to you so that you can file it with the court to prove that your spouse received the paperwork to start the divorce. Usually this acknowledgment form is available along with the rest of the divorce forms you get from the court or online. Have someone else drop the divorce papers in the mailbox—you're not allowed to do it, because it's part of serving the papers.

Service by Mail for Motion Papers

If you've already served the initial divorce papers and all you need to deliver is paperwork seeking temporary support or custody orders, you can usually serve these motion papers by mail—you don't need the other person's agreement like you do for serving the initial divorce papers. But check with the court clerk or your state's rules of court to be sure what's legally right in your court. (See "Rules of Court and Local Rules," above.) You must then be sure to prepare a document called a proof of service, signed (by the person who sent the papers) under penalty of perjury and showing that the papers were mailed far enough in advance of the hearing that your spouse got the required amount of notice. Typically, a court might require that a parent get 15 to 30 days' notice of any hearing involving custody or support.

Proof of Service

Whether you're serving all of your divorce paperwork or just motion papers, you must let the court know that service has been accomplished in a way that complies with the law. In other words, the court wants to know that the other parent has gotten adequate notice of the hearing and knows what you're asking for from the court. You do this by filing a form called a "proof of service" or "declaration of service" with the court clerk. (You'll find the proof of service wherever you've obtained your other forms—either from the court clerk or online.) On this form, the person who served the papers enters information about where, when, and how service was accomplished, and then signs the form. It's your responsibility to file it. In some places, there is a different form for proof of service of the initial paperwork, and for proof of service of later documents. Check the forms carefully to be sure you are using the right one.

Gathering Evidence: Disclosures and Discovery

In every divorce case, the spouses are required to provide each other with certain financial information designated by the court—this is usually called making mandatory disclosures. And in a court case, the term "discovery" means the part of the process in which everyone involved can ask the other people involved for relevant information before the trial. The idea of discovery is that a trial is more efficient and fair if everyone has the same information and no one is surprised by information the other side withheld. The mandatory financial disclosures and information you gather in discovery should also help get the case settled—the more information both spouses have, the more likely it is you'll be able to reach a solution that works for both.

Mandatory Financial Disclosures

Family courts usually require that each spouse tells the other everything about their respective financial situations. This means each person tells the other about assets, debts, income, and property. You might already know a lot of the information that your spouse will give you, but you also might be surprised by some of it, especially if your spouse has separate accounts or a business that you're not much involved in. The information will be most relevant to your property settlement, but it will also be important if you're in a dispute about support. Both of you will be required to provide the other person with:

- pay stubs and anything else related to income, like employment contracts
- bank and brokerage statements showing current assets
- tax returns
- statements and plan information for retirement and benefit plans
- insurance coverage, and
- credit card statements and information about other debts.

You may be reluctant to give some of your own financial information to your spouse, but you don't have a choice, and there's no point in resisting.

Discovery Requests

The information required by the mandatory disclosures may not get you everything you need, or perhaps your court doesn't require the exchange of financial information. In that case, you can use discovery procedures to get the information you need. You can also get other types of information that will help you in a custody dispute. There are a few different ways that you can ask for information from the other parent.

Interrogatories are written questions that you send to your spouse, who then has a specified time (usually 30 days) to respond with answers or object to the questions. You can ask about anything relevant to your disputes, from when stock options will vest (for the purpose of determining income for support) to who stays with the children when your spouse has evening meetings.

A request for admissions is a yes-or-no question in which you ask your spouse to confirm or deny a certain fact. For example, you might ask the other parent to admit that "Sarah didn't get to ballet class on Tuesday, May 22 or Tuesday, May 29," and "Sarah was in your custody on May 22 and May 29." Once someone admits a fact by responding to a request for admission, you can use the response to challenge any contradictory testimony that comes up at trial.

Requests for production can be used to ask the other parent for written documents. You can ask for anything that will provide information you need to engage in an informed negotiation, including financial records or something relating to your kids. If you need to get records from a person or entity outside of the case, you can use a subpoena—an order you ask the judge to issue, requiring the person or entity (for example, your child's school) to turn over the documentation.

At a deposition, a person answers questions under oath. You can have your spouse appear and answer questions under oath about anything related to the divorce, and you can also ask other people, like a child's teacher or an expert witness, to come to a deposition. Depositions take place in a lawyer's office (usually the lawyer who has requested the deposition), not in court, but the person being questioned is under oath, and everything said is taken down by a court reporter just as in a courtroom.

Depositions are really expensive, so they should be used sparingly. Your lawyer will definitely want to take your spouse's deposition if you suspect that your spouse is hiding assets or engaging in some other type of financial wrongdoing that is keeping you from getting the child support you're entitled to. More likely, you'll take depositions of anyone that either of you has hired to evaluate your kids and make a recommendation about what custody arrangement would be in their best interests.

Preparing for the Hearing

Going to court can be an intimidating experience whether or not you have a lawyer advocating for you. So try to remember that the lawyers and judges don't own the courts—in fact, you do. You have every right to be there seeking the court's assistance with a question you are unable to resolve any other way. (Of course, it's always better to settle matters out of court! See Chapters 1 and 5, which discuss mediation and collaboration.)

Here's some general advice about getting ready to go to court. If you are working with a lawyer, your lawyer will advise you about how things generally go in your local court.

Organize Your Paperwork

It's very important that your documents, including everything you've filed with the court, are organized and easily available to you. You might think that the judge will have at hand all the documents you've already submitted. This isn't necessarily so, and you never know when you may be asked to show a document or a piece of evidence to the judge. Just as important, you need to remember what you've submitted and be familiar with all of the documentation. If the judge asks you what your monthly income is, your answer needs to be the same as what you wrote on the financial declaration that you submitted.

Get a three-ring binder and put all of your papers in it. You can either separate papers you submitted from those submitted by the other parent, or put all the documents in the order they were filed. Either way, label the documents clearly by title and date, using dividers with tabs or even small sticky notes with the writing on the edge so it can be seen.

If you are using any "exhibits" as evidence—for example, your child's report cards to show that there's been a decline in grades since your spouse started working a second job—to support your request for a change in custody, make sure you have at least two extra copies of everything you want the judge to consider. You may need to provide one to the judge and one to the other parent or the opposing lawyer while you are in court. Again, even if you've already provided the documents, make sure you have extra copies with you. (There's more about exhibits in Chapter 7, "Going to Trial.")

Make a list of everything you need to prove, so that you won't forget anything. On the list, make a note of the evidence you're going to use to prove each fact or legal theory.

Do Some Advance Scouting

Before your hearing date, make sure you know where the courthouse is, how you'll get there, and if you're driving, where you'll park. If you have time, make a dry run and find the courtroom to which your hearing is assigned. Most court proceedings are public, and you can go in and watch the judge who will be hearing your case to see how the courtroom is run. It will make the process at least a little familiar when it's your turn.

Check In With Your Witnesses

For most short-cause hearings, you won't be allowed to bring witnesses. But some judges may allow it, and it shouldn't be a problem at an extended or long cause hearing or a trial. (A long cause hearing is a court hearing that's longer than the 15 to 30 minutes to allotted for short-cause hearings in most courts.) If you have arranged for any witnesses to testify on your behalf, remind them of the time and location of the court hearing, and make everything as easy as possible for them by letting them know where to park and what to expect. If there are any witnesses that you're worried won't show up, you can serve them with a subpoena, which is a court document that requires them to be in court at the time and place you specify. There's more about that in Chapter 7.

At the Hearing

First and foremost, be on time! Remember that many courthouses now have security procedures at the entrance, so think of it like a trip to the airport. Be sure to leave time to park, stand in a security line, and put your belt and shoes back on after you get through it.

Courtroom Attire and Etiquette

You're not required to wear a suit or other formal clothes to court if you don't have them or aren't comfortable dressing like that, but you should dress in a way that shows respect to the court. Dress as though you're going on an important job interview, and you should be fine. Turn off your cell phone, pager, and any other electronic device you have with you, unless you have the court's permission to use a laptop computer.

Address the judge as "Your Honor." Never address the other parent directly while you're standing in front of the judge, unless both of you are representing yourselves. Even then, confine your comments to procedural matters, like "Do you need a copy of the babysitter's declaration?" Don't argue any of the points you're trying to make with your spouse—your entire courtroom presentation should be directed to the judge.

If you want to show the judge a document or other piece of evidence, ask permission to "approach the bench." Never move toward the judge's bench without permission. Most of the time you will hand things to the clerk who sits next to the judge rather than directly to the judge.

Everything that is said in court will be taken down by a court reporter or recorded on tape. It's important that you speak clearly, audibly, and slowly so that the court reporter can hear and understand what you say.

If you need to, you will be able to get a transcript of your court hearing later. You might need one if the judge makes a ruling that you find confusing and you want to be sure that the written order following it up is correct, or if you want to know exactly what the other parent said about something.

Argument and Testimony

When your case is called, meaning that the clerk calls out your name and case number, you'll go to the counsel table, which is usually a long table directly across from the judge's seat on the bench. There's usually a sign on each table saying "petitioner" or "complainant" or "respondent," so that you know where to sit. The court clerk will ask you to raise your right hand and swear to tell the truth. Greet the judge by saying "Good morning, Your Honor," and wait for the judge to tell you what to do. The judge will let you know who should begin, and may ask you some questions. This is your chance to argue your case. Generally, the judge will allow you to tell your story, either from where you are already sitting at the counsel table or by taking the witness stand. If you're at the counsel table, stand up to speak to the judge. If you're on the witness stand, you'll be seated.

In a short motion hearing, it's very unlikely that you'll present any witnesses other than your own testimony. You will have submitted your papers beforehand, and the judge most likely will have read them, or at least reviewed them very quickly just before the hearing. If the judge asks you to state what you're asking for and what evidence it's based on, don't say that it's all in the documents you've already submitted—just answer the question. The whole thing will probably be over quickly. Most short-cause hearings are scheduled for about 20 minutes, though some can go longer.

When you're speaking to the court about what you want and why, the same rules apply that applied to your declaration—keep it short and simple, don't trash the other parent, say what you're asking for and why, and be honest. If the judge asks you questions, answer as succinctly as possible.

Don't try to avoid the question, don't answer the question you wish had been asked, and don't editorialize. Just respond to exactly what the judge asks you.

If you have a longer hearing on the calendar, it's possible you might be allowed to present witnesses if you want to. You don't have to, and some judges don't want live testimony, just written declarations. If you go to trial, you'll almost certainly present witnesses. See Chapter 7 for more about testimony in court and the rules of evidence that apply—these are the rules about what you're allowed to say in court and what type of documents and witnesses you can present. You don't need to know much about evidence rules for most short-cause hearings, especially if the other parent also doesn't have a lawyer.

The Judge's Decision

After you and your spouse have argued your sides, the judge will make a decision. In motion hearings, most often the judge will make a ruling on the spot. If the judge gives you everything you asked for, and you prepared a proposed order as described in "Documents You Might Need," above, you can just ask the judge to sign your order. The same is true for the other parent if the ruling goes against you.

If there's no proposed order, or if the judge's ruling is very different from what either of you asked for, try to write down very carefully what the ruling is. If the judge goes too fast or you don't understand something, you can ask for clarification—but don't interrupt the judge. Wait until the judge is finished and then say, "Excuse me, Your Honor, may I be sure I got all of that correctly?" or something along those lines. Also, be sure that you get a business card from the court reporter, in case you need to get a transcript of the hearing later.

You might think that the judge would prepare a written version of the order stated in court, but that's not usually the case—the lawyers (or a party without a lawyer) must do it, and then have the judge sign it. Usually, the job of preparing the order falls to the person who won at the hearing. However, if the other parent has an attorney, it's quite likely that the attorney will offer to prepare the order regardless of who won. Go ahead and accept the offer—you'll get a chance to review the order before it's submitted to the judge for a signature. When you do have that opportunity, review the order very carefully before you sign that you accept it. If it's not consistent with what the judge said, send it back to the attorney with a polite note pointing out the inconsistency, and don't sign it until it's right. If you end up in a fight about this with the other parent or the attorney, you might have to go back and ask the judge to finalize the order.

After the Hearing

Once the judge issues an order, you must follow it, even if you think it's completely wrong. If you do disagree with it, you will have a chance to argue about if your case goes to trial. (If you think the judge made a legal mistake and you want to challenge it immediately, there is a procedure for doing that. In many places it's called filing a "writ of mandamus." You will most likely need an attorney to help you with that.)

Try to keep an open mind about the temporary orders even if they didn't go your way, and see whether you can make the arrangement work for you, or come up with some approximation of it that your spouse will accept. In other words, do whatever you can to avoid a trial. ●

Going to Trial

A lot has to happen before you end up in a courtroom, in front of a judge, presenting your evidence and then waiting for the final decision about whatever you and your spouse are arguing about. Almost certainly, you have already attended at least one pendente lite hearing (described in Chapter 6) and tried to negotiate with your spouse (possibly with help from mediators and lawyers), in an effort to settle your case. Going to trial is admitting that you've given up on reaching a settlement and need the judge to make decisions for you. At trial, the judge will rule on all the issues that haven't been permanently settled yet.

A trial is best avoided at nearly all costs, but you may not be able to stay away from the courtroom in the end. If you feel strongly that your children's welfare is being threatened by what your spouse considers a reasonable parenting plan, or that your temporary child support award was based on an inaccurate assessment of your spouse's income, then you may simply have no choice other than to have your day in court.

Chapter 6 covered the basics of dealing with court clerks, filing papers, and going to court for hearings to establish temporary custody or support orders. All the information there about interacting with the court system and the judge still applies. Here, we'll delve deeper into courtroom procedures, with a focus on what will happen if you actually get to a trial.

Should You Have a Lawyer?

Most people who go to trial in their divorce case hire a lawyer. Conducting a trial is a complicated matter, entailing presenting evidence, questioning witnesses, and objecting to the other side's questions or evidence. A good lawyer can be an enormous help.

If, however, you represented yourself at earlier hearings and felt comfortable, the same may be true about a trial. But because a trial results in a final judgment that will bind you and your spouse, there is more at stake. The process is different, too; the court generally will allow a day or even longer for the trial, instead of 20 minutes or an hour for a hearing. You're more likely to present witnesses at a trial than at a temporary hearing, and you'll probably use more evidence. For the same reasons listed above, the other parent is also more likely to have a lawyer, so you have to consider the impact of being on your own when there's a lawyer on the other side.

You'll probably at least want to consult a lawyer who can coach you through the complicated spots. Chapter 12 has much more about hiring a lawyer and the different ways of working with attorneys.

Getting a Trial Date

Most states have a form that you must file to request a trial date. It's commonly called an "at-issue memorandum," "request to set trial," "notice of intention to request entry of divorce," or something along those lines. Different courts' forms look different, but most of them ask for certain information:

- The date you filed your case and the date that the other spouse (respondent) was served with process (legally received the divorce petition)
- Whether you have completed all of your discovery (information-gathering), and if not, what is left to do
- Whether you have attended any pretrial or settlement conferences (explained below)
- What issues you are asking the court to decide, and
- How long you think the trial will take (if you have a lawyer helping you, the lawyer can help you estimate; if not, request one day if you expect to present more than one witness or a number of exhibits, and two or three hours if only you and the other parent will testify).

Even when you're asking for a trial date, the court still wants you to settle your case. So before you can have your case heard in front of a judge, you might be required to attend a status conference, a settlement conference, or both.

A **status conference** determines whether the case is ready for trial. It is a short hearing at which the judge makes sure that all of your discovery is complete and that you are actually ready to go to trial. If it turns out there's still something you need to do—for example, you still need financial information from the other parent before you can seriously negotiate about child support—the judge will make orders that should result in the case being ready soon. Not all courts use status conferences so don't be surprised if there isn't one and you just go directly to the settlement conference.

A **settlement conference** is an in-person meeting with a judge or possibly a court-appointed mediator. The neutral person's job is to help the parents try to settle the case.

Some courts schedule the settlement conference and give you a trial date only if you don't settle at that time. Other courts give you a trial date and set a settlement conference date a week or so before that date. Still others plan the trial date and have you meet with a settlement judge or mediator on that very day, immediately before you're scheduled to go into court.

High-Conflict Cases

Some courts have special programs to handle high-conflict custody cases, meaning those in which the parents can't seem to agree on anything and end up back in court repeatedly, asking the judge to decide everything from where the kids should go to school to what after-school activities they should participate in to who can care for them when a parent isn't available. These cases are characterized by ongoing and powerful hostility between the parents, a complete or near-complete inability to communicate effectively about parenting, and a tendency to bring every issue, large or small, to court for a long, drawn-out fight.

If you are one of these parents, you may find yourself under the scrutiny of your court system. Usually these programs assign parents to one judge who follows the case from start to finish. (Otherwise, it's more likely you'd appear in front of a number of different judges over multiple court dates.) In addition, you might be required to participate in counseling and parenting skills training before you can schedule your trial.

Some judges appoint "parenting coordinators" to meet with battling parents regularly to monitor how things are going in terms of day-to-day compliance with existing court orders. This keeps the judges from having to micromanage arguments over whether the kids were dropped off on time and with the right clothes in their backpacks.

If You're Stuck in a High-Conflict Divorce

It only takes one determined spouse to create a high-conflict divorce case. Usually, it happens when a parent:

- is extremely controlling about the children or feels that there's only one way to be a good parent
- is very angry and wants to punish the parent who left the relationship, or
- is emotionally or physically abusive and continues the abuse by forcing the other parent into ongoing court proceedings.

The other factor that is present in nearly all high-conflict divorces is money. It is very expensive to return to court over and over again, and the sad truth is that sometimes the person with more resources wears down the other parent and wins the day.

If you are in a high-conflict divorce that you attribute to one or more of the motives listed above on the part of the other parent, you may find it very difficult to get out. You may be completely dedicated to the idea of mediation or using a collaborative process, but if the other parent won't participate in good faith, there isn't a lot you can do except enter the playing field that's been chosen for you—the courtroom.

Often, the only thing that ends a high-conflict divorce—and the only thing that a high-conflict parent will respect—is a decision from a judge. Unfortunately, even that doesn't stop some parents, and you may find yourself back in court repeatedly over the years that you are parenting together. If this is how it goes, it may be that the most important thing you can do to deal with it is to get some help for your children. Being dragged through a high-conflict divorce can be extremely damaging for them, and you should do everything you can to help them work through it.

Getting Divorced Before All Issues Are Resolved: Bifurcation

What if you want to be officially divorced, either so that you can remarry or so that you don't go into another tax year as a married person, but you're not ready to begin your trial yet? In this case, the court can bifurcate, or separate, the issue of your marital status from the other issues in your divorce, and grant the divorce as to status only, without making a final decision on custody or support. Often the form that you file to ask for a trial date will have a place to note if you are seeking a "status only" divorce and still intend to come to court for a trial on support or custody when you are ready to present your case.

To get a status-only judgment, you have to show that the responding party was properly served with the complaint or petition, and that the appropriate amount of time has passed. You may also have to file some special paperwork related to retirement plans, usually called "joinder" papers. If you are considering bifurcation, check with an attorney about whether you need to protect yourself in this way.

Commissioners and Judges

Your divorce case may be heard by a "commissioner" instead of a judge. The difference between the two is that judges are usually appointed by a governor or other official or elected by the public, while commissioners are attorneys who are hired by the court to perform the same function. They have the same authority as a judge. Commissioners are needed because in most courts, there aren't enough judges to handle the workload. In some states, however, a spouse who doesn't like a commissioner's decision can ask to have the matter reheard by a judge. Most people go ahead and accept the commissioner, for obvious reasons of efficiency.

Your case won't be heard by a commissioner unless you agree to it. If you are asked to stipulate (agree) to have a commissioner hear your case, there's no reason to object unless you have reason to believe that the particular commissioner won't be fair in your case. In that case, you can refuse to agree, and you will be given a court date with a judge—but be prepared to wait for it.

Issues in Child Custody Trials

Custody cases are decided by the judge evaluating what is in the best interests of the child. Parents bring an enormous variety of conflicts to custody trials, including:

- Which parent should have legal custody or whether it should be joint
- Which parent should have physical custody or whether it should be joint
- How much parenting time each parent should have
- How that parenting time should be scheduled
- How a child should be educated (home-schooling, choice of private or public schools)
- What type of medical care a child should receive, and
- What type of religious education a child should receive and how parents should deal with differences in religious beliefs or activities.

The Best Interests of the Child

All courts use the "best interests of the child" standard to decide issues of child custody. (See Chapter 2.) In other words, every state's laws say that the judge must put the child's best interests above everything else in making custody decisions. That said, custody laws do differ. A few states don't list any specific factors, simply stating that the judge must do what's in the child's best interests. Others list factors (a few or many) for the judge to consider. The "State Custody Best Interest Statutes" in the appendix lists each state's statute (or relevant case law) setting out the factors that judges consider important in evaluating a child's best interests; you can look up your state and see what you'll have to prove. (Chapter 12 explains how to find and read statutes.)

One of the most important factors in a custody determination, included in the laws of nearly every state that lists specific factors, is which parent will do more to support the child's relationship with the other parent. Unless there is domestic violence or other abuse, all judges consider it important that a child have a relationship with both parents.

If the evidence shows that one parent is clearly more likely to cooperate and is committed to fostering a good relationship between the child and the other parent, that supportive parent will have a significant advantage in a custody dispute. The judge will also look at what the relationship was between parents and children before the divorce. It's not at all uncommon for a parent who was uninvolved to develop a sudden interest in parenting when the divorce is filed, and courts will look closely at a parent's motivation for deciding to get more involved in children's lives.

Those are far from the only factors, though. Others include:

- The child's age (an infant, especially one who's nursing, will usually spend more time with the mother, but the "tender years" doctrine, in which very young children were always awarded to the mother, is a thing of the past)
- The child's physical, emotional, mental, and social needs, and each parent's ability to meet those needs
- The child's preference, if old enough (some states specify 12 or 14, and others leave it to the judge; the judge can learn about the child's opinions by speaking to the child directly or from an evaluator's report, if there is one)
- Whether the status quo is working well for the child, especially if one parent has been the primary caretaker
- Each parent's living situation and how well it meets the child's needs (this includes what kind of space the children have in each home and how close each place is to their everyday activities and to the other parent)
- Domestic violence, abuse, or neglect, which will always weigh in favor of the nonabusive parent and may give rise to an order for supervised visitation
- Substance abuse by either parent or anyone in the parent's household, and
- The child's relationships with family members and friends of each parent.

In some places, the court takes into account whether a parent was convicted of making false accusations of child abuse, as well as whether one parent coerced the other into a parenting agreement.

Most states agree that a parent's military deployment can't be used as a factor in rendering a decision about permanent custody, and many states have enacted new laws in recent years governing how deployment affects custody and visitation in the short term. There's more about that in Chapter 11, which deals with military families.

Custody Evaluations

Most judges agree that they do not always have all of the information, or the ability to assess it, that they need to make a decision about a child's best interests. For this reason, most state laws authorize judges to seek the opinion of child custody specialists. Most often, this means requiring the parents to pay for a custody evaluation that the judge will use in making a decision. In this instance, the court will appoint the evaluator (even though you are required to pay for the evaluator's services).

You and your spouse can also agree to hire an evaluator at any point in your case, even if the judge does not order it. A child custody evaluator is almost always a licensed therapist with significant experience working with children and a deep understanding of developmental and emotional issues facing children in divorce. However, in some states, judges instead appoint someone called a "guardian ad litem" (GAL), often an attorney, to represent the interests of the child during a custody dispute. If the GAL is an attorney and not a therapist, then the GAL will be authorized to hire a therapist to conduct the psychological evaluation. A court-appointed custody evaluator and a GAL serve the same function, which is to gather information and provide the judge with an unbiased assessment of the child's best interests.

A custody evaluator's recommendation is never binding on the court, but as a rule, judges give it a lot of weight, especially if they asked for it themselves. In many cases, it's the only information they have about your family that isn't presented through the filter of one parent's argument.

How to Choose an Evaluator

If the judge orders an evaluation, it's possible you'll be given the name of the evaluator and that will be that. It's also possible that the judge might give you and your spouse a list of a few evaluators and have you choose—usually, with the help of your lawyer. If you and the other parent agree on an evaluator recommended by one of your lawyers, the judge will probably go along with your choice.

If you're choosing an evaluator yourselves, or if you're choosing from among options given to you by the judge, ask your lawyer to get some information so you're comfortable with the person. (Don't meet with the evaluator directly to ask questions or make a decision. You shouldn't have any contact with the evaluator outside of the actual evaluation, both to avoid looking like you're trying to influence the evaluation, and also to try to avoid doing anything that might reflect negatively on you with the evaluator.) Find out about the evaluator's experience generally, and if your family has special issues (for example, a relocation question or a child with special needs), about whether the evaluator has dealt with similar issues before. It's also appropriate to ask whether the evaluator has a history of recommending in favor of either fathers or mothers.

In the unlikely event that you don't want to agree to any of the evaluators that the court suggested, you can ask the court to give you more options—but don't count on getting any, and keep in mind that you risk making the judge think that you are difficult, which won't do you any good when the judge is making a decision in your case. If you and your spouse have agreed to an evaluation but can't agree on the evaluator, you can hire competing evaluators. But paying the full cost of an evaluation isn't a very attractive option, nor do you want to put yourself and your kids through the process twice.

Cost of the Evaluation

How much the evaluation costs will depend on whether it's court-ordered or voluntary. If the court orders the evaluation and chooses the evaluator, you'll pay a much lower hourly rate than if you hire a private evaluator. An evaluation ordered by the judge will probably cost between $2,000 and $7,500. You could pay well over $10,000 for a private evaluation.

The Evaluation Process

Evaluators have differences in style, approach, and emphasis, and sometimes those things will depend on your family and the disagreements you're having. No matter what, though, the evaluator will:

- interview both you and your spouse up to three times (interviews will be planned, not unannounced visits)
- interview each child once or twice
- spend time with you and the other parent with each child, to observe your interactions (at the evaluator's office, your home, or both)
- speak to teachers, caregivers, doctors, therapists, and other witnesses, and
- look over your court file.

Many evaluators use psychological testing as well—for both children and parents. Some do the testing themselves and some (including a guardian ad litem who might be a lawyer, not a mental health professional) send you to another professional for testing.

If you become worried during the course of the evaluation that the evaluator is biased in favor of your spouse, or if you feel that any of the questions asked of you are inappropriate, talk to your lawyer immediately, before the report is submitted. The timing is really important, because complaints about the evaluator that you submit after the report goes against you won't be as believable as ones submitted before the recommendations are made. If you're representing yourself, send a letter to the judge, and make absolutely sure you send a copy of that letter to your spouse or your spouse's attorney, because you're not allowed to communicate with the judge without letting them know.

Your Role in the Evaluation

There is no doubt that you will be stressed out by the custody evaluation. After all, a stranger is coming to your home and talking with your children about your parenting skills and the environment you've created for your children. Try to stay as calm as you can, and think of the evaluation as a good opportunity to show the judge your side of the story. No matter how nervous and anxious you are, try to be yourself, and always be completely honest, even if you think it makes you look bad.

The most important tip of all is to be sure not to try to manipulate the evaluator. You can spend a lot of time searching for information on the Internet about this type of evaluation, and you might think that this self-education will allow you to shape things so that the evaluation goes in your favor—in fact, some of the websites dealing with this question promise just that. In reality, you've got enough problems without bending yourself out of shape to try to meet some imaginary standard or create a particular impression. Staying focused on what's best for the kids means acknowledging that the input of an experienced evaluator might actually be helpful to you and your family. Try to see the evaluator as someone with something to teach you—something that could help your family function better.

Talking to Your Kids About the Evaluation

Even though you undoubtedly believe you are doing what's best for your kids by fighting over the parenting plan, you have to accept that the evaluation process will not be pleasant for them. They're likely to find it confusing and scary, and to feel a lot of pressure about what they say—probably believing that whatever they say will control the outcome or get one parent in trouble. You can't avoid the difficult truth—in any event, if you think your kids don't already know there's a lot of conflict between you and the other parent, you are kidding yourself. So be honest with them, but keep it simple. Explain that the evaluator is going to ask questions of everyone in the family to help you work out a way to be good parents after the divorce.

Whatever you do, you absolutely must not tell your children what to say to the evaluator, even if they ask you—and in case it's not obvious, don't coach them to say negative things about their other parent. Just tell them that their only job is to tell the truth, and that that's all anyone expects from them. If they're worried about the effect their input might have, remind them that the evaluator is going to talk to a lot of different people and take everyone's views into account.

Ten Tips for Dealing With a Custody Evaluation

1. Be on time for appointments with the evaluator. If you really have an emergency, be sure to call rather than just not showing up.

2. Answer questions honestly, and answer only the question the evaluator asks, not the question you wish you could answer. Don't bring an agenda to your answers.

3. Don't argue your side or try to influence what the evaluator puts in the report; just provide the information the evaluator wants.

4. Acknowledge that you want your children to have a positive relationship with the other parent.

5. Be willing to consider various custody and visitation arrangements, but clearly explain why you prefer one over another.

6. Follow up promptly if the evaluator asks for more information—for example, verification of your employment or medical information about your children.

7. If you're asked about your spouse's strengths and weaknesses as a parent, be as fair as you can. If you're asked about your own parenting skills, acknowledge both your strengths and your weaknesses as a parent. If you're asked about how you think the kids are doing, be honest about what's going on with them, even if you are worried that problems they have might reflect badly on you.

8. Don't ask the evaluator for advice on how to deal with a family problem or try to find out what's going to be in the report.

9. Never coach your kids about what to say or do when they're dealing with the evaluator. Tell them to tell the truth and reassure them that they won't get in trouble no matter what they say.

10. Concentrate on what's best for the kids.

The Evaluator's Report

You'll get a copy of the evaluator's report at the same time it's delivered to your spouse and to the judge. It's possible that the evaluator might come and speak to you, around the same time, about the report and the recommendations. The report will certainly include recommendations on custody, visitation, and time sharing. Depending on what the judge asked for or what you and your spouse identified as your conflicts, it might also cover:

- contact between the children and people outside the nuclear family, like grandparents, aunts and uncles, and friends of either parent
- education or activities
- whether therapy is appropriate for the family together or for any individuals or subsets of the family
- how you and your spouse should deal with conflicts in the future and whether either or both of you should attend parenting classes or anger management classes, or take other measures to help you be a better parent, and
- how to deal with specific issues like substance abuse.

The level of detail in the report will probably depend on how much trouble you and your spouse have communicating and agreeing on parenting issues. If you fight over everything, then the recommendations are likely to be extremely specific, even down to stating the precise time when a nonresidential parent is allowed to call the child who's with the other parent, and how long the phone call can be. If you're able to work out some things, the evaluation might leave some room for you to continue to do that, to bolster your ability to cooperate. The report might recommend a reevaluation at a specific time in the future, especially if your children are very young.

Read the entire report carefully when you get it. Whether it's favorable to you or not, don't do anything right away. (In other words, don't call your spouse and gloat, and don't call the evaluator and heap abuse on the ridiculous findings.) If you have a lawyer, schedule an appointment to discuss the evaluation and recommendations. If you can live with the recommendations, even if they're not ideal, you can save yourself the possibility of a judge's decision that you like even less—not to mention a lot of additional time, money, and heartache—by agreeing to what the evaluator suggests instead of disputing the findings at a trial. Of course, if your spouse doesn't agree as well, you'll have to go to court anyway.

Look at the report with your children in mind, and stay focused on their needs instead of getting your ego involved in what the evaluator said about you. If you can, take advantage of the fact that a skilled, experienced professional spent time with your family and made suggestions for moving forward into your postdivorce family life. If the evaluator made suggestions about your parenting style or specifics about how your household is run or how you interact with your children, consider learning from them, even if they're uncomfortable to you. You don't get many opportunities to get feedback about your parenting from neutral parties, so take advantage of whatever positives you can find.

Your Children and the Trial Process

Ideally, your children's contact with the court process should be minimized. But they can't be protected completely from something so important, and something that will affect their future so profoundly.

Talking to Your Kids About the Trial

Unless your children are very young, you won't be able to keep them in the dark about the fact that there's a trial going on—nor do you want to, given that the outcome may cause changes in their daily routine. As is true in most things involving kids, it's important to tell them the truth in a way that is developmentally appropriate. Even teenagers shouldn't be given a lot of detail.

The core message is that you and their other parent haven't been able to agree about certain things related to parenting, and you're going to both tell a judge what you think and then the judge will decide what's best for your family. Children are mostly concerned about the concrete details that will affect them, but you don't want to go into a lot of detail about who wants what or what the various possible outcomes are. The judge may decide on something entirely different from what either you or your spouse has asked for.

Children's Role in the Trial

It's probably obvious that you want to do everything you can to avoid having your children testify at trial. Very few children, regardless of their age, will relish the prospect of taking sides in a public legal fight between their parents, and many will find it quite traumatic. In addition, the testimony of younger children isn't necessarily reliable or predictable.

It's also not a good idea from a strategic standpoint. Judges do not want to see kids testifying in court. They don't think it's good for the kids and don't believe that children always know what's in their best interests—for example, the judge won't give a lot of weight to the testimony of a child who prefers living with the parent who doesn't require chores, homework, or a consistent bedtime. Some courts require you to file a motion with the court requesting permission for the child to testify and explaining why the information the child will present can't be produced in any other way.

If you insist on having a child testify, the judge may see it as a mark against you when considering whether you have your child's best interests at heart or are more focused on your own agenda. In fact, some states' lists of the factors to be considered in a best interest evaluation include whether either parent has involved the child in custody litigation or has protected the child from it. In these places, you will gain no advantage from your child's testimony, no matter what the child says.

It's rarely truly necessary to have a child testify. If the point you want to make is that the child is happy in school (to prove that no change in school should be made), you can present report cards, evidence of extracurricular activities, and written statements from teachers or others at the school. If you want to show that your child is not close to the other parent, ask relatives and close friends to testify about what they have observed.

If a judge considers a child's testimony necessary—as might be the case where one parent claims the other has abused the child—there are alternatives to having the child testify in open court. It's possible to have the child interviewed by a doctor or custody evaluator in a much less threatening environment, and then have those adults report to the court. Judges can also interview children outside of the courtroom, in chambers (the judge's office), about the child's preferences and about the facts of the case, without any questioning from lawyers.

Some states require that the parents or their attorneys be allowed to be present at the interview, but many allow the judge to interview the child privately, to allow for a more frank discussion. In some states, there's no court reporter present and no record made of the conversation.

Others require that a court reporter take down the conversation, but say that no transcription can be made unless there's an appeal. While your child may be intimidated by this prospect, it will not be as scary as testifying in open court, and you can prepare your child in the same way you did for the custody evaluation, by explaining that the judge is going to try to help your family function better and that your child's thoughts may be helpful. Remind the child that all that's necessary is to answer the judge's questions truthfully.

Some judges always require children's testimony to be taken in chambers rather than in open court. But if you have the option, and you really feel your child must testify, at least do your best to make it short and limit the questioning to whatever specific information you can't present in any other way. Make sure your lawyer knows that you don't want your child subjected to lengthy questioning, which could open the door to a challenging cross-examination by the other side.

If your spouse presents your child as a witness, you may want to forgo cross-examination. It will show the judge that you care more about your child's welfare than you do about making a point.

Issues in Child Support Trials

In some ways, arguing about money might seem easier than arguing about who your children will be living with. On the other hand, an argument about child support is actually an argument about your children—what resources they'll have available to them and what each parent's responsibility is. There's no question that both parents have a legal obligation to support their children until the children reach the age of majority (and sometimes longer), but there can be many questions about how to calculate support.

State Child Support Guidelines

Every state has child support guidelines that calculate an amount of child support to be paid, based largely on the parents' income and the way parenting time is shared. For many couples, the guidelines are the beginning and the end of the support issue. But questions—and court cases—arise when it's not clear what numbers should be used for the guideline calculations, or when one parent believes the other is misstating income.

Judges always go to the guidelines first, and you should too. (See Chapter 3 for how to find an online calculator for your state.) If you don't have accurate information from your spouse about income or other important issues (like tax liability), you'll have to ask the judge to decide what numbers are to be used.

Chapter 3 discusses some of the issues that will lead you to a support trial if you can't resolve them: what constitutes income for purposes of support, when it's appropriate to deviate from guideline support, how much a parent is actually earning, how long support lasts, whether a parent's ability to earn should be considered along with the parent's actual earnings, and more.

Proving Your Support Case

In some child support cases, everyone agrees on the facts, but not on how the law should apply to them. For example, if your spouse receives disbursements from a trust, there's no argument about the existence of the trust. But there might be a question about whether the money should be counted as income for purposes of calculating child support. In a case like this, your spouse would probably stipulate (agree) to the facts that the trust exists and the approximate amount received from the trust each year. The question you would argue about to the court is whether or not the income should be counted.

Many other cases, though, aren't so cut and dried in terms of the facts. Perhaps your spouse owns a small business, and during your marriage deposited a certain amount into your house account each month to pay your family's expenses. You have no idea whether that amount is all of your spouse's business income—as your spouse is arguing—or whether there's a great deal more money coming out of the business that could be used to pay child support. If you believe that your spouse is hiding money in the business (see "Ways to Hide Income," below), then you'll probably hire a forensic accountant to investigate the situation. That person will testify at trial about your spouse's business and projected income, and you will ask the judge to make a decision about support based on the amounts your forensic expert says are reasonable.

Ways to Hide Income

You might be surprised at how many ways there are to hide income and assets. It's particularly easy for someone who owns a business, but there are other frequently used methods as well. Here are some common asset-hiding tricks:

- open accounts in one person's name, in another state or offshore
- ask a trustee to delay distribution of income under trusts
- cash checks and hide the cash, rather than putting it in the bank
- transfer cash into accounts held in another person's name
- create balances that can be used for purchases by overpaying credit cards
- overpay estimated tax payments, which will lead to future (postseparation, postdivorce) refunds
- ask an employer to delay a bonus or vesting of stock options
- a business person can hide money by "hiring" fake employees, "writing off" or understating accounts receivable, overstating accounts payable, and delaying bonuses or other forms of compensation
- move valuable jewelry, art work, coins, or other items to undisclosed locations, or
- purchase valuable items for a business, like art or furniture, in order to tie up or hide available cash.

There are also ways to create the illusion of less money or avoid disclosing income or assets that don't involve hiding the actual funds, but do involve hiding the facts—for example, concealing a transaction that could result in an increase in the value of stock options.

Not all of these assets and sources of income are necessarily relevant to child support. For example, there's an ongoing debate about whether stock options constitute an asset or an income stream—or a combination of the two—after they are vested and can be exercised. The point is that it's important that both parents' financial situation be disclosed fully so that anything that is relevant can be counted and the children can benefit from the support that's truly payable.

Forensic Accountants

If you haven't been in the loop on financial matters and you're concerned that the other parent may be hiding assets, you have two ways of dealing with your concerns. First, you (or a lawyer) can use the discovery process (described in Chapter 6) to try to find out what's going on by gathering all the financial information that's available. If the other parent is financially sophisticated, however, or if the finances are particularly complex, you might be best served by hiring a forensic accountant—a professional whose job is to review financial information looking for irregularities and bad practices. There are a surprising (to the novice) number of ways these professionals can find hidden assets, including analyzing computers for hidden data. You can also hire a private investigator to search for assets.

Whatever you do, be sure you stay within the law. Don't invade the other parent's privacy illegally, no matter how tempting it might seem. For one thing, it's wrong, and for another, you probably wouldn't be able to use any evidence you obtained through illegal means.

Courtroom Procedures at Your Trial

It's very unusual for any legal case, whether a divorce or anything else, to make it all the way to trial. Even most cases that appear destined for trial get settled before the trial date—sometimes only hours or days before. But if yours is one of the few that actually gets there, you need to know how a trial happens.

The closer you get to the trial date, the more you'll have to do. Your lawyer, if you have one, will spend many hours preparing a trial brief (the document that lays out your arguments for the judge), an opening statement to be made in court, and all of the evidence to present to the judge—as well as preparing witnesses if you are going to present any. You may have to spend a good chunk of time at the lawyer's office, working with the lawyer and the staff to be sure that all of you are well prepared. If you're not working with your lawyer, either in person or by phone, then you need to ask why. If it's because of your schedule, then you need to make time. If it's because the lawyer hasn't asked you to contribute to the preparations, then you need to have a talk with your lawyer to make sure that the two of you are on the same page about what issues are important and how they're going to be presented in court. More than ever as you get closer to trial, this is your case and you need to be in close touch with what's going on.

Most trials follow a similar pattern, one you've probably seen on television (in a very condensed form) many times. But unlike TV trials, there's no jury in a divorce case; in almost every state, the judge will make the final decisions alone. (Texas and Georgia are the only states that allow jury trials in divorce cases if you request it.) You're generally better off that way, too—a judge is less likely to get caught up in your personal drama than a juror who may have been through something similar, and you only have to persuade one person of your position, instead of six or 12.

If You Are Your Own Lawyer

If you're representing yourself at trial, you have a lot to think about and a great deal to do—much more than can be covered here. This chapter will give you some guidance on what a trial looks like and some basics of evidence rules and dealing with witnesses, but you'll also need some resources that go into much greater detail.

Definitely check out *Represent Yourself in Court: How to Prepare and Try a Winning Case,* by Paul Bergman and Sara Berman (Nolo), and *Legal Research: How to Find & Understand the Law,* by Stephen Elias and the Editors of Nolo (Nolo).

Also consider getting some help from a lawyer—possibly with your trial brief, your plan for examining witnesses, or the important evidence rules that might apply to the exhibits (documents) you want to present. (See "Unbundled Representation," in Chapter 12, for more about having a lawyer help you with just part of your case.)

There are a lot of moving parts in a trial, but even with all the back and forth that's described below, a trial can last an hour, a day, or much longer. It depends on whether you and your spouse settled any of your issues before going to trial or the judge has to decide every single thing. It also turns on how complicated your legal and financial issues are. If there is a lot of forensic evidence relating to a support dispute, or an evaluator with lengthy testimony about custody, you're unlikely to finish in a day. In other words, the more you have left to resolve and the more complicated the issues are, the more witnesses and evidence you'll need to present, and that means more trial time.

Opening Statements

For these purposes we'll assume that you are the person who filed for divorce—called either the petitioner or the complainant, depending on your state—and that a lawyer is representing you. The trial will begin with your lawyer telling the judge what you are asking for and how the evidence will show that you are entitled to it. Next, your spouse's lawyer will have a chance to do the same thing on behalf of your spouse. The lawyers aren't supposed to argue in their opening statements, only to tell the judge what the evidence will show and what they want the judge to decide. In divorce trials, opening statements tend to be brief—there's no jury to talk to, and the judge has probably heard most of your factual contentions before, in the declarations you've submitted before trial and in the trial brief.

Petitioner's Case: Evidence and Testimony

The person who filed for divorce goes first in court. Your lawyer will present evidence, both by submitting documents and by having witnesses testify. You will most likely be one of the witnesses, unless the case is purely about child support and the witnesses are all financial types. (See "Your Testimony," below.) Other witnesses might include a custody evaluator if you had an evaluation, as well as your spouse, and if absolutely necessary, your kids. You may also have hired expert witnesses to testify about things like the best interests of your children or, if one party's income is in dispute in a support trial, financial issues. Friends and family members may testify about things they've observed that are in dispute—for example, who has been the children's primary caretaker or the date that your spouse moved out of the house. (See "Testimony of Other Witnesses," below.)

How to Be a Good Listener

You'll spend a lot of your courtroom time just sitting at a table next to your lawyer, listening to the lawyers argue and the witnesses testify. While you're sitting there, practice your best poker face—in other words, don't shake your head, raise your eyebrows, or roll your eyes if someone says something you don't agree with. If what's being said is wrong or untrue, write a note and give it to your lawyer. Don't whisper to your lawyer, and don't address the witness, the judge, your spouse, or your spouse's lawyer unless you have the judge's permission. Keeping your cool can only help your cause, and losing it can really hurt you.

The testimony that your witnesses give under your lawyer's questioning is called "direct" testimony. After the direct testimony, the other lawyer will get a chance to cross-examine each person. Your lawyer then gets to question each person again in what's called "redirect" examination. This can go on as long as the judge will let it, except that each time the lawyers can only ask follow-up questions on topics that have been covered before. They can't go over the same ground or bring in something new, so the process gets shorter with each round.

Any documents that you want to submit to the judge as evidence must be submitted through the testimony of a witness. There's more about this process in "Exhibits," below.

Your Testimony

It's likely that you will testify at your trial, to tell the judge in your own words the facts that support your position. But more and more judges now require that direct testimony (your version of the facts) be submitted in writing, meaning that the lawyers write up all the things each person would say in court in the form of sworn declarations, and submit them to the judge and the other side. At trial, each lawyer can ask the other side's witnesses questions about their declarations, as though the person had testified out loud to what's in it. But if the other parent's lawyer doesn't choose to cross-examine you in this way, you will not take the stand at all.

Some people don't think this is fair, because it doesn't give you your day in court in the same way that in-person testimony does. Some states, including California, require that people be allowed to testify live in court if they wish to. But if you don't live in a state with that rule and the judge wants your testimony in writing, you'll have to submit it that way. In that case, you and your lawyer will go over what the declaration says, and you'll know everything that's in it.

If you do take the stand, your testimony will start with your own lawyer asking you questions. You should have been well prepared for this by your attorney. The lawyer will use the questions to show all the reasons why the judge should adopt your position. The other side's lawyer can object to the questions or the answers if there's something about them that the lawyer thinks isn't fair under the evidence rules. If that happens, your lawyer will answer the objection and then tell you what to do—either answer the question or move on to something else. If you're representing yourself, you will take the witness stand and simply tell your story and say what order you want the court to make. The judge might ask you some questions to help make sure your testimony is complete. The other side is unlikely to make many objections, as it doesn't look good for a lawyer to bully a self-represented witness in court.

After your initial testimony is complete, the other parent's lawyer (or the other parent, if there's no lawyer on the other side) may cross-examine you. The goal of the cross-examination is to show that some or all of what you have said is not true or is incomplete or misleading. Be prepared to be challenged on every aspect of your testimony, as well as to be insulted by the lawyer's implications or outright accusations. Stay calm, and never be sarcastic or rude, no matter how awful your spouse's attorney is to you. Your lawyer will prepare you for the cross-examination before you go into court, probably by playing the role of the other lawyer and asking you the questions the other lawyer is likely to ask you. But expect the unexpected—there's no way that you or your lawyer can anticipate every question the lawyer might ask you.

Testifying in court can be quite anxiety producing, no matter how certain you are of your position and no matter how much time you spend preparing. The single most important thing to remember is to stay calm and focused. Take your time in answering the questions; think about the answers before you speak. Always tell the truth, even if it doesn't make you look good. If you don't understand a question, say so. The lawyer will repeat or rephrase it until you know what you are answering. Keep your answers as brief as you can while still being truthful and complete. Don't lose your temper, exaggerate, or be overly dramatic.

If you get very nervous, try looking at a friendly face in the courtroom—in fact, if you can, bring a friend to sit in the front row. You can also direct your answers to the judge, who will be listening attentively and may be a calming influence. You can pour yourself a drink of water, which will almost always be handy when you are testifying. If you are shaking, put your hands in your lap and take a deep breath to try to calm down. And if you feel faint or sick, ask the judge for a short break to pull yourself together.

Testimony of Other Witnesses

You have an important role in the trial, and it's possible that you might be the only witness in your case. But there may be other witnesses as well.

Expert Witnesses

Expert witnesses are people who have experience and knowledge in a particular field that makes their testimony useful to the judge. For example, you might hire a child development expert to testify to an opinion about why your child isn't progressing in school as expected, or a learning disability specialist who can explain your child's special needs and how they would be best served. If your dispute is over child support, a forensic accountant might be involved, or a vocational expert who can testify about your spouse's employment prospects and earning capacity if you're arguing that child support should be based on earning potential instead of actual earnings.

Expert witnesses are paid a fee by the person who hires them. It's entirely possible that you and your spouse would each hire an expert on the same topic, and leave the judge to decide whose testimony is more credible.

Your lawyer will make most of the decisions about whether to use expert witnesses. But remember, it's your money and you have a say in how it's used in your trial. Make sure the expert's testimony is necessary, and that it's limited to the most important and relevant topics. You could also choose to submit the expert's testimony in writing (by declaration or report) instead of in person, which would be much less expensive. The other side would still be able to cross-examine the witness, but the expert's time in court would be shorter.

Testimony by a Child's Lawyer or Custody Evaluator

In contested custody cases, the most likely expert witness is the child custody evaluator or guardian ad litem who evaluated your family. The guardian ad litem or custody evaluator will testify not for one side or the other, but for the benefit of the judge, usually after both sides have already presented their testimony.

Percipient Witnesses

In addition to your own testimony and that of experts, you may present witnesses who are called "lay witnesses" or "percipient witnesses." These are people who saw something with their own eyes that you think is important to your case, and you've asked them to tell the judge about it. A typical percipient witness might be your day care provider, who might testify that on the days that your son is dropped off by the other parent, his clothes are dirty and he says he is hungry and hasn't had breakfast.

Testimony by Declaration

Ideally, you want your percipient witnesses to testify in person. But some judges won't allow this for all witnesses—as discussed above in "Your Testimony," there's something of a trend these days for judges to keep witnesses out of the courtroom and require written statements from them instead. It's a sign of how crowded the courts have become, because only a really overworked judge would prefer written testimony to a real live witness. Judges' primary job, after all, is to gauge the truthfulness of the people who testify before them. There's no contest between seeing a person in the flesh, with facial expressions, vocal inflections and tics, and hesitations or certainty in speaking, and seeing the same witness's words on paper, most likely drafted or at least vetted by a lawyer.

However, many harried judges simply find it more efficient to review declarations and then ask questions of the attorney and, possibly, the spouse. If you don't live in one of the states where the law requires the judge to allow testimony if you insist upon it, then you'll have to follow the judge's instructions.

If you're getting a declaration from a witness (described in Chapter 6), there are a few things to remember. First, if you have a lawyer, don't contact your witnesses—let the lawyer do it. If you're on your own and you need to arrange for the witnesses to come to court:

- Don't try to influence the witness's testimony in any way. Ask a neutral question about whether the person would be willing to tell the judge about what they've observed. For example, don't say, "Could you come to court and say how late Bobby is getting to school every day?" Instead, ask "Would you be willing to tell the judge what you've observed about what time Bobby gets to school in the morning?"

- Offer to subpoena the witness if you think the person might have a problem getting off work or might feel uncomfortable coming to court voluntarily—a subpoena is a notice that a person has to come to court. (See "Using Subpoenas," below.)

- Have the witness write the declaration, if possible. If you think it won't get done, offer to type up whatever the witness wants to say and then have the person sign it.

Using Subpoenas

A subpoena is a legal order that requires a person to show up in court to testify or, sometimes, to bring certain documents to court. A subpoena has to be issued by the court clerk and served on (delivered to) the witness in person. (See Chapter 6 for information about serving legal papers.)

You can sometimes get the subpoena form online, fill it out, and take it to the clerk, who will stamp it to show that it's been approved and that the weight of the court is behind it. Once the clerk has issued the subpoena, a person who doesn't come to court can face potential charges of contempt of court. If the form's not available online, go to the clerk's office and ask for it, then fill it out by hand and have the clerk issue it then.

Why would you need a subpoena? Obviously, you don't need one for your own expert witnesses, whom you're paying to come to court. And you might think you don't need one for your child's day care provider, but think again. First off, it's good for the witness to have something in writing to present at work, kind of like a doctor's note. Second, any witness who has a relationship with both parents might be afraid that testifying for one parent would anger the other. A subpoena lets the witness truthfully say that there was no choice but to go to court.

What about using a subpoena to compel a witness you know is reluctant? If you really need the testimony, then by all means use a subpoena to make sure the person shows up. But think twice; reluctant witnesses don't always provide the best testimony.

Exhibits

If some part of your case can be proved by written evidence, you can submit exhibits to the judge. In a custody case, typical exhibits could include a child's school report cards, medical records, or other documents showing how the child is progressing or demonstrating changes that are relevant to the case. In a support trial, you might submit pay stubs, small business records, bank records, or the report of a forensic accountant who has examined your family finances or one spouse's financial information.

All exhibits must be "authenticated" before the judge will accept them, meaning that someone with personal knowledge about the item must testify that it is either the original or an accurate photocopy. Any time you are going to submit an exhibit, you must give a copy to the judge and a copy to the other lawyer, and formally "offer" the exhibit into evidence. ("Your Honor, I offer Exhibit A, Maggie's report card from the most recent semester.") In most cases, everyone knows what the exhibits are going to be before the trial, because many of them have been passed back and forth during the discovery process.

If your lawyer knows beforehand that the other side has some evidence that shouldn't be allowed, there's something called a "motion in limine" (pronounced "lim-in-nee") through which your lawyer can ask the judge to exclude the evidence. These motions are used much more in jury trials, because in those cases the judge can actually prevent the jurors from seeing the evidence. In a judge trial, when you ask the judge to exclude evidence the judge is, of course, getting a look at the evidence.

Sometimes it's easier to simply allow the other side to submit the evidence, and then argue that the judge shouldn't consider it. Either way, the judge will first see the evidence and then decide whether or not to ignore it.

Respondent's Case: Evidence and Testimony

After your lawyer has questioned all your witnesses and submitted all your evidence, your spouse gets the chance to do the same thing. The other side will probably have expert witnesses of its own, and your spouse will likely testify just as you did. The direct and cross-examination process will happen just as it did when your lawyer presented your case.

"Fathers' Rights" as a Trial Strategy

Some divorcing fathers argue that the court system is biased in favor of women in custody decisions. It is true that in the past, a rule called the "tender years doctrine" directed judges in many places to always place young children with their mothers after a divorce, on the principle that children of tender years need the nurturing of a mother. However, almost all states now have laws explicitly stating that no advantage should go to either parent on account of sex. Many states also presume that joint custody is in a child's best interests and that fathers and mothers should be equally involved in child-rearing.

Still, some men feel that they are treated unfairly by the system, and numerous websites are devoted to trial strategies for winning more parenting time. If you are likely to face these strategies, be sure that your lawyer knows about them.

Petitioner's Rebuttal

After your spouse's first presentation of evidence, you will have a chance to respond by putting on witnesses and submitting evidence to contradict (rebut) what your spouse's witnesses said. Your witnesses can't repeat what they said earlier, but can respond only to what the other side's witnesses said. You may not need to call your witnesses back if you can rebut the testimony yourself.

Respondent's Surrebuttal

Sometimes, a judge gives the respondent the opportunity for what's called "surrebuttal," which is where the respondent's witnesses respond to what your witnesses said on rebuttal. Again, they can't bring up anything new or repeat themselves—they must limit their testimony to contradicting what was said in the rebuttal case.

Closing Arguments

After all the testimony has been heard and all the evidence presented, the lawyers each get a chance to make a last statement to the judge. This time, they can argue all they want. Sometimes, the judge asks for closing arguments in writing—this is more likely if there are sticky legal issues that the judge wants time to consider, or if the trial has gone on for a long time.

The Judge's Ruling

It's very unlikely that you'll know the result of your trial right away, in the courtroom, unless you're in one of the rare places that a jury trial is allowed and you chose one. Nearly always, the judge will take some time to consider all the evidence and arguments before making a written ruling. You may, though, have a sense of what's coming from comments the judge made during the trial. You'll receive the written decision in the mail, usually in a couple of weeks.

If the judge does tell you the ruling from the bench in court, one of the lawyers will have to prepare a written order based on what the judge says. The other lawyer will get a chance to review it before the judge signs it, to make sure it's complete and accurate. Once both lawyers have agreed on the language, they'll submit the order to the judge for signature, and it will become the final decision in your case.

Appeals

It's likely that the judge's decision isn't going to sit right with the parent who lost. And for the most part, that person is just going to have to live with it—a judge has the right to make decisions based on the facts of the case, and the only reason for appealing a decision is if the judge in your trial made a serious mistake in applying the law. If you think (and an appellate lawyer agrees) that the judge has made such a mistake in your case, you have the right to appeal the judgment to a higher court, called a court of appeal or appellate court.

It's very unlikely that you'll have a basis for an appeal, because legal errors aren't that common. And even if there was a mistake, it has to have affected the outcome of the trial. Because it's hard to meet these standards, and because appeals are expensive and take a long time to resolve, they aren't very common.

Any orders that the judge made will stay in effect during your appeal. If you win your appeal, the appellate court will either reverse the judge's orders or send you back for another trial.

If you're considering an appeal, you absolutely must consult an appellate lawyer about whether it's worthwhile given the enormous expense and time commitment. You'll have to weigh your sense of how wrong the ruling was, how likely you are to win an appeal, and whether you have the money and time to do it.

After the Trial

Even if your hearing or trial didn't come out the way you wanted, it's still a relief to have it over. At least you can relax and enjoy the absence of such a big drain on your time, energy, and bank account. If all goes well, you'll never have to see the inside of a courtroom again. Still, getting a decision doesn't mean the end to the challenges of coparenting. The next two chapters cover what happens after the dust settles.

Custody Orders: Living With, Enforcing, and Changing Them

t's not uncommon for divorced parents to find themselves dealing with ongoing parenting issues, especially when either parent's life changes significantly. If you've been through court hearings and maybe even a trial, you're probably willing to do a lot to avoid another trip to the courthouse. So when the other parent comes to you with a possible wrinkle in the parenting schedule, don't hit the ceiling right away. Sit down and talk about it and see whether you can work something out. If you reach an impasse, you always have the option of returning to court to deal with the change—or to enforce the order you already have, if the other parent isn't complying with it. This chapter explains how to deal with those situations, both outside of court and if you have to return to the judge for changes or enforcement. The next chapter covers enforcing and modifying orders for child support.

If you need to go to court to enforce or change a custody order, the process is the same whether your existing order resulted from a settlement agreement with your ex, from a hearing that resulted in a temporary order, or from a full trial. Any judge's order, whether made after a contested hearing or at the request of both parents, is subject to enforcement by the court.

In reality, most parents who get a court-ordered parenting plan after a hearing end up changing some or all of it without ever going back to court. For one thing, by definition a court order issued by a judge after a hearing (as opposed to an agreement that was turned into an order upon request) wasn't agreed on, and often doesn't really meet the needs of the family when it comes to day-to-day life. For another thing, families are constantly changing, and as children grow their needs change. What worked for your daughter when she was six might not make sense when she's nine and involved in a whole different set of activities.

Sharing Parenting After a Custody Hearing or Trial

Nobody really wins when there's a custody trial, but the nature of a trial means that there is a winner and a loser. It's possible to get a ruling that neither of you wants (this is one of the reasons to avoid the crapshoot of a trial), but a great deal of the time, the parents' positions are so polarized that it really is a choice of one or the other. After all, if one parent wants to move away or the parents disagree about what school the child should go to, only one person is going to be satisfied with the outcome.

If You're the "Winner"

Good for you—now try to be gracious. Even if the goal you accomplished was to strictly limit the time your kids spend with the other parent or to get an order for supervised visitation, the kids will probably still be seeing and spending time with your spouse. Try to make that time as good for them as possible. See "Lessons for Both Parents," below, for more about how.

If You're the "Loser"

Maybe the trial didn't come out the way you wanted it to at all, and you're feeling like the world is against you and your kids are going to suffer for it. You may even be right about the last part, at least. But for now, you can't change the situation, so you will need to make the best of it. Here are a few additional considerations for you in the aftermath of your court case.

Don't complain to your kids about how unfair the judge was. Before and during the trial, you probably tried to keep your kids' involvement to a minimum. The same should be true afterwards. Explain the judge's decision to them in terms they can understand and with a focus on the things that affect them the most and that they care about. For example, "The judge said that you're going to be at Daddy's house all the time except on every other weekend and then you'll be with me. When it's time to come here to my house I'll pick you up at school on Friday and bring you back to Daddy's on Sunday after dinner. When you're with me you'll still have soccer and swimming like you usually do."

If the kids complain about the schedule or ask how you feel about it, tell them that the judge made the decision that he or she thought was best for your whole family, and you all need to try hard to make it work. Don't tell the kids that the judge was wrong or unfair, and don't promise that you're going to go back to court to change things. Even if your lawyer has told you that you have a good cause for appeal (which is very unlikely), keep it to yourself until it's a done deal.

Do what the judge said to do. Whether you like it or not, you need to do what the judge ordered. Don't act as if you won—for example, by trying to keep the kids longer than the order says or trying to avoid a supervision requirement. If the judge said a certain person can't be in your household when the kids are around, make sure that person stays away. If the judge said your son needs tutoring for a learning disability that you don't believe he has, take him to tutoring anyway. Violating a court order will create all kinds of problems. First, you'll find yourself back in court with your spouse filing an enforcement action, possibly resulting in a contempt ruling against you. Second, you'll be a lot less likely to succeed if you ask for a change in the order in the future. Finally, you'll be teaching your kids that authorities like the court are not to be respected, and that will not turn out well for you later.

Learn to be a better parent. Let's face it, if you didn't get what you wanted in court there may be a reason for it. Yes, it's possible the judge was biased against you for some reason—but it's just as likely that the judge or the custody evaluator saw something that you are not acknowledging. Are there ways that you can be a better parent and meet your kids' needs more effectively? Do you need to practice putting the children's needs before your own? Do you need anger management classes, parenting training, or treatment for substance abuse? Face your own realities and step up to your responsibilities. Doing so will guarantee you a better relationship with your kids.

Lessons for Both Parents

As you're undoubtedly well aware by now, your relationship with the other parent does not end just because you're not living together anymore. In fact, some of the stresses you may have experienced during your marriage, especially conflicts over parenting styles and beliefs, can be exacerbated when you separate. However, your divorce is an opportunity to achieve greater clarity about what you can and can't control, and to let go of the latter in a way that will improve the quality of your life.

> **RESOURCE**
>
> **Highly recommended.** Even if your ex doesn't drive you crazy, get two copies of *Custody Chaos, Personal Peace: Sharing Custody With an Ex Who Drives You Crazy*, by Jeffrey P. Wittman, Ph.D. (Perigree)—one for you and one for your ex. It's full of concrete ways to transform your experience of coparenting with someone you no longer want to live with by taking responsibility for your own actions, determining what problems are (and aren't) yours to solve, and behaving in a way that reflects your own moral values, instead of getting sucked into conflicts that cause you to act in ways you feel bad about later. There's also good advice on how to look at your parenting relationship as a business partnership, how to choose your battles, and how to communicate about challenging topics.
>
> One of the most important lessons in Wittman's book, and one that you will do well to learn, is that you cannot control or change your ex. The only behavior that you can control is your own. It's possible, and entirely likely, that if you begin treating the other parent with respect you will eventually get more respect in return—but you shouldn't do it for that reason. If you choose to behave reasonably, to always put your kids first, to try to focus on appreciating positive things your ex does, and to communicate respectfully, do it because you think it's right, not because you hope it will cause the other parent to do the same.

Remember that your children observe everything that you do. You can't tell them to solve their problems by using their words and their inside voices if they see you scream curses when your ex drops them off half an hour late, or throw a muddy shoe at the car because the kids came home dirty and tired again. That doesn't mean you can't set healthy boundaries—in fact, it's a great lesson for your kids when they see you doing that. For example, letting the other parent know—calmly and without anger—that you'll no longer intervene in conflicts between her and your nine-year-old son during their time together will give both of them the important message that they have their own relationship and they'll have to work things out for themselves.

Here are some concrete tips for working toward a productive and reasonably harmonious relationship with your kids' other parent.

Make sure your children understand that even though time is not shared equally, they still have two parents. This may be a challenge, especially if you are the primary (and therefore, you may feel, superior) parent. It may be even more challenging if you've lost custody and feel that you're being shut out of your children's lives. But kids need both of their parents, and most important, they need to know that both parents love them. Whether you are the primary caretaker or have limited contact, make sure your children know that their relationship with you is secure and that you will be there for them.

Don't bad-mouth the other parent to your kids or in front of your kids. It is truly harmful to your children to hear that someone they love and rely on for their care is a loser, a louse, or whatever other pejorative you want to lay on your ex. And don't think that the kids aren't listening while you complain to your best friend on the telephone. If you must express your frustration, do it when you know the kids are nowhere to be found. Better still, try not to do it at all. There's a saying that resentment is like eating rat poison and then waiting for the rat to die—every minute you spend putting down your ex-spouse is a minute you don't spend thinking about how to be a better parent yourself, or considering all that you have to be grateful for in your own life, or simply doing something you consider fun. Keeping that type of negative thinking out of your daily life will improve it.

And if your ex gets a new love interest at some point, refrain from saying negative things about that person, too. All of the same rules apply.

Never ask your kids to take messages to the other parent or to inform on the other parent. There's always a way to get information to the other parent without asking the kids to carry it. Chapter 2 lists a number of ways to communicate with your ex-spouse, including websites that allow you to deal with scheduling changes and information-sharing over the Internet. Better to practice the ways that don't involve the kids. And never ask your kids to tell you anything about the other parent's life. They will feel trapped and confused about what's the right thing to say. If they volunteer information, respond as neutrally (or positively) as you can, and don't pump them for more information.

Don't ask your kids to lie about or keep secret anything that happens in your house. "Don't mention to your mother that we had ice cream before dinner" might seem harmless, but it will stress your kids out to have to think about what they can and can't say in each household. You might think that certain things, like whether your new love interest spent the night at your house, is your business alone—but while your kids are young, you are still sharing your life with their other parent. The only way to keep events in your personal life private is to make sure they happen when you're not with the kids.

Let your kids contact the other parent any time they want to, privately. These days, many kids have constant access not only to a phone, but to texting and email—all good ways for them to be in touch with their other parent. Feel free to monitor your kids' use of electronic devices in general, but don't interfere with their regular, reasonable contact with the other parent. If your kids are young and have to rely on you to make contact with the other parent, don't be stingy. It will only backfire on you when you find them ever more anxious to speak to your ex. Of course, if there is a court order in place about the parameters of contact between the kids and the other parent during your parenting time, make sure you comply with the order.

Try to have a good attitude about sending your kids to the other parent. It can be hard to deal with the transition between households—either because the kids want to go or because they don't. Most kids do look forward to spending time with their other parent and in their other household. Let them have their anticipation and their appreciation of the other parent. Maybe they don't have the best dental hygiene when they're there, or perhaps they are allowed to stay up later than you think is appropriate. But no matter how frustrating you may find the other parent, there is absolutely nothing you can do about that. Unless there's something truly dangerous or abusive going on, let it go. Acknowledge that the kids have a relationship with their other parent that is separate from their relationship with you, and also separate from your relationship with your ex-spouse. What to do when the kids resist going to visitation is covered in "When The Kids Don't Want to Go," below.

Dating and New Relationships

Dating after a divorce when you have kids isn't always easy. Especially if you're in a high-conflict divorce that very likely causes stress for your children, it's important to wait until they're prepared before you bring home anyone you're dating. Even where there is a great deal of conflict, kids hold onto the possibility of reconciliation for a surprisingly long time. You can try talking them out of it, but you'll probably do better if you just wait and continue to talk to them honestly about the divorce.

Be cautious. Your kids have been through a big loss, and you don't want to keep repeating it as you search for the right relationship. Especially if you share custody with your former spouse, you have a ready-made schedule for dating: For a while, do it when the kids are with your ex.

It's also likely that both you and your ex will be challenged when the other begins dating—no matter how ready you both are to be away from each other. You probably want to maintain your privacy, but you also want to be sure your ex hears about any serious relationship directly from you, rather than from another source (especially your kids).

If there's a big problem with your ex's new partner, like substance abuse or physical abuse, of course you'll need to deal with it. But if you just don't take to the new friend, keep it to yourself. You may find that those feelings fade as you get to know the new person—and you won't be able to avoid that. Try to take the high road as much as you can, in hopes of establishing a decent relationship in the future.

When the Other Parent Violates a Court Order

A court order is a piece of paper that is worthy of respect, but there are many ways that parents don't treat it that way. Being chronically late (or early) to pick up or drop off the kids, leaving them in the care of others, abusing drugs or alcohol in the children's presence, not taking the kids to court-ordered medical or counseling appointments, violating orders regarding religious training or education, interfering with the other parent's visitation time … the list could go on. Perhaps some of these violations are familiar to you, and perhaps you have a list of your own.

It may help with your frustration to make (in your head or on paper) two lists. One can be titled "Violations of Court Orders," and the other "Things That Drive Me Nuts but Aren't Violations of Court Orders." You are likely to find that the second list is much longer than the first. You may also find that some of the things on the first list are going to be challenging to enforce. It's not like the court has people whose job it is to follow parents around making sure they're doing what their court order says they're supposed to do. It's very difficult for a judge to change the habits of a parent who is chronically late picking up the children or who fails to make their lunch for school.

When the other parent violates a court order, your first impulse may be to report the transgression to the judge. But take some time first to assess whether it's likely that the court would be helpful in enforcement, and consider trying negotiation first. Talk to your ex, ask for mediation, and see whether you can move toward greater compliance with the order, perhaps by negotiating adjustments that work for both of you.

In the end, though, the reason you put your custody and support agreements with the other parent in writing and got a judge's signature—or fought hard in court for the order you wanted—was to get enforceable orders so that if either parent doesn't do what the order says, the judge has the authority to make them do it. And when the other parent frequently violates the court's order, you can ask the court to intervene by punishing the other parent or revising the order to something that might be more likely to get compliance.

To get the court to enforce an order, you'll have to document everything that happens. While being late a few times isn't going to get the court's attention, a clear pattern of flouting the court's orders might. On your "Violations" list, note the dates and times of every instance of the other parent not complying with the court's orders. Also keep records of any email you send or phone call you make to try to remedy the situation. Once you have a documented record of meaningful violations of your order, you can ask the court to change the orders, in hopes that a different order will generate more compliance. In most cases, this will mean some kind of adjustment to the parenting schedule or some new rules about what parents can or can't do when they're with the kids. In extreme situations—for example, if one parent persistently interferes with the other's visitation rights—the court may switch custody from one parent to the other. (See "Changing Your Custody Arrangements," below.)

You can also file a motion to have your ex found in contempt of court, which means that a person has ignored a court order. But a contempt action isn't always the best way to deal with a custody or visitation problem, because what the court can do is limited. (Contempt can work well if you have a child support problem, as described in Chapter 9.) In the case of repeated violations, especially violations that put the children at risk, a contempt order can put a person in jail. This could feel like a good solution in the moment, and will certainly give you some temporary relief, but it's not going to do much to improve your long-term relationship with the other parent, or to help your kids. It's more likely that the judge will remind the other parent of the obligations under the court order, and possibly require that your ex pay your attorneys' fees.

With any court proceeding, there's the issue of cost. Every time you go into court, you can expect to spend hundreds of dollars, if not more, in attorneys' fees. If you don't have an attorney, you'll suffer the cost of your time, effort, and energy. You may be able to get the other parent to pay some of your attorneys' fees, though, especially if there are egregious violations of the orders. (See Chapter 12.)

THE LAW IN REAL LIFE

A New Hampshire mother lost custody of her children after five years of making unfounded allegations of sexual abuse and domestic violence against their father. The trial court ruled that she should keep custody because the children had lived with her for most of their lives, but the appeals court said that she should not benefit from her bad behavior in keeping the children from having contact with their father by making false allegations against him. The court held that she was obviously unable to meet the important custody criteria of fostering a positive relationship between the children and their other parent.

In a case that has been litigated between Vermont and Virginia since 2003, two women have been fighting over custody of a child born into their Vermont civil union in 2000. Lisa Miller originally received custody, with an order for visitation by Janet, the child's other legal parent. After fighting the visitation order in every possible court, Lisa simply refused to cooperate, and denied Janet any visitation. Finally, in 2007 the Vermont court modified its original order and awarded sole custody to Janet, on the ground that Lisa's "willful and calculated noncompliance resulted in a ... change of circumstances." The court also ordered reunification therapy for Janet and the child, who had barely seen each other for years. After losing an appeal, and before the new order could be enforced, Lisa Miller fled the country with the child and has not been seen since.

When the Other Parent Is Just Annoying

What about that other list, the list of things that don't actually go against a judge's order but that you probably feel are just as outrageous? Here's where the work of Jeffrey Wittman, described in "Lessons for Both Parents," above, will come in handy. When your ex sends the kids home with dirty hair and clothes, exhausted and hyped up from staying up too late and eating too much junk food, you're going to have to figure out a way to deal with it short of asking a judge to intervene.

Your best option, if your kids aren't actually being abused or neglected, is to ignore it and spend your energy on feeding, clothing, and educating them the ways you think are best when they are with you. Remember, you cannot control what your ex does—and you have to accept that the children have a relationship with their other parent that is separate from the one they have with you.

If you have serious concerns about your kids' health and welfare, and you really want some modifications in the other parents' behavior, try to persuade the other parent to attend some mediation or coparent counseling sessions. Even if you've tried it before, give it another shot in hopes that the passage of time might help the two of you to communicate better with the help of a skilled facilitator.

When the Kids Don't Want to Go

What happens if your ex is scheduled to pick up the kids at nine on a Saturday morning, and on Friday night they begin a lobbying campaign to be excused from visitation? In most cases, the answer is that they must go anyway; your job is to stand firm. For one thing, it's important for kids to have a relationship with both of their parents, even if they don't like the way things are done over at the other parent's house. For another, you too are under court order to have the children ready and to send them with their other parent when the order says you must. You may have to resort to saying, "Because the judge said so!"

At the same time, however, and without giving any indication that the answer will make a difference in their obligation to go with the other parent, it's worthwhile to inquire about why they don't want to go. It may be something as simple as wanting to play with the friend next door instead of going ten miles away to where they don't know any other kids the same age, or it may be something more significant, like an objection to being left with a babysitter the majority of the time instead of actually spending time with the other parent. Stick to your position and tell your children that they're going. If the problem is one you consider important enough to follow up on, do so. Talk to the other parent and, if necessary, seek help in mediation or even from a judge. If it's more in the nature of just the child's preference, you can validate their feelings to a point, but this is a good opportunity to remember that problems in the relationship between your kids and their other parent aren't necessarily your problem.

However, if it sounds like real abuse or neglect is going on, you'll need to take steps.

If You Suspect Abuse

If your children are telling you things that raise concerns about the possibility of abuse or other serious harm, start by talking with the other parent before sending the kids off for visitation. You may find out that your child isn't being completely accurate about everything that's going on, or that the other parent isn't aware of something. Unless you are certain the children would be in danger with the other parent, even if you're not satisfied with what you learn, you still need to send the kids— you can't unilaterally cancel a scheduled visitation. If you do have clear proof that there's a dangerous situation, you can keep the kids with you.

Whether you send them despite your misgivings or whether you refuse, if you're worried about abuse you should immediately contact your attorney, and follow the attorney's advice about the best way to proceed. If you don't have a lawyer, this might be the time to get one. If you're going to refuse to send your kids for visitation because you believe it's not safe for them, you will be the one who's not complying with a court order, and you might be well served by having an advocate who knows how to talk to the judge about what's going on, as well as how to put together the evidence in the most persuasive way.

If you can't find help right away or you decide not to hire an attorney, you will need to figure out your court's procedure for emergency orders. This kind of motion is often called "ex parte," meaning "without notice," because you don't give the other person 15 or 30 days' notice of your request. You simply prepare the paperwork, submit it to the court, fax or hand-deliver a copy to the other parent or the other attorney, and follow up with a phone call telling them you're seeking an emergency order. In many places you'll get in front of a judge within a day or two. Other places might make you wait longer. It's likely that your court has a special forms packet with the forms and instructions for getting emergency orders; usually there will be a particular judge assigned each day to hear ex parte cases.

There's more about dealing with abuse in Chapter 10.

When the Other Parent Doesn't Take the Children

While most court fights involve parents competing over who gets more time with the children, a sad reality of shared custody is that some parents, even after winning an order for shared custody, don't actually spend all of the parenting time they're given with their kids. They call and cancel, or they don't show up, or they abbreviate the time from a full weekend to one day and night—leaving disappointed children and a frustrated former spouse whose plans have been disrupted as well.

If this describes your situation, you may not mind having the extra time with your kids, but you probably do mind their sadness or sense of rejection when the other parent doesn't show up. There isn't a lot you can do about the lack of relationship—a court can't force a parent to spend time with the children. But if it becomes chronic, you could try to adjust the parenting schedule to conform more to reality, so that you and the kids at least won't be living with disappointed expectations over and over again. (It would also adjust child support.) Try to negotiate (See "Agreeing to a Change," below), and if that doesn't work, you can go back to court and ask for a modification, as long as the required amount of time has passed. (See "Going to Court to Argue Changed Circumstances," below.) Meanwhile, keep good records about how visitation actually happens—or doesn't. You're much more likely to get a change if you have documentation that the other parent isn't complying with the schedule.

In a few states, including California, you can ask the court to order the other parent to compensate you for costs you incur when the other parent fails to take the kids as the schedule calls for. For example, you could ask for compensation for expenses such as child care, transportation, or even meals, but not payment for any inconvenience you suffered. The court may also order your ex to reimburse you for the cost (attorneys' fees) of having to file for compensation. But a Tennessee appeals court reversed a lower court's order that a father pay the mother an additional $50 every time he failed to exercise his visitation rights on a weekend, and an extra $25 on top of that when he failed to visit on a holiday or during the summer. The court noted that the state's child support guidelines already called for modification of support if a parent's parenting time changed by more than 15%, making it inappropriate to set a specific amount as a penalty.

TIP

The failure to exercise visitation rights doesn't reduce support obligations. Most child support orders are based on how much time each parent spends with the children, and the parents' income. Don't let your ex persuade you that support should be lower because less parenting time is actually happening. It actually works the other way—a paying parent's support obligation would increase if time with the children were to decrease.

Traveling With Your Child

Assuming that your custody order doesn't prohibit you from traveling with your child, then it's likely that at some point you'll want to go somewhere. Traveling within the United States will be no problem, but if you are going abroad you need to do some planning ahead. Because of the frequency of international kidnapping by parents, you may find yourself under scrutiny at the airport when you're traveling alone with your child.

To avoid problems at the airport, be sure you have four things with you:

- A written consent from the other parent or an order of the family court making it clear that you have the authority to travel with the child. If you expect to travel frequently with your child, make sure your final court order is consistent with your plans, or get a special order that addresses travel. (If you have sole legal and physical custody, then you automatically have that authority and you only need to bring the order granting that custody to you.) Otherwise, ask the other parent to sign a document that sets out your travel plans and states the other parent's consent. Have the document notarized.

- A valid passport for the child. If your kids don't have passports yet, you must apply to the U.S. State Department, and both parents must sign the application. (See Chapter 10 for more about passports and preventing kidnapping.)
- A travel visa issued by the country you are going to.
- The child's birth certificate. This is a backup in case there is any question about your parent-child relationship.

Some airlines and airports are more attentive than others to making sure parents have the appropriate documentation, so you may carry all of these documents and never be asked for them at all. But parental kidnapping is a federal offense in the United States, and State Department officials are working to increase awareness among airlines—so be prepared to prove your right to travel with your child. (See Chapter 10 for more about kidnapping.)

Changing Your Custody Arrangements

It's very unusual for the custody order that's entered after a hearing or trial to be the last word on how any given family operates. Parenting arrangements change all the time, either because the parents agree that the status quo isn't working or because one asks the court to order a change.

Agreeing to a Change

You and your ex are free to change your parenting arrangements any time you want to—if you can agree on the changes. If the court gave you sole physical custody with the other parent having parenting time every other weekend and every Wednesday night, and you find that Tuesday works better for both of you, you can go ahead and change to Tuesday. You don't have to ask the court's permission or even tell the court.

If you're making a bigger change, like reversing the percentage of time that your children spend with each parent, you should get a court order. For one thing, you want to get the change in writing so that the parent who first had primary custody doesn't force a return to the original order, causing stress to everyone from too much change. For another, you want the court record to show a change that significant.

A lot of changes fall somewhere in between minor and major. The vast majority of parents don't bother getting a new court order for most changes; they just adjust things as they go along. It's never a bad idea, however, to at least write down what you've decided, with a date and both of your signatures. That way, if there's any confusion later about what you agreed to, you'll have an easy way to refresh both of your memories. This document won't be enforceable in court, but it may help keep you from landing there.

CAUTION
Don't use an informal agreement for changes in child support. If you agree to a change, be absolutely sure to get a new court order. Chapter 9 explains why and how.

If you do want a new court order, getting one shouldn't be particularly complicated. You and the other parent will write up a stipulation (agreement) stating your new arrangement and file it with the court. There may be a minimal filing fee, but it won't be too significant. Along with the stipulation you'll file a proposed order for the judge to sign. You won't have to appear in court; you'll just get the signed order back in the mail. Even if you used a lawyer for your divorce, you don't necessarily need one for this. A book like *Represent Yourself in Court: How to Prepare & Try a Winning Case*, by Paul Bergman and Sara Berman (Nolo), contains everything you need to know to prepare and file a simple stipulation and order.

Agreeing to a change is the best-case scenario, especially it if improves your children's experience and helps communication between you and your ex. If you're having trouble agreeing when one parent seeks a change, it's a great idea to seek help from a mediator or parenting counselor before going to court. You'll find yourself in mediation once you submit your motion to court, anyway—mediation is almost always mandatory in disputes over custody and visitation, whether you've been to court before or not.

Going to Court to Argue Changed Circumstances

If you and your former spouse find yourselves at loggerheads, you will have to ask the judge to rule on whether a change is appropriate or not. There are some barriers to asking for modification to a custody or visitation order. Because it's believed that frequent custody changes are detrimental to kids (as well as not being a good use of the court's time), most states require that a certain amount of time pass after the court's final custody order—a year or as long as two—before a parent can seek a change of custody unless the child is in danger of being harmed.

All states require a showing that there has been a significant change in circumstances in order to make a change. The proposed new custody arrangement must also be in the child's best interest, and some states require that the parent seeking the change prove that the current arrangement is actually detrimental to the child.

Your opinion that the parenting order isn't working out doesn't count as changed circumstances, nor does the fact that your child started taking piano lessons or wants to join the baseball team. Even things that might seem to be game-changers aren't always seen that way by the courts. In one Georgia case, for example, a father's no-contest plea to a charge of cruelty toward a child wasn't considered a change of circumstances sufficient to warrant a change of custody, because the child in question wasn't his child. Likewise, remarriage of either parent, while obviously affecting the child, isn't necessarily considered a material change.

THE LAW IN REAL LIFE

An Ohio appeals court held that a change isn't a change until it happens. A lower court changed custody from the mother to the father based on the mother's stated intent to move to Wyoming. But because she had not actually moved, and said that she would not go without her son, the trial court was wrong to change custody to the father in advance of the actual move—there was no real change of circumstances.

In separate cases, courts in Oklahoma and Iowa held that the parents' inability to cooperate in their parenting duties was a change of circumstances that justified giving sole custody to one parent, instead of continuing joint custody.

The Alaska Supreme Court held that an out-of-state move is always a change of circumstances, even in a case where a child already lives some distance from a noncustodial parent. The parents lived 600 miles apart in Alaska, so the visitation plan already required long-distance travel, but when the custodial father moved to Arizona with the child, the mother petitioned for a change in custody based on the move. The trial court said that because of the distance between the parties' homes in Alaska, the move to Arizona wasn't a change of circumstances, but the Supreme Court disagreed and required a hearing on the child's best interests.

A mother's immigration status didn't qualify as a change of circumstances, said the Arkansas Supreme Court, when it was the same as it had been at the time of the divorce. The father asked for a change in custody based on the fact that the mother was undocumented and faced a risk of deportation, which could result in the child being placed with nonparents, at least temporarily. Noting that the mother had not taken steps to change her legal status since the divorce five years before, the judge changed custody to the father; the Supreme Court said there was no actual change in circumstances that would justify the switch.

But something like moving to a larger home or a better neighborhood, when a parent's living situation was considered as a factor in the original custody determination, could be a change of circumstance justifying a modification; so could a parent starting a job that would require significant travel, making the parent less available to care for the children. A parent's move out of state is generally considered a change of circumstances if it would have a significant effect on the other parent's parenting time. (See "When One Parent Wants to Move Away," below.)

Many states have laws explicitly stating that a temporary military deployment does not warrant a permanent change in the parenting schedule. However, a temporary change in the schedule is, obviously, likely if the deployed parent won't be around to spend time with the child. (Chapter 11 has more about military families.)

In short, the change must be meaningful and it must affect the child, not just the adults. As always, the proposed change in custody must be in the child's best interest. This means that there's a two-step analysis. First, is the change in circumstances significant to the child, and second, is the proposed modification of the parenting plan in the child's best interest? Pretty much every request for a modification of custody is decided based on the specific facts of the case, using that analysis.

The "State Custody Modification Statutes" chart in the appendix lists each state's statutes (or cases) governing changes in child custody. You can start there to find your own state's rules about when a parent can request a change in custody; Chapter 12 explains how to find and read statutes and cases.

A court hearing on modification of custody or visitation will be very much like any other hearing you've attended so far. The process will start with one parent filing papers with the court; it's possible you'll be required to return to mediation or show that you've already been through mediation on this particular conflict and haven't been able to resolve it. If mediation again fails to bring you to agreement, you'll go to court and present your evidence, and the judge will make a decision.

Modifying Visitation
In most states, it isn't as hard to modify visitation as it is to make a change in custody. When it comes to custody, small differences won't suffice to justify a modification, but there's a less restrictive, more expansive definition of what constitutes a change for purposes of adjusting a visitation schedule, as long as the adjustment doesn't change which parent has primary custody (or change the arrangement from a joint to a sole custody situation, or vice versa). Other than the lower standard, the rules and procedures for seeking a change of visitation are the same as everything discussed here about custody.

When One Parent Wants to Move Away

Every year, approximately one in five Americans changes where they live, and a parent's desire to relocate is one of the most common reasons for custody cases to return to court. This may be because a moveaway dispute often appears to offer very little room for compromise, and because both parents almost always have a good argument. Most frequently, the move is to take advantage of opportunities that will benefit the child as well as the moving parent, but the interest of the other parent and the children in maintaining a close relationship is also significant.

No matter how polarized things seem, though, it's always worth trying to come to an agreement before heading off to court. Situations that sometimes seem incapable of being resolved can end in a compromise that works for everyone—for example, agreements about vacation time, webcams, travel expenses, and support adjustments can make a move seem more palatable and avert an expensive and upsetting trip to see the judge.

Communication Tips

If you've had a parenting arrangement that's been working well for the kids and you're considering a move, start by inviting your ex-spouse to a session with a therapist, mediator, or parenting counselor, and raise the possibility of the move. Listen carefully to what your ex has to say, and present your reasons for wanting to go without acting like it's the only possible outcome that could work for you or the kids. Be patient with your ex's reaction.

If you're the parent who fears losing your kids, try to keep your mind open too. There may be ways to keep in close contact with your children even if they move away, and it's possible that the move will have benefits for them. Being open-minded may not get you all the way to an agreement, and you may be in for a court fight—but at least give it a try.

State Laws and the Burden of Proof

If you're not able to reach an agreement through discussions or mediation, prepare to learn a lot about your state's rules regarding relocation cases. This is an area where states can have very different rules—both about when a parent will be allowed to relocate with the child, and also about who has to prove what. The concept of the "burden of proof" is very important in relocation cases. The phrase refers to which party in a lawsuit must prove something—a particular fact or legal theory— in order to move ahead with the lawsuit or win the case. For example, in a criminal case the prosecution must show "beyond a reasonable doubt" that the accused committed the crime—that's the burden of proof, and if the prosecution doesn't meet it, the person goes free.

In relocation cases, the burden of proof is different in different states. In some places, the parent who wants to move has the burden of showing why the move will be in the child's best interests. If the parent can't show that, the move can't happen. (At least, it can't happen with the kids. No court can prevent an adult from moving—that would violate constitutional rights. But the court can say that if the parent wants to move, the result will be a change in primary custody to the other parent.)

But other states presume that a parent with sole physical custody has the right to move with the child, and put the burden on the noncustodial parent to prove that a move would be detrimental to the child or is being made in bad faith. For example, Tennessee says that a custodial parent who wants to move with a child can do so unless the noncustodial parent can prove that the move has no reasonable purpose, would pose a threat to the child, or is made for vindictive reasons on the moving parent's part. That's the burden of proof on the objecting parent.

Here's an example of how one state treats the burden of proof and considers the evidence. Oklahoma's law places the burden on the noncustodial parent, requiring that parent to show that consideration of these five factors, taken together, weighs against the move:
- the reason for the relocation
- the educational, health, and leisure opportunities available where the custodial parent and children will relocate
- the visitation and communication schedule for the noncustodial parent
- the effect of the move on the extended family relationships in the new location, and
- preference of the child, including the age, maturity, and the reasons given by the child.

Other states have similar requirements, with different details.

Some states have what's called a "shifting burden." That means that the parent who wants to move starts with the burden of proving something—in some states they must prove that the move will be in the children's best interest, and in others only that the move is made for legitimate reasons. If the parent can meet that burden, then the burden shifts to the other parent, who can only prevent the move by proving that it will be harmful to the child.

If the judge thinks that you're moving just so you can keep the kids away from your former spouse, watch out. You're likely to get an earful as well as have your request denied.

> ! CAUTION
>
> **Don't go unrepresented to a moveaway hearing.** There is so much at stake in a battle like this that you almost certainly want a lawyer representing you, whether or not you hired one during your divorce.

The "State Relocation Statutes" chart in the appendix lists each state's statute that applies to relocation cases, and identifies which parent has the burden of proof. If there's nothing listed in the "burden" column, then there's no specific rule in that state. If there's a case listed in the last column, that means that the case law is important or unusual and worth reading. Chapter 12 explains how to find and read statutes and cases.

Issues and Arguments

If you're the custodial parent who wants to move, you'll argue that stability and continuity are paramount and that changing custody as a result of the move would be detrimental to the child. You'll also try to show the ways that the move would benefit the child, because of greater financial opportunities for you, better educational options for the child, or more opportunities for contact with extended family. Most important, you should emphasize that you will do everything in your power to maintain the child's relationship with the noncustodial parent. If you are financially able to offer to pay for travel expenses, all the better. Even if you aren't, explain what you will do to support the relationship and maximize contact between the child and the other parent.

If you're the noncustodial parent seeking to prevent the move or persuade the court to transfer primary custody to you, you have to show why the move doesn't benefit the child. You also need to show that you are an appropriate choice as primary caretaker. The fact that you're currently the nonresidential parent will work against you, so you may have to explain the reasons for that original decision and say why those reasons don't preclude you from becoming the custodial parent now. This means showing that you are an involved parent with intimate knowledge of your children's activities, needs, likes, and dislikes. If there have been problems with the current custody arrangement or you think the other parent is a less than perfect custodian for the child, you can also present that argument, but be careful about denigrating the other parent too much, unless you have hard evidence. For example, if you can show that the custodial parent leaves the child with a babysitter frequently, that the custodial parent's new spouse is hostile to the child, or that the custodial parent does not take care of the child's physical or emotional needs in some way, you may make some headway.

THE LAW IN REAL LIFE

An Alabama court ruled that if a mother decided to move to Michigan, custody would be shifted to the father, because the child had a close relationship with the father and the father's family in Alabama but had no family in Michigan and would suffer from moving there.

An Indiana court changed custody from the mother to the father after the mother moved to New York with the children without notifying either the court or the father, and where the mother moved frequently while the father's residence was stable. The mother also failed to take care of the children properly.

The Minnesota court of appeals held it was appropriate to change custody from a father to the mother where the father moved with his son to Omaha without informing the mother or even giving the son a chance to say good-bye to her. In addition, the father gave a false forwarding address and made other efforts to hide his whereabouts. In contrast, the mother was willing to support the child's relationship with his father if custody changed.

No change of custody was ordered where a mother in Louisiana met her burden of proving that her request to relocate was made in good faith and not to deprive the father of parenting time, that she wanted to move closer to her parents and to take a higher-paying job.

A mother was permitted to relocate from Rhode Island to Indiana with her children because her desire to move was in good faith and motivated by better job prospects in her new home and the proximity of her parents; the court also took into account the father's bad temper and alcoholism and the fact that the children had been exposed to "dysfunctional behavior" in the father's home.

When One Parent Is Out of State

Most of the time, a divorce is handled in the local court where the family has been living, and child custody issues are decided as part of the divorce. But what if one parent is living in another state because there has been a long separation, or one parent moves during or after the divorce? Which state's court decides custody issues?

The answer comes from a law called the Uniform Child Custody Jurisdiction and Enforcement Act (UCCJEA). The UCCJEA is designed to do two things: prevent parental kidnapping, and give the court information so it can determine a child's "home state." Courts in the home state have authority (jurisdiction) over custody litigation involving that child. The home state is the place where the child has lived with at least one parent for the six months just before the beginning of the divorce or custody case. The home state court is the only one that can hear a custody case for this child.

The home state court's jurisdiction continues until one of two things happens:

1. The home state court determines that neither the child, the child's parents, nor any person acting as a parent has a significant connection with that state and that state no longer has access to substantial evidence concerning the child's care, protection, training, and personal relationships, or

2. A court (in the home state court or another state) determines that the child, the child's parents, and any person acting as a parent does not presently reside in the state that initially made the child custody order.

If the child has not lived in one state for at least six months, then the court determines which state has "significant connections" with the child and at least one parent *and* "substantial evidence concerning the child's care, protection, training, and personal relationships." If more than one state meets this test—for example, where a child has lived with one parent in one state and the other in another in the six months before the court action—then judges in the two states must contact each other and discuss which state has the most significant connections to the child. If two states have issued valid child custody orders because the child has lived in each of them at some point in the past, the order from the child's current home state is the one that will be enforced.

The UCCJEA discourages what is sometimes called "forum shopping," where one parent moves to a state in hopes it will be friendlier to his or her case—for example, because the new state is more conservative and its courts might disapprove of the other parent for some reason—or tries to enter an order in the new state simply because it's more convenient.

If you are having a dispute not only about custody but also about which state will make the decision about custody, you'll need a lawyer. The law about which state gets to decide custody issues is complex, and the decision is important. Once a state has jurisdiction over a child custody dispute, it's hard to move the case to another state.

THE LAW IN REAL LIFE

A mother took her son to Pakistan for what was supposed to be a four-week visit, and then stated her intention not to return. The father filed for divorce in California, where the family had been living, and the California court granted him sole legal and physical custody. The mother filed for custody in Pakistan and received an order there (after the father's order was entered). The father went to Pakistan and filed suit to enforce the California order; the Pakistani court granted him visitation, but said he could not take the child back to California. The mother argued that the California court had lost jurisdiction when the father went to Pakistan, but the California court said that as long as the father continued to have a home in California, he was a resident there and the court's order was still in force.

If You Move to Another State: Registering Your Custody Order

If you move to a new state with your children, you can ensure that your new home state has the ability to enforce your custody order by registering or, as it's sometimes called, "domesticating" the judgment with the new state. Most states have forms for doing this; the forms often refer to "foreign" judgments, which means judgments from another state (though it could also apply to a judgment from a foreign country). You may need to have your signature on the form notarized. Look for this form in the same places you'd find other family law forms—on the website or from the court clerk in the new state's court.

You'll have to submit at least one certified copy of your existing order. You can get a certified copy from the clerk of the court that issued the order. A certified copy usually has an embossed (raised) seal or a purple seal with the clerk's original signature on it. You'll generally have to pay for certified copies—anywhere from about a dollar a page to $25 for the whole document.

You must serve the request to register the judgment on the other parent, to give that parent a chance to object. As with any other document where service is required, you will need to file a "proof of service" with the clerk's office, usually along with the request to register the judgment. Most states don't require personal service for this document, so you will probably be allowed to mail it to the other parent or the attorney for the other parent. But make sure you check first in case there are requirements about how service must be made. (Chapter 6 explains service.)

THE LAW IN REAL LIFE

An Alabama court of appeals rejected a request to register a Mississippi custody order because the grandparents, who had custody, failed to comply with the UCCJEA requirements for registration (they didn't include the right number of certified copies of the order, and didn't prove to the court that the original Mississippi order hadn't been subsequently modified). The court didn't say what the effect of the failure to register would be, though— most likely the grandparents would be allowed to refile the registration request with the proper information included. In the meantime, however, jurisdiction remained in Mississippi and the mother, who objected to the Alabama registration, could petition for modification there.

Child Support Orders: Living With, Enforcing, and Changing Them

Whether you and the other parent agreed to an amount of support and the court entered an order based on that agreement, or you went through a hearing or trial and came out with a support order, you now have a final child support order. Once there's a court order, whether your divorce is final or not, the recipient parent can enforce the support order if the other parent doesn't pay support on time or as agreed. Still, an enormous percentage of child support goes unpaid every year in this country.

If you're the paying parent, it's in your power to pay on time and make things simple, or not follow the court order and make them more challenging. If you're the parent receiving support, your job is to make sure you keep getting support payments for as long as the children need them. Making sure you can collect the payments regularly and on time can be a challenge, especially if the paying parent is self-employed or has a sporadic income stream.

Arranging for Payment

Once the amount of support is set, either by agreement or by court order, your next step is to figure out how it will be paid. These are the options:

- paying through an income withholding order (IWO), also called a wage garnishment
- paying directly, or
- paying through a state child support enforcement agency.

Each of these options is discussed in detail below.

Income Withholding Orders

All child support orders, in all states, automatically allow the recipient parent to arrange for automatic deductions from the paying parent's paycheck, through an income withholding order (IWO). You'll also hear an IWO called a wage garnishment, and it is a form of garnishment— one that has priority over any other type of wage garnishment. The only withholding that takes precedence over child support is a federal tax levy issued before the child support order was established—all other debts are secondary. It's up to the parent receiving support to decide whether or not to ask the employer to garnish the other parent's wages.

Automatic deductions are an easy way for parents to make sure support arrives on time each month. They're a necessity if there are concerns about whether the paying parent will send checks on time or at all.

If you're the paying parent, an IWO may seem intrusive or embarrassing. But your employer can't fire you or take any kind of action against you because of your first wage garnishment (there aren't as many protections when you're subject to garnishments for multiple debts). And now that income withholding orders are automatic and fairly common, there's no implication that you are a deadbeat. An IWO makes things easy for you, too—you don't have to mail checks or worry about being late or where the money is going to come from.

Limitations on Income Withholding

Having child support automatically deducted from the paying parent's paycheck under an IWO requires that the paying parent have an employer. You can't garnish the wages of a self-employed person.

Federal law limits how much can be taken from each paycheck (Consumer Credit Protection Act). For a child support order, 60% of "disposable earnings" can be taken out of each paycheck (50% if the employee is also supporting a current spouse or a child who is not the subject of the child support order involved in the garnishment). An additional 5% may be taken for any support payment that's over 12 weeks late.

"Disposable earnings" means what's left after deductions that are required by law, like Social Security, federal and state taxes, unemployment insurance, and contributions required by state retirement systems. Deductions for things like union dues and employee benefits aren't deducted before the limit is calculated. Even though they may be mandatory, like some retirement payments and union dues, they're not required by law, so they don't count as an offset.

Multiple Support Orders

If the paying spouse owes support to a child from another relationship under a different child support order, the orders aren't paid on a first-come, first-served basis—instead, the employer must pay something toward each child support order. Each state has enacted its own laws relating to how funds are to be apportioned between the different orders.

How the Process Works

Once there's a court order stating the amount and terms of payment and providing for income withholding, the recipient parent must deal with getting the garnishment in place. This involves sending a copy of the court order and an IWO form to the paying parent's employer. You can probably find the Income Withholding Order form from the same source that you got the rest of your court forms, but you can also use the federal Department of Health Services form on which the state forms are modeled—that's available at www.acf.hhs.gov/programs/cse/forms/OMB-0970-0154.pdf. Or, you can turn over collection to your state's child support enforcement agency, described below.

Once you send the IWO to the employer, the employer then becomes responsible for taking the money out of the paying parent's paycheck and paying it to the recipient parent or to the child support enforcement agency (see below). The employer also is required to notify the recipient if the paying parent changes jobs within the company or leaves the job. (This is another advantage of wage garnishment, if it might be hard to keep track of the other parent.)

For information about how to institute an IWO, check out your state's child support enforcement agency website, listed in the appendix. You can also get help from staffers at the agency—in fact one of the things a child support enforcement agency does is to prepare IWOs and transmit them to employers.

Direct Payment

If you and the other parent agree to direct payments instead of an IWO, you can simply follow the court order as far as the amount and date of the payments and go from there. It's up to you to decide how the direct payment will be made—for example, by check, money order, or electronic funds transfer.

That keeps things simple, but it means that if the paying parent stops sending checks or making deposits, the other parent will have to establish an IWO or start a relationship with the state child enforcement agency. The recipient parent will always be able to institute the IWO, because the support order allows for garnishment at any time. But there's bound to be some delay—getting the IWO after some time has passed takes longer than if it's done as soon as the court issues the support order.

An easy way to make direct payments without sending a check is to set up an automatic bill payment or electronic funds transfer through your bank's online banking system. This allows for a fast, regularly scheduled transfer of funds and is a lot easier for the recipient parent to verify than the old "the check's in the mail" promise. If the paying parent is self-employed, and the recipient parent is concerned about a steady flow of checks, there are a couple of ways to create a safety net with the terms of your child support order, discussed in "Securing Payment" in Chapter 3.

State Child Support Enforcement Agencies

Federal law requires that every state have an agency dedicated to child support enforcement. A state child support enforcement agency (CSEA) can:

- help the recipient get an income withholding order prepared and mailed to the paying parent's employer
- receive payments from the paying parent and distribute them to the recipient
- keep track of the payment history in your case
- if payments aren't made on time, follow up and enforce support through wage garnishments, taking money directly out of the

paying parent's bank accounts, intercepting tax refunds, invalidating the paying parent's passport, suspending the paying parent's driver's license and professional licenses, and going to court for a contempt order that could subject the parent to criminal prosecution

- ensure that health insurance for your children is in place and continuing under the support order by helping the recipient prepare the appropriate medical support order (see Chapter 3)
- monitor the paying parent's efforts to get work if that parent isn't paying because of loss of a job, and
- work with both parents to come up with a plan to pay overdue support (arrearages), if all payments haven't been made.

You may have to pay a small administrative fee or a tiny percentage of your support payment to the agency for these services, but it's well worth it. To find out how to get an account with your state's support enforcement agency, go to the website for your state, which is listed in the "State Child Support Enforcement Agencies" chart in the appendix.

If you ask your state agency to prepare and deliver an IWO to the employer, the employer will send payments to the CSEA, which will in turn forward them to you. The advantage to this is that the agency will take care of the paperwork and keep track of payments, and will follow up if payments are late or don't come. If the paying parent is self-employed, you can still arrange for payments to be made through the agency rather than directly to you. You might want to do this, for example, if there's a history of domestic violence and you don't want the other parent to know where you live, or if you expect payments to be sporadic and you want to be sure there are unassailable records and that you will have help with enforcement.

When you get in touch with the enforcement agency, be prepared to provide the information it will need, most of which you should be able to get from the order providing for support. To start, you'll need basic identifying information for you, the paying parent, and each of your children, including each person's date of birth, Social Security number, and current contact information. (Some courts have forms specifically for the purpose of collecting information that's required for child support enforcement—these forms are protected from disclosure, so that

Social Security numbers don't go into the public record with the rest of the divorce papers.) In addition, you'll need to give the agency:

- your court case number
- a copy of the order of support
- information about the paying parent's employment, including contact information for the employer, and
- the paying parent's driver's license number, passport number, and the identifying information for any professional license (for example, if the paying parent is a doctor, lawyer, architect, or contractor).

Establish a good relationship with the folks at your child support office from the start by being organized and providing the information they need to do their jobs. You'll probably be assigned to one worker who will be in charge of your case, but keep track of every contact you have with the agency and whom you talked to so that you can always trace the history of your case. It's also possible that you'll be able to follow your case through an online tracker—some states have them now, and more will in the future. You can see whether payments are on their way to you and, if the paying parent is behind, see what the current arrearage is.

State agencies can be an enormous help to you. At the same time, they're working with a lot of cases, so be patient and don't expect immediate results.

If You're Paying Support: Changing the Amount

You may find it frustrating to use most of your paycheck to support your children, especially if you think the other parent and the kids are living much better than you are or are worried that your former spouse is misusing the money. Stay focused on the fact that the money is to support your children, just as you probably used most of your income to support them when you lived with them full time. It's not easy to go from helping to support one household to helping to support two, but your first responsibility is always to your kids.

If you find that you really can't pay the amount that has been ordered, or your financial situation changes in a meaningful way, you'll need to ask the court to modify your support obligation. (See "When Circumstances Change," below.) Never alter your child support payments without the court's permission—even if the other parent says it's okay to lower the payments or take your time paying. If the parent ever has a change of heart, he or she could go to court at any time to collect the arrearage (the amount that was due under the order and is now officially late). The court won't care that you had a promise that it was okay to modify the payment, and you'll be subject to the various punishments that can apply.

In one New Hampshire case, for example, a judge rejected a written agreement between the parents because it had never been filed with the court. The state child support enforcement department sought to enforce the original order, and the judge said it was still in full force. The judge rejected the father's argument that the parents were free to make a contract to change the original order, saying that if a judge doesn't approve modifications to child support agreements there is a danger of collusion (for example, the parents agree to a lower amount than the court ordered, to the children's detriment) or of one party being pressured by the other into an unwanted agreement.

Whatever you do, *don't stop paying before the court issues a new order*. Failure to pay court-ordered child support is a crime. That means that under certain circumstances, a warrant could be issued for your arrest and you could be put in jail for up to six months for a first offense, and two years if you're a repeat offender.

There are a lot of other possibilities short of jail that could make your life miserable, including having money taken directly out of your bank account or having your professional licenses suspended, your passport denied, or your tax refund intercepted. Your credit rating could be affected as well, because most states report nonpayment to the credit bureaus. All states report to the federal "new hire database," which means that if you try to change jobs, your prospective new employer can find out that you are behind in your child support. Some states also list deadbeat parents on public websites. And if you live in a different state from your child and you haven't paid for over a year or your arrearage is

$5,000 or more, the federal government can get involved and you can be fined and even put in jail—in addition to having to pay the arrearage.

Child support obligations don't go away, either—in most states there's no limit on how many years can pass between the order and collection of the support payments. In one Texas case, a mother successfully went to court seeking payment of arrearages for her daughter, who was 39 years old. Most states have "dormancy" laws that say that judgments can't be enforced after too much time has passed, but the court in this case said these laws don't apply to child support judgments.

Even filing for bankruptcy doesn't wipe out your obligation to support your children. Almost all other debts may go away, but you'll still be on the hook for anything you owe the other parent for child support.

> **TIP**
> **It's not a good idea to make any kind of change in how you deal with supporting your kids without discussing it with the other parent.** One Ohio father changed his kids' health insurance coverage from their mother's policy to his new wife's insurance, causing him to be held in contempt of court because the existing court order said he had to consult his ex-wife about "major health care issues." In the end, an appellate court agreed with the dad that the term "health care issues" didn't include insurance, and reversed the contempt order. But this was after the case went all the way to the appellate court, undoubtedly costing both parents significant sums of money. Better to communicate from the beginning.

How Long Child Support Lasts

Child support obligations usually end when the child becomes an adult in the eyes of the law. Most states consider 18 the age of majority, but a few use 21. Some states require parents to continue paying child support as long as the child is a full-time student in high school, college, or trade school, up to a certain age—or under "exceptional circumstances." Some parents are required to pay even longer—see "College Expenses," in Chapter 3.

THE LAW IN REAL LIFE

In South Carolina, a court held that college expenses didn't qualify as "exceptional circumstances" under the state's rules about postmajority support, so that a father who hadn't previously been paying support didn't have to start when his son went to college. The court made a distinction between cases where there was already a child support order—in which case the law allowed for continuation of support for the adult child's education—and cases where there was no order. In the latter case, the court said there was no authority to create a new court order for a legally adult child who wanted to attend college.

An Arizona father asked the court to relieve him of the responsibility to pay support for his college-age son, who was on what the father called a "five-year plan" in high school because of poor grades and absences. The judge said that the state rule that parents must support their children through high school still applied, and that because the son was now making a "sincere effort" to graduate, the father must continue paying. Likewise, in Georgia, a court held that online high school courses satisfied the requirement that the child be "enrolled in and attending a secondary school" in order to continue receiving support.

In Kansas, a mother asked the court to extend indefinitely her ex-husband's support obligation for their disabled son. The trial court ordered lifetime support, but that decision was overturned on appeal because Kansas law doesn't require a parent to provide support for an adult child in these circumstances.

An Illinois appellate court determined that incarceration isn't the same as emancipation. A trial court ruled that a father no longer had any obligation to support his incarcerated 20-year-old son. But when the decision was appealed, an appellate court said that because the divorce order required the parents to contribute to the son's college expenses unless he became emancipated, they were responsible for those expenses even if the son was in jail, where he had the opportunity to continue his education.

Certain events mean that your child support obligation is over, no matter what else is going on in your child's life or yours. You are no longer obligated to pay support if your child:

- becomes emancipated, meaning that before the legal age of adulthood in your state, the child goes to court and is declared an "emancipated minor"—someone with the same rights and autonomy as a legal adult
- joins the military, or
- gets married.

THE LAW IN REAL LIFE

Two divorcing parents agreed that the husband would relinquish parental rights in exchange for not having to pay child support. The divorce judge allowed the agreement, but after the state child support enforcement agency intervened the appeals court said no, ruling that the termination of the father's rights was not in the child's best interest, no matter what the parents agreed. As a matter of public policy, courts want kids to have two parents who are responsible for their welfare, if at all possible.

When Circumstances Change

Whether you agreed on an amount of support or had the amount decided for you by the court, the best-case scenario is that the amount will work for your family for some time to come. As described in Chapter 3, the child support order might incorporate some regular increases or events that would cause a change in the amount of support. However, it's also possible that changes you didn't anticipate will occur—you or the other parent could lose a job, get a new one that pays more, or experience some other change in your financial circumstances. Your child could also turn out to have special needs or a special talent that needs nurturing. You and the other parent may agree to a change in how the kids split their time between households.

If the time comes that your current support arrangement is no longer appropriate, either parent can seek a change in the amount of child support. The court has authority to change child support until your kids reach adulthood, so if you can't work something out with your former spouse, you can always ask the judge to decide.

In most places, the judge will start by determining whether or not there's been a change in circumstances that's significant enough to justify changing the support amount. A small change in your income or a minor shift in the time share between the parents won't be adequate to support an adjustment. The change must be a permanent one that has actually happened, not just something you expect to happen. It also can't be a change that you made purposely to avoid paying support or to qualify for a higher support payment—for example, voluntarily leaving your job or taking a lower-paying position.

In many states, even a significant change in one parent's income is not enough enough to justify a change in support unless the child's needs have also increased.

Some examples of meaningful changes of circumstances justifying an adjustment in child support include:

- A change of a certain percentage in the amount of guideline child support based on both parents' current income and the current time share. Many states use 15% as the benchmark; others use 10%, and some are as high as 25%. Some states also use a dollar amount—you can't seek a modification unless the change pursuant to guidelines would be more than a certain amount. For example, Iowa law provides that there has been a substantial change of circumstances when an existing child support order varies by 10% from the amount that would be due based on current guidelines and the parents' current incomes—so if the original child support order called for $300 per month in child support, and changes in the parents' income or the guidelines meant that a recalculation would set support at $350, the 10% threshold has been met and the amount must be changed.

- A major change in the amount of time the child spends with each parent

- The loss of a job without immediate prospects of reemployment
- A change in either parent's actual income, earning capacity, or overall resources
- Disability or serious illness of one parent, or significant changes in the physical, mental, or emotional health of either parent
- Remarriage of either parent, or support of either party by another person
- Significant change in the child's needs, such as extensive orthodontia or uninsured medical care
- Receipt by either parent of an inheritance or other gift, and
- Incarceration of the paying parent.

A parent can also seek a one-time or temporary offset or reduction. For example, a father in Indiana successfully petitioned for an offset for his contribution to his son's college expenses because his ex-wife received a $4,000 tax credit for her own contributions—the court accepted his argument that the initial calculations didn't take the tax credit into account and that once the mother received it, she was paying $4,000 less than what was agreed to.

A parent can always seek a modification based on changed circumstances, no matter how much or how little time has passed. If there's no change of circumstances, however, most states limit how often you can seek a modification on the basis that a current calculation would result in a different amount of guideline support. In essence, the court doesn't want the paying parent coming back every time union dues go up, or the recipient parent petitioning whenever the paying parent gets an incremental raise, to make minor adjustments. Many state CSEAs review each child support order at least every three years if either parent asks for review, and some do it automatically.

If you are the paying parent and you lose your job or your income is reduced, you're probably going to tell the other parent right away and go to court to try to get a downward adjustment in support. If you're the parent receiving support, however, how will you know if there's an increase in the other parent's income that would justify a support increase? Some state laws require that parents keep each other informed of any changes in employment, incomes, or benefits; in other states, such a provision can be included in your support order. If you don't have that provision in your existing order and you believe there's been a substantial change in the other parent's income, you may have to use discovery procedures to get the relevant financial information. If it turns out you're right and you get a new support order, try to have the notification provision included in your modified order.

Enforcing Support Orders Across State Lines

When one parent moves out of state, does the child support order need to be changed to apply in the new state? The answer is: sometimes. It's determined by the Uniform Interstate Family Support Act (UIFSA), a law that's been adopted by all 50 states.

The UIFSA controls when and where child support orders can be issued and enforced. The goal is to have just one child support order for each child. So if there are multiple children in a family, there may also be multiple orders, and these could even be in different states—but for each child, there must be only one.

The law says which court has jurisdiction—the right to make decisions—over a child support order by defining what is a child's home state. The home state is the place where the child has lived with at least one parent for the six months just before the beginning of the divorce or child support case.

Once a home state issues an initial child support order, it has what the UISFA calls "continuing exclusive jurisdiction" (CEJ) over that order. As long as one of the parents or the child lives in the original home state, that state continues to have CEJ—including authority to enforce the order under its laws and to modify the order.

If both parents and the child move to another state, it is possible to transfer jurisdiction to the new state. There are two ways to give a new state CEJ:

- If both parents agree in writing that another state where one of them lives may take control of the case, that new state will be able to enforce or modify the original order. Once a new state modifies an order, the original state loses CEJ, and the new state gets it.

- A parent who wants to change a child support order in a different state than the one that has CEJ, but can't get the other parent's agreement, can register the order in a new state for purposes of modifying the order. (Registration is discussed below.) The new state then has CEJ.

A state that takes over CEJ by modifying support then is responsible for collecting amounts owed under the new support order. However, the state that originally had CEJ can still collect past-due support under the order made in that state. If the paying parent failed to meet other provisions in the original order, like paying for child care or health insurance, the original state can seek repayment for those arrearages as well.

An order must be registered in a new state before the new state can enforce or modify it. To register an order, the enforcement agency of the state that originally issued the order must send copies of the order and any related paperwork, like an income withholding order, to the new state's UIFSA agency (the state's child support enforcement agency). That agency will send a notice to the other parent, who has 20 days to object to the registration in the new state. If the other parent does object in good time, the agency in the new state will schedule a hearing.

Note that even if you've been representing yourself up to this point in your divorce or support action, you'll probably have to turn things over to your state's child support enforcement agency if you want to register your child support order—federal policy says that the new state should communicate with the issuing state's enforcement agency, not with individuals.

UIFSA isn't easy to understand, and it can be hard to know how it would apply to your particular situation. Because you'll need to turn your case over to the child support agency in the state where it was issued, you really only need to know the basics.

If you're the parent receiving support, even if you haven't had problems with getting your child support so far, it is a good idea to register your order when you move, so that your new state has the order on record and can intervene if it does become necessary. If you're the paying parent, don't ignore notices about efforts to register the order in a new state—this could mean that the other parent is seeking to modify the order. If you think the registration is inappropriate, see a lawyer to find out whether you have grounds to object.

If Your Spouse Goes Missing

One of the most frustrating things for a parent who is supposed to be receiving child support is for the paying parent to stop paying and disappear from sight. If this happens and you don't already have a relationship with your CSEA, establish one—they will help you look for the missing parent in order to collect support. You'll need to give them as much personal information about the other spouse as you have, including:

- name, any former names, and nicknames
- Social Security number
- date and place of birth
- last known address (and any previous addresses, if they're recent)
- last known employer (and previous employers, if recent)
- photograph
- names and addresses of relatives
- names and addresses of close friends
- military record (there's information about finding military servicemembers in Chapter 11)
- assets (home, business, cars, and boats, and where assets are kept), and
- favorite places, hobbies, and any club memberships.

The CSEA will use the information you provide, especially the Social Security number, to try to locate the other parent. The CSEA will also use the Federal Parent Locator Service if it looks like the other parent has moved to another state. The FPLS compares data from various databases to try to locate the missing parent by checking whether the missing parent has a new job or is claiming unemployment insurance benefits anywhere.

You can also try on your own to find the other parent. You can check the last known address and employer, as well as checking with relatives and friends, to find out whether anyone knows where the other parent went. If your spouse owned property, like a house, you can ask the county tax assessor for the owner's last known address. Use search engines. You can also pay a small fee to an Internet search service, or a larger fee to a private investigator.

Bankruptcy and Child Support

If your former spouse files for bankruptcy, it has no effect on your right to child support. It could, however, affect a settlement agreement that obligates your ex to pay certain joint debts. (See *Nolo's Essential Guide to Divorce*, by Emily Doskow (Nolo), or get advice from a bankruptcy attorney.)

The most common type of bankruptcy is Chapter 7, also called "liquidation" bankruptcy. In a Chapter 7 case, the debtor (the person who filed for bankruptcy) is allowed to keep certain specific items of property, while everything else is sold and used to pay creditors. Debts that aren't paid in full are discharged, meaning they're wiped out and simply don't exist anymore. The debtor can use Chapter 7 bankruptcy to discharge almost any kind of personal debts *except* student loans, money owed to the government (like back taxes), or "domestic support obligations," including past-due child and spousal support. Because these are not dischargeable in bankruptcy, they continue to exist after the bankruptcy is over. And you don't have to worry about the bankruptcy affecting your future payments—it has no effect on your child support order. So not only is past-due support not dischargeable, but your current and future support is secure—unless the other parent gets a court to agree to a change, of course.

Even though the rules about child support and bankruptcy are pretty clear, if your spouse does file for bankruptcy, you should contact a lawyer for some advice. In most cases, you're better off cooperating with the bankruptcy than you would be fighting it—the rules are in your favor, and the court will take your interests into account. You probably won't need to do anything except make sure the bankruptcy petition accurately describes the other parent's obligations to you.

The fact that past-due support obligations aren't discharged in bankruptcy doesn't mean you're going to have any easier time enforcing them than you did before the bankruptcy was filed. After the bankruptcy filing, you can continue trying to get past-due support using an income withholding order. You will be first in line (of all your spouse's creditors) for any property that your former spouse is not, by law, allowed to keep after filing for bankruptcy. So, if your former spouse owns any such property, the bankruptcy trustee (the person appointed by the court to handle your spouse's property during the bankruptcy) will pay your claim before any others. The bankruptcy trustee has a legal obligation to notify you if your spouse files for bankruptcy. ●

All divorces are difficult. But some involve scenarios that are far beyond the standard-issue divorce conflicts, including:

- Kidnapping
- Child abuse or neglect
- Interference with parental relationship (sometimes also called parental alienation), or
- Domestic violence.

It's very likely that if you find yourself in any of these situations, you'll need to hire an attorney. But to help you get the lay of the land, here are the basics you should know and some advice on how to get the help you will need.

Getting Help

All of the situations that are discussed in this chapter are enormously stressful. If you can afford a lawyer's help, find one and turn over the legal aspects so you can focus on your own and your children's emotional health. Look back at Chapter 4 for resources and advice for dealing with stress, and at Chapter 12 for advice on finding a lawyer. If you can't afford a lawyer, your local court may help you with do-it-yourself restraining orders and other emergency orders, and if you've been battered by your spouse and go to a shelter, the shelter workers may be able to connect you with services. Low-cost legal services are difficult to find, but your local bar association should be able to direct you to services in your area.

Kidnapping

It's far more common than you might think for one parent to take the children and leave without the other parent's consent. According to the Department of Justice, each year more than 200,000 children are kidnapped by a family member. Kidnapping isn't always a sudden thing, where you wake up and find that the other parent has spirited the kids away. It can also happen when a parent has permission to travel with the children but fails to bring them back. It's important to be vigilant if you believe there's any risk of abduction, and you may have particular reason to worry if your children's other parent has family in another country and wants to take the children to visit.

If your spouse takes your children outside of the area that your custody agreement covers without your permission, contact your local police or sheriff right away. Also call the National Center for Missing and Exploited Children, 800-843-5678, www.missingkids.com. The organization has a 24-hour hotline to report a missing child and receive assistance with the search; other services include reunification services once a child is found, and referrals to experienced professionals who can help with the emotional fallout of an abduction.

If you think your spouse may try to leave the country with the kids in the near future—or if it's already happened—contact the federal Office of Children's Issues at 888-407-4747. The agency provides prevention tips and information, and assists with international abduction cases by assigning a case officer who helps you deal with your local law enforcement agencies and with the search for your child. You should also contact your lawyer right away, so you can get accurate information about your custody rights and advice on how to proceed.

Preventing Abduction

If you suspect that your children's other parent is likely to remove them to another location, take steps to try to prevent abduction and to prepare yourself for the possibility:

- Make sure you have current contact information for the other parent's relatives, friends, and business associates both here and abroad.
- Keep a record of identifying information about the other parent, including physical description and a current photograph, passport number (a copy of the passport is even better), Social Security number, bank information, driver's license number, and automobile make, model, and license number.

- Maintain a current written description of your kids, including hair and eye color, height, weight, and any special physical characteristics. Keep it updated as they grow.
- Take color pictures or videos of your children every six months.
- Go to your local police department and get a set of fingerprints for each of your children, so that there's a set that can be transmitted to another state or country to help identify the kids.
- Teach your children how to use the phone, including how to make collect calls, and make sure they know your phone numbers. Tell them to call you immediately if anything unusual happens and give them a second person to call if they're unable to reach you.

If you have very strong suspicions that the other parent may take the kids in the very near future, you could hire someone (there are private investigators with this specialty) to follow along on visits. But if the person you hire interferes with the visitation and there's no actual threat, it will be you who's in trouble. If you do decide the risk is worth it, find someone who has experience in dealing with potential parental abduction cases.

Domestic Child Abduction by Parents

Thousands of children are abducted by their parents each year, and many of them never leave the United States. In fact, most of them are found within hours, which means it's critical to report an abduction or suspected abduction immediately. Some children are kidnapped for the express purpose of bringing them to a state that the parent believes will be more friendly to a custody petition. The Uniform Child Custody Jurisdiction and Enforcement Act (UCCJEA, discussed in Chapter 8) and the Parental Kidnapping Prevention Act seek to deter kidnapping by providing for exclusive jurisdiction over child custody matters in a child's home state.

The "AMBER Alert" program is a U.S. Department of Justice program that brings together police and other law enforcement agencies with media broadcasters, transportation agencies, and wireless phone carriers to help find abducted children. When a report is made to the AMBER Alert program, all available information about the child and the abductor are transmitted to these agencies and then disseminated as an urgent bulletin on highway signs, over television and radio, and through wireless communication, in hopes that individuals will join law enforcement in searching for the missing child. All 50 states, the District of Columbia, Puerto Rico, and the U.S. Virgin Islands have AMBER Alert plans, and the program has also been adopted in Canada and parts of Mexico.

The AMBER Alert program does have criteria for issuing an alert. There must be a confirmation from law enforcement that an abduction has taken place, and the child must be at risk of serious harm or death. If the abductor is a parent, it may be more challenging to meet the risk criteria. To learn more about the AMBER Alert program, see www.amberalert.gov/factsheet.htm.

International Abduction and the Hague Convention

An international law, called the Hague Convention, governs the custody of children across international borders and provides a procedure to help get abducted children home quickly. The Convention doesn't provide an enforcement mechanism for dealing with child abduction—rather, it's a collection of rules that countries must follow when a child has been abducted.

Defining Child Abduction

Child abduction doesn't always mean taking a child from one place to another (removal); it can also mean keeping a child in another country after a legitimate period of custody or visitation (wrongful retention). To meet the definition of child abduction under the Hague Convention, all of the following must be true:

1. The child must be habitually resident in the country of origin—in other words, the country where the child was living before being removed. While this seems like a clear rule, it can become muddy when a child is kept in another country long enough to create a habitual residence there.

2. The move has to go against someone else's custody rights. Usually, this is a parent with a court order. If the court case is still pending and there's no final decision about custody, then the Hague Convention considers the court to have "rights of custody," so moving outside of the court's jurisdiction is considered abduction.

3. The parent with custody rights must be exercising the rights at the time of the move. This just means the parent must spend some amount of time with the child—there's no requirement of how much, but a parent who has moved away and not been in contact with a child couldn't bring a Hague Convention action.

How the Convention Works

The United States and approximately 79 foreign states and countries are members of the Hague Convention. You can find a list at www.hcch. net/index_en.php?act=conventions.status&cid=24. Each country must designate its own "Central Authority" that deals with Hague issues; in the United States, it's the State Department. This is the agency you would contact if you fear or are in the midst of an international abduction, or want more information about it. The contact information is:

> Office of Children's Issues (CA/OCS/CI)
> U.S. Department of State, SA-29
> 2100 Pennsylvania Ave. NW, 4th Floor
> Washington, DC 20037
> Telephone: 202-736-9130
> Fax: 202-736-9132
> www.travel.state.gov/content/childabduction/english.html

If your children are wrongfully abducted to a country that participates in the Convention, you can expect that country to cooperate with the United States' efforts to locate your children and return them to their home.

THE LAW IN REAL LIFE

The United Kingdom was found to be the habitual residence of two children who were born in the United States but subsequently lived in England for more than two years—during which time their father initiated a divorce action there and an English court issued a custody order. After the father traveled back to the United States for a vacation with the children, he informed the mother he wasn't bringing the children back to the U.K. The Maryland court determined that the children's habitual residence was England and that they were enrolled in school and fully integrated into their lives there, and that the mother had custody rights there. The children were ordered returned there.

A mother was not allowed to keep her children in the United States, but had to return them to Cyprus, where they were born and had lived for their entire lives until the mother brought them to Maine for a vacation and then kept them there. The mother argued that their son was at risk of abuse from corporal punishment in the father's extended family, and also said that because she had fought the father on custody, she would not be safe returning to Cyprus—so returning the children there would mean she might lose contact with them. The Maine court found that possibility "horribly sad," but still held Cyprus was the children's habitual residence, and ordered them returned there.

A father who wrongfully retained his daughter in the United States after a weeklong visit was ordered to return the girl to El Salvador even though the mother didn't file her Hague Convention petition within the one-year window. The court said that the father shouldn't benefit from his own wrongful actions in retaining the girl, especially where the mother's delay in filing her petition was based in part on ongoing negotiations between the parents about the girl's return. Reaching the opposite result, an Ohio court wouldn't order an American mother to return her children to their Australian father, even though he filed his petition in a timely way. The mother had kept the children in the United States for 26 months after the parents agreed to a six-month stay; by the time the mother served the father with divorce papers, the children were well-settled in Ohio, and the father could no longer prove that Australia was their habitual residence.

The Hague Convention does not concern itself with the child's best interests. Instead, it regulates which country has the jurisdiction—meaning the right to decide—over where the child should live. The rules say the deciding country must determine the country where the child was habitually resident, and either return or allow the child to remain there. If the child is returned to a country of habitual residence, the parent who removed the child can still argue there that it's not in the child's best interests to stay there, and the courts there may give the parent permission to relocate later on—but those courts have the right to decide.

The fact that Hague rules only call for a child to end up in the country of habitual residence can lead to some very surprising results.

Controlling Passports

One way to try to prevent an international abduction is to control your children's passports. If your children already have passports and you fear an abduction, you may want to ask your attorney or another trustworthy person to hold them and not release them to either of you without the consent of the other parent. In addition, there are laws and agencies that might help.

U.S. Passports

To have a U.S. passport issued for a child under 16, the child and both parents must appear in person to apply for the passport. If one parent can't be present in person, the parent who is there must bring a notarized form called DS-3053, *Statement of Consent*, from the parent who isn't there. This law applies whether the application is made in the United States or at a U.S. consular office abroad.

If you register with the Department of State's Children's Passport Issuance Alert Program, you'll be notified if the other parent applies for new passports for your kids—or for renewal of an existing passport—any time until they turn 18. You can register with CPIAP by submitting an application and proof of your identity and your parent-child relationship to the Charleston Passport Center (part of Passport Services). Go to www.travel.state.gov and search for CPIAP for the details on how to participate in this program.

Once a passport is issued, though, the Department of State doesn't provide any tracking of its use, and there are no exit controls for American citizens leaving the United States. Other countries may have controls at entry points—for example, Mexico requires that a parent traveling alone with a child produce the child's birth certificate and written proof that the other parent has given permission for the travel. But not all countries do this.

Passports and Visas Issued by Other Countries

If your children have dual citizenship, you have more reason to worry and watch, because they may have more than one passport—and because dual-national children are the most frequently abducted by parents. Even if you have the children's U.S. passports, the other parent might be able to take them out of the country on their second passport.

If the kids don't already have a second passport, you can try to prevent the other parent from getting one. You don't have a right to make another country refrain from issuing a passport for your child, but you can try to persuade them, especially if you have a court order that says the other parent can't take the kids out of the country. Send a letter to the country's consulate, enclosing certified copies of the custody orders in your case. Tell the foreign agency that you'll send a copy of the request to the Office of Children's Issues of the U.S. Department of State. (See the sample, below.) You can find the address of the country's consulate online by searching for "[country] U.S. consulate."

If your child doesn't have dual citizenship, then you can send a similar letter asking the other country not to issue a visa for travel there. Again, there's no law that requires other countries to comply with such requests, but some countries may.

Sample Letter to Foreign Embassy

French Consulate
Attn: Passport Services
10390 Santa Monica Blvd, Suite 410
Los Angeles, CA 90025
Re: Sharon Allman, dob 29-05-2007, and Brad Allman, dob 14-01-2009

Dear Passport Services:

I am the mother of Sharon and Brad Allman, both minor children of my marriage to Jacques Barden, who holds dual American and French citizenship. M. Barden and I have recently divorced and our divorce decree prohibits him from taking the children out of the country. I have the children's American passports, but I am concerned that he may attempt to get French passports for them based on his French citizenship. I write to ask you to decline to issue such passports if M. Barden requests them, and to notify me if he does make such a request.

I am enclosing the following documentation:

1. Certified copies of birth certificates for both of the children

2. Photocopies of the children's U.S. passports

3. A photocopy of my passport and driver's license

4. A certified copy of the final decree of divorce between me and M. Barden

5. Photocopies of M. Barden's French and United States passports.

I am also sending a copy of this letter to the United States Department of State, Office of Children's Issues. Please advise me whether you can comply with this request and protect my children from potential international abduction. Thank you very much for your attention.

Sincerely,

Caroline Allman
4545 Excelsior Street
Boulder, Colorado
333-555-1212

Child Abuse

There's not much that's more distressing than learning, or even suspecting, that your children are being abused. The four major categories of child abuse identified by the Centers for Disease Prevention are:

- neglect
- physical abuse
- psychological/emotional abuse, and
- sexual abuse.

Any of these forms of abuse cause significant harm to a child. If you suspect or discover physical or sexual abuse, take the child to a doctor right away, both for treatment and for documentation of whatever is happening. You should also see a doctor if you think your child is being neglected to the point that it's harming the child physically.

If you're concerned about psychological or emotional abuse, find an experienced child therapist.

Neglect is a form of abuse that's challenging to deal with, because the line can be fuzzy. Many children live in conditions that some people would consider neglectful, but that wouldn't raise a concern for a court or social worker. For example, if your children eat nothing but pizza and ice cream when they're with the other parent, you won't get very far with a claim of neglect, no matter how much evidence there is about the negative consequences of that diet. But if the other parent were failing to give your child a daily dose of a prescription medicine and the child's health was at risk as a result, there's a much greater likelihood a court would find neglect and make an adjustment to the parenting plan. Other forms of neglect include failing to send a child to school, failing to get needed medical care for a child, exposing the child to illegal drugs or abuse of alcohol, or leaving a young child unattended.

What Do Courts Consider Abuse?

Every state considers child abuse as a significant factor in making decisions about custody and visitation. But states have different laws about what constitutes child abuse, and allegations of abuse in the context of a high-conflict divorce are subject to a particular kind of scrutiny. There are no hard and fast universal rules for what courts consider abuse. A review of some of the cases shows that.

THE LAW IN REAL LIFE

An Oregon court held that a father's previous possession of pornography, including child pornography, did not endanger the welfare of his children. The court took into account the fact that he no longer owned the computers that contained the pornography and also stated that the fact that his behavior might negatively affect his parenting wasn't enough to create a current threat of harm.

A father's use of a paddle to discipline his 12-year-old son was not "physical abuse" under state law in Minnesota. The court said that the punishment didn't meet the definition of abuse because it wasn't "malicious punishment" (defined as "unreasonable force or cruel discipline that is excessive under the circumstances"). The child, who was 5'2" and weighed 195 pounds, was warned that his behavior would result in the punishment, and while the court stated the punishment might not have been totally appropriate, it did not rise to the level of abuse.

A North Carolina court held that a father's punishment of his son by hitting him with a belt didn't constitute abuse because bruising on his arm and buttocks weren't a "serious physical injury."

A New York court held that a man who was in prison for molesting several boys in a school where he was a teacher could still have visitation with his 18-month-old daughter while he was incarcerated. The trial court granted him four visits per year at the prison, said that the child must be accompanied by an adult other than the mother, and ordered counseling for the child and the companion following the visits, at the mother's expense. After the mother appealed the decision, the appellate court upheld it, saying that the fact that the child was young and lived three hours from the prison wasn't reason enough to preclude visitation. The appellate court did stress that the father should never be unsupervised with the child, and it reversed the part of the decision requiring the mother to pay for the counseling and for telephone calls between father and daughter.

Gathering Proof

It's crucial that you be able to back up any claim that your children are being abused. Allegations of abuse that are made during the course of a divorce proceeding are automatically suspected of being strategic rather than truthful. And it is certainly true that parents are sometimes wrongly accused, with terrible consequences.

You will probably need to get testimony or sworn written statements from witnesses and experts to prove your accusations in court. You may need to look to:

- health care workers
- child therapists
- teachers or child care workers
- household workers in your home
- your child's friends, if they're old enough, and
- anyone else who comes in regular contact with your child or has reason to know about the abuse.

You need to do everything possible to protect your child, and this may be the time that you hire a lawyer if you aren't already working with one. These issues are highly emotional for everyone, so that representing yourself may simply be too much to deal with. An attorney can help you gather testimony from the type of witnesses described above, and present it to the court in the most effective way.

Dealing With the Court

You can ask the court for whatever would keep your children safe: a restraining order keeping the other parent away from you and the kids, a change in your permanent custody arrangements or parenting schedule, supervised visitation, or an emergency order giving you sole custody.

Don't do anything illegal while you're trying to deal with the situation. If you hide your children, it may leave you open to charges of kidnapping or interfering with custody. If you need to get your children to safety right away, ask the court for an emergency custody order that gives you sole custody until a hearing can be held to determine whether a permanent change should be made. You'll need evidence to back up your story; the judge and other court personnel or child protective services workers, like mediators and social workers who may be called in to investigate the allegations, are very unlikely to believe your story without it, especially if the other parent hasn't ever been found to have abused or neglected the children before.

The court may appoint an evaluator to talk to you, the children, and the other parent. There's much more detail about custody evaluations in Chapter 7.

Dealing With the Kids

If you've discovered that your children are being abused, there is no doubt that you are upset, angry, and worried. You now have the exceptionally challenging job of managing your own feelings while helping the kids to manage theirs. Even if you've never considered sending your child to see a counselor or therapist, consider it now. Talking to someone outside the family can be a lifesaver for a child who's dealing not only with divorcing parents but with having been abused by a trusted adult. Whether it's talk therapy, working with a sand tray, using art as therapeutic treatment, or any other legitimate method, make sure your child has a way to express feelings and get help. Chapter 4 has advice about finding a therapist for your child.

Interference With Parental Relationship

In most shared custody situations, separated parents each try to help support the other parent's relationship with the children. Some do it because they—correctly—think it will be best for the kids; others cooperate because they know the courts approve of and reward cooperation. But other parents won't make any effort at all to nurture their children's relationship with the other parent, and often fail to comply with the parenting plan.

Returning the kids late, changing plans at the last minute, and refusing to communicate about scheduling are all ways that one parent can interfere with the other's relationship with the kids.

Some parents go further and attempt to undermine the relationship by persistently denigrating the other parent in front of the children. When a parent repeatedly presents a negative view of the other parent and manipulates the child into fearing the other parent or not wanting to spend time with the other parent, it is sometimes called "Parental Alienation Syndrome." Only a few states have laws or cases that specifically refer to Parental Alienation Syndrome, and some judges question the existence of such a syndrome. (In 2008, the American Psychological Association declined to take a position on whether it exists or not.)

Whether it's truly a psychological syndrome or not, however, custodial parents have a great deal of influence over the children who live with them most of the time. When they tell a child, "Daddy didn't want to come and see you today" when in fact they told the father not to come, or say something like "Mommy won't get a job or find a good place to live, and that's why you live with me," these parents are creating a terrible conflict for their children, who love both of their parents and, in the vast majority of cases, want to spend time with both. They can become confused and stressed by the conflicts.

If your child's other parent is interfering with your custody rights or your relationship with your children, do everything you can to improve the situation using mediation and counseling, but if it does not improve, go to court and argue for a change in custody. Make sure you document the problems as they arise—keep a calendar of your parenting schedule, and note on every day whether things happened as they were supposed to and, if they didn't, what the other parent did to get in the way. Try to get as much proof as you can, using email and online scheduling tools (described in Chapter 2) if possible. Records that you keep at the time the events happen are more reliable than reports you make later from memory.

THE LAW IN REAL LIFE

In a New York case, a judge declined to grant a father's motion for a custody evaluation of his 14-year-old daughter, but did make a number of orders designed to prevent the mother from continuing to interfere with the father's relationship with the girl. The court's orders make clear the ways that the mother was interfering. The judge ordered the mother to: refrain from sending or responding to text messages or making or receiving phone calls with the daughter during the father's parenting time; refrain from making plans or buying tickets to events that occur during the father's parenting time; refrain from scheduling social activities or classes for the girl during the father's parenting time, unless the father agrees to transport her to the events; and refrain from showing up at the father's house or at activities planned for the father and daughter during his parenting time, including refraining from bringing the daughter items that she "forgot" to bring with her. In addition, both parents were prohibited from allowing the child to read any of the court paperwork, and were ordered to discuss with the daughter the importance of her time with her father.

Showing how seriously the courts take any expression of negativity toward another parent or that parent's rights, an Indiana judge used disparaging remarks that a father made about a mother (his phone calls had been recorded) as a basis for granting custody to the mother, even though the statements weren't made in front of the mother or the child. (The father called her names, made threats, and said he would tell the child that her mother had kidnapped her.)

An Alabama judge refused to allow evidence of parental alienation syndrome because it wasn't generally accepted, but did change custody to the father based on the mother's actions damaging the relationship between the father and children.

If the problems stem entirely from ways that the other parent undermines your relationship with your child, keep records of that as well. For example, make a note when your child tells you that the other parent spoke disparagingly of you or resists visitation because of things the other parent said. Your child may say things that you know came from the other parent, even if the child doesn't say so specifically—keep a record of that. You can bring this type of interference to the judge if it's pervasive and if you can prove it. Because one of the most important factors in custody decisions is which parent is more likely to support the other parent's relationship with the child, you may have some persuasive evidence.

If you can show that the other parent is interfering with your parenting time, you are very likely to persuade a judge to take action. This could mean anything from fining the parent for contempt of court (if the parenting order is violated), to adjusting parenting time, to appointing a supervisor—see "Supervised Visitation for Difficult Situations," below—to ordering a change in custody so that you have primary custody.

Domestic Violence

If you are in a violent relationship, you have a whole separate set of issues, especially in relation to your children. You may have been thinking about getting out for a long time, and are finally ready—or close to ready—to take the final step. As long as you are still living with your spouse or partner, keep careful records of every incident of physical or emotional abuse that involves you or your kids. Write down the date, time, and place of every event, along with a description of what happened and any injuries to you or your children.

Once you make the decision to get out, do some planning if you can—you're in the most danger at the point when you actually leave the relationship, so if you can create a safety net for that period, do it. Try to save some cash, preferably in a place outside of your house, and stash some clothes for yourself and your kids with a friend. Most important, find a place you can stay when you do leave, one that isn't somewhere your partner would immediately think to look for you. Don't go to your best friend's house, your mom's, or somewhere else that would be predictable. Try a shelter or a hotel, or ask a coworker or a friend your spouse doesn't know to put you up for a short while.

! CAUTION

Don't risk kidnapping charges. If you have to leave your home quickly with your kids to get away from an abusive spouse, go to court immediately for an emergency order giving you custody as well as a restraining order that requires your spouse to stay away from you. Otherwise, you may be accused of kidnapping.

If you have the resources, hire a lawyer to help you make this important transition. If you go to a shelter, the staff should be able to help you find legal assistance quickly to file the necessary papers, possibly at low or no cost. Many courts offer help to women experiencing domestic violence. Your local courthouse may provide restraining order packets with instructions, in-person assistance from clerks who can help you with the paperwork, and judges who are available to sign restraining orders and custody orders on very short notice—in some places, 24 hours a day. In general, you also will be able to find immediate help with delivering legal documents to your spouse—the local sheriff's office is usually charged with this task. Your spouse has to receive the papers before they take effect, so that's an important step. If you're afraid of your spouse and you're filing for a restraining order, you have the right to keep your address and telephone number confidential by leaving it off of the court paperwork.

It might seem strange for a batterer to get to see the kids, but as long as the parent hasn't abused them, it's not unusual for a violent parent to get visitation rights. If it's appropriate, though, you can ask for the visitation to be supervised, or for the court to require that the other parent not drink, or that certain other people can't be around the kids. You can also make arrangements to deliver the kids at a neutral pickup site or to have third parties pick up and drop off your kids. If you are dropping off the kids yourself and you don't feel safe, you can agree to meet at the local police station, a restaurant, or some other very public place. You can also ask the court to appoint a supervisor for the visitation—see "Supervised Visitation for Difficult Situations," below. If you have other creative ideas, propose them to the judge. Most judges will consider any plan that will keep everyone safe and facilitate visitation at the same time.

THE LAW IN REAL LIFE

A father succeeded in getting a restraining order against his child's maternal grandfather, with whom the child lived, after the grandfather had slapped the mother. The grandfather argued against the order because the mother, rather than the child, was the victim of the abuse; the court held that the law covered harm to other people in the household from the abuse of one household member.

A woman was allowed to extend a restraining order against her ex-husband after he accessed her email account. The California court said that the husband's use of the information amounted to "disturbing the peace" of his ex-wife, and that violent assault or physical injury weren't necessary to constitute domestic abuse.

Stalking is a crime just like domestic violence, and if your spouse stalks you after you separate, get the police and the courts involved as soon as you begin to feel concern. Just as you would if you were dealing with domestic violence, make sure people around you know what's going on and can support you, and have a safety plan. Check out the website of the National Center for Victims of Crime: Stalking Center at www.ncvc.org/SRC.

 RESOURCE

You are not alone. Look online or check your phone book under "domestic violence" for local agencies, or contact one of these national resources for advice and help locating services in your area:

- The National Domestic Violence Hotline, 800-799-SAFE (7233), www.thehotline.org, provides advice and assistance.
- The National Coalition Against Domestic Violence, www.ncadv.org, 303-839-1852, has a list of state coalitions that can help you find local services.

Most divorce websites have information about dealing with domestic violence.

Supervised Visitation for Difficult Situations

Courts working with families where there's a proven risk of abduction, a history of abuse, serious interference with a parent-child relationship, or substance abuse problems often establish a plan for supervision of one parent's parenting time. Supervision can be done by an agency or an individual third party, or in rare cases, by a therapist.

In some cases, it isn't necessary for the entire visit to be supervised, but there is a need for the transitions between parents to involve a third party. In domestic violence situations where it isn't considered safe for the parents to have direct contact, the court can appoint a monitor and arrange for the dropoff and pickup to be staggered in time, with the monitor watching the kids in between. This can also work well in extremely high-conflict cases where transitions create opportunities for problems to occur.

Supervision by a Friend, Relative, or Other Third Party

When supervision doesn't need to be quite as strict as what would be provided by an agency, as described below, or is intended to be a more short-term intervention, the court may approve an agreed-upon friend or relative—or even a willing child care worker or teacher—to monitor visitation. Some situations where third-party supervision might be appropriate include:

- where the parent's living situation isn't appropriate for exercising parenting time
- where the parent has been in treatment for substance abuse but hasn't yet demonstrated consistent sobriety, and
- where the parent and child have spent little time together and need to become reacquainted, and the presence of a third person would be reassuring to the child.

Parents will be asked to agree on the supervisor, who needs to be not just willing, but also mature enough to handle the responsibility of intervening if necessary. Ideally, the parents can agree to someone they both trust; if they can't, the court may ask them each to submit some names to each other and to the judge or someone the court appoints (like a family court services mediator), who can review the names, consider each parent's objections to the other parent's suggestions, and make a decision.

While agency supervision generally means the entire visit takes place with the supervisor present and in visual contact with the parent and child at all times, the ground rules for third-party visitation might be less stringent—for example, the visits might take place at the third party's home, where the parent and child could play in the yard while the supervisor is in the house. Whether the visit is in the supervisor's immediate presence or simply requires the presence of the supervisor at the location of the visit would be up to the parents and the judge.

Agency Supervision

Private or court-affiliated agencies are available to supervise parenting time where the children's safety is considered to be at risk, as in cases of child abuse, substance abuse, or domestic violence. The agency could be the same family court services agency that provides mediation services in disputed custody and visitation cases, or a separate counseling center, or even a substance abuse program. The main purpose of the supervision is to make sure that the children are safe, but there could also be a component of helping with a parent's substance abuse treatment, or with helping parents learn better parenting skills with the idea of transitioning to unsupervised visitation.

The supervisor, generally a social worker or another employee of the agency, monitors the child's physical safety, but also makes sure that other parameters are in place. For example, the supervisor would:

- ensure the parent does not try to communicate privately with the child through passing a concealed note or whispering—and speaks only in a language that the supervisor also speaks
- ensure that any physical contact between parent and child is initiated by the child, and is age-appropriate, nonsexual, and nonviolent

- check out and approve in advance any gift that the parent wants to give the child
- where domestic violence or abduction is an issue, make sure that the parent doesn't question the child about where the child lives or goes to school
- ensure the parent doesn't engage the child in unauthorized discussions of the court proceedings, disagreements between the parents, or the possibility of future changes in the child's living arrangements or how parenting time is exercised (such conversations could be authorized if there is a plan for some kind of transition, however)
- ensure that the parent doesn't ask the child to carry messages to the other parent or other family members, and
- ensure the parent doesn't make any negative comments about the other parent or try to question the child about the other parent.

Supervision by a Therapist

Therapist-supervised visitation is reserved for situations where the parent and child need professional intervention in the relationship. The therapist might observe the relationship between a parent and child who have been separated for a time (perhaps because the parent was incarcerated or was deemed not safe to be around the child), and then work with both the parent and child to improve and strengthen the relationship. A therapist might also supervise visitation in cases where one parent has attempted to alienate the child from the other parent.

All of the situations that are discussed in this chapter are enormously stressful. If you can afford a lawyer's help, find one and turn over the legal aspects so you can focus on your own and your children's emotional health. Look back at Chapter 5 for resources and advice for dealing with stress. ●

Custody and Support in Military Families

I f you or your spouse is in the military or a veteran, you have some special concerns. This chapter focuses on the unique custody and support issues military families face and what you can expect in terms of dealing with them. In the end, you are likely to need an attorney to help you. Especially if you're dealing with property division issues as part of the divorce process, don't negotiate your divorce or sign a settlement agreement without at least consulting a lawyer experienced in military divorce. But even if you're only dealing with issues related to your kids, you'll probably want a lawyer representing you. Things like getting a service member served with legal papers, negotiating (or fighting about) the timing of hearings under the Servicemembers Civil Relief Act, understanding the Leave and Earnings statement, and other issues are specialized and can be challenging, and the help of an expert can be valuable. (There may be some free legal help available through the military; see the resource list at the end of the chapter.)

Delaying Court Decisions: The Servicemembers Civil Relief Act

The Servicemembers Civil Relief Act (SCRA) is a federal law that provides for special treatment of service members in court proceedings in the United States. You will need to understand its basics because it can affect your custody or child support case in significant ways.

The law applies to all proceedings connected with your divorce, including requests for custody, support, or property division. The idea of the SCRA is to protect service members from drama at home so that they can focus on their important tasks at hand. The law allows service members to get a delay in any court or agency proceeding that might affect their rights. (50 U.S.C. Appendix § 502(2).) A service member can get a delay by showing that harm would result if the case went forward.

If you're in the military, the SCRA is your friend—it can prevent a judge from issuing court orders that could affect your relationship with your children in important ways. If you're the nonmilitary spouse, you may feel frustrated by the delays, because the law gives service members extra time to respond to legal papers and lets scheduled hearings be postponed until the service member can arrange to be there. As a result, an order for support or for a change in custody may take a lot longer than the civilian spouse had hoped. In fact, the entire divorce case may be delayed, making the final judgment take a lot longer as well.

THE LAW IN REAL LIFE

A service member had custody of her daughter while she was deployed to Germany; her former spouse, also in the service, was deployed to Afghanistan. Their agreement was that when the father returned to Texas, the mother would also return there for a hearing. But when she did so, the court rescheduled the hearing because of its own conflict. The mother returned to Germany with the child and asked for an SCRA delay of the custody proceeding, saying she could not be in Texas on the new hearing date. The trial judge denied her request, but the appeals court overturned the ruling, deciding instead that a delay (a "stay," in legal terms) is mandatory where the service member complies with all the rules of the SCRA by filing the appropriate documentation about why the stay is needed. The appellate court said that a service member should always get the benefit of the doubt if there's something confusing about the fact situation or how the law applies.

On the other hand, a Nebraska judge denied a request for an SCRA stay because the service member parent did not present enough evidence that her military service would prevent her from showing up for the custody modification hearing.

The SCRA provides other protections to military families as well, including preventing eviction and foreclosure and limiting interest on consumer credit card debt, among other things. To learn how the SCRA can protect your family, see www.military.com/benefits/military-legal-matters/scra.

Again, if the SCRA is going to come into play in your divorce or custody case, regardless of whether you're the military spouse or a civilian, you need the help of a family law attorney who's an expert in military cases.

Custody and Visitation

Sharing parenting responsibilities after a divorce or separation can be challenging for anyone. For military service members, the issues can be complicated by uncertainty about future deployments overseas or stateside assignments.

Parenting Plans and Family Care Plans

All divorcing parents are required to have a parenting plan describing how they will share time and care of their children after the divorce. (Chapter 2 discusses parenting plans in detail.) If you are in the military and uncertain about where you'll be deployed and for how long, it's practical for you to develop alternate parenting plans for various possibilities. For example, if the service member might remain at a base that's close to where the children live, prepare a plan that calls for visitation consistent with expected free time for that parent. At the same time, prepare a plan that you'll implement if the service member is deployed overseas or transferred farther away. Communication is really important—often service members don't know exactly what's going to happen, but it's important to convey to the other parent all the information that is available, and make contingency plans that will cover your family whatever happens.

Where only one parent is in the military and the parents have joint custody, the civilian parent will generally take care of the child when the service member is unavailable. When the military parent has sole custody, however, many states consider a transfer of custody to the other parent to be a change of custody, and it's not uncommon for the court to allow the military parent's new spouse or another family member, like an aunt or uncle or grandparent, to take over as the child's guardian during deployment.

THE LAW IN REAL LIFE

In a New Jersey case, a court held that the service member's new wife, the child's stepparent, was an appropriate person to care for the child while the father was deployed, despite the objections of the boy's mother, who wanted primary custody during the deployment.

A Texas court likewise refused to transfer custody to a father in anticipation of the mother's deployment, on the ground that the child was safe and comfortable with her stepfather and the state's custody modification law required that the change of circumstance must have lasted six months before a request for modification could be heard—the court wouldn't make the move prospectively, before the deployment began.

A Maryland court ordered a child's custody transferred to his civilian father when his mother was deployed, despite her wish that the boy stay with her own parents. Although the mother had sole legal custody, the parents' court order stated that the father should be included in all major decisions, and he had significant visitation rights, which the court deemed to be the equivalent of custodial rights for the purpose of dealing with the mother's deployment.

Who Must Have a Family Care Plan?

The military also has its own rules for situations in which a child's sole caretaker, or both caretakers if there are two parents, might be deployed. A Family Care Plan is required in these situations:

- A service member is a single parent who has custody of a child under age 19, or shares custody with another parent to whom the service member is not currently married.
- Both parents are service members and have custody of children under 19. (Both parents must sign the same Family Care Plan.)
- A service member is the sole caretaker for a child under 19 or an adult family member who's unable to provide his or her own care, including a disabled spouse or other family member.

A service member who is in any of these situations is required to advise the military immediately. The service member then has 60 days (active duty members) or 90 days (reserve members) to give a commanding officer a formal Family Care Plan.

What's in a Family Care Plan

The plan must set out what will happen to the service member's children if the service member is deployed or must be absent, whether for the short term or for a longer period (31 days or more). Specific requirements may vary among different branches of the service, but the basics are the same. The plan must include:

- Name and contact information for the person who would care for the child, who must be a civilian at least 21 years old, along with a certification that the caregiver has all the necessary information to care for the child and has accepted the responsibility. The plan must also name an alternate caregiver in case the primary person isn't able to do it when the time comes. Because the plan must provide for both short-term and long-term absences, in some cases that will mean naming different caregivers for different situations. A short-term caregiver would most likely be someone living in the local area who could step in when the service member is away for a six-week training period or brief educational program. A longer-term caregiver might live farther away but be more appropriate if the parent is deployed for a significant period of time. For example, a service member who has primary custody of a child might designate a relative who lives nearby as a short-term caregiver, but agree to send the child to live with the other parent across the country in the event of a long-term absence.
- Information about the child's other parent, including written consent if the other parent is not named as caregiver.
- Information about how the child will be supported financially during the service member's absence, and proof that the service member has provided powers of attorney to the caregiver or other responsible adult (powers of attorney are documents that allow another person to deal with financial matters on your behalf).

- Information about transporting family members if the Family Care Plan goes into effect—the military requires the plan to include details as small as how airline tickets will be paid for and how the caregiver and child will get to the airport. The plan also must include the arrangements for transferring care of a child from a short-term to a long-term caregiver if the service member is deployed with very little notice.
- The name of the person the service member wishes to take custody of the child in the event of the service member's death. If there's another legal parent, that person will automatically take custody in almost all cases, but if you believe that's not appropriate (for example, the other parent doesn't have visitation because of abuse or has abandoned the child), you would designate another person and include the reasons for doing so.

To learn more about Family Care Plans, the service member can ask a supervisor or commander for resources or go to a Legal Assistance Office or Family Support Center on base (if there is one). There's a great deal of detailed information at www.militaryonesource.mil; search "family care plan."

Custody, Visitation, and the SCRA

Service members can invoke the SCRA to delay hearings and extend their time to respond to legal papers, but there are often issues related to children that need to be resolved so that the children can have some stability and predictability. Courts do a balancing act between the important protections provided by the SCRA and the needs of the family at home. Often, children's needs come before the SCRA rules in judges' orders.

For example, if a service member successfully requests an SCRA delay, the court can still make a temporary custody order. This avoids making the civilian parent and child wait for resolution of their postseparation living situation, and also prevents service members from abusing the SCRA just to prevent the civilian parent from exercising parental rights. For example, one military parent left her child, who was under a joint custody order, with her new spouse instead of her ex-husband, who had parenting rights. The court wouldn't allow her to use the SCRA to prevent a change of custody, instead giving the father primary custody.

One issue that comes up often in military cases is which state has control (jurisdiction) over decisions involving the children. The Uniform Child Custody Jurisdiction and Enforcement Act (UCCJEA), discussed in Chapter 8, sets out rules about jurisdiction for all children, including service members' children. The UCCJEA rules are complicated, as they require figuring out where a child has lived for the six months before the action is brought—sometimes a harder task than it might seem. These rules can be hard on service members, especially those who are deployed overseas. If they stay away longer than six months, the other parent can establish residency in a state where the service member has no ties, and the rest of the case will have to be handled there. A good idea when you are deployed overseas is to ask the other parent to sign an agreement about where the child will live and where the permanent home is. Then you won't end up in a battle about where to argue about custody.

RESOURCE

More about custody. There's more about the UCCJEA in Chapter 10 and at www.ncjrs.gov/pdffiles1/ojjdp/189181.pdf.

A service member's protection against default judgments (a court judgment issued against a person when the person wasn't present) also applies to child custody proceedings. This is a new rule, and there aren't many court decisions to provide guidance. But it appears to mean that while a service member is deployed, a civilian spouse can't persuade a court to enter a permanent child custody order if the service member parent fails to appear and argue against the change. Some states also bar their courts from entering permanent orders involving children while the service member is deployed. Also, a growing number of states now have rules that a service member's absence from parenting because of deployment or other military service can't be used as a factor in deciding custody.

If you're a civilian and it seems like everything is weighted in favor of the service member, remember that you have the enormous advantage of proximity—to the children as well as to the courts. Don't give up without an argument if you think the service member parent is taking advantage of the SCRA unfairly. For example, if the service member is invoking the SCRA to delay a hearing by saying there's no leave available, you can check the Leave and Earning Statement (LES), which provides information about accrued leave, and see whether it's just a delaying tactic. (See "Calculating a Service Member's Income," below.)

When the Service Member Can't Visit

A few courts have held in recent years that close relatives of a service member may exercise the service member's visitation rights while the service member is stationed or deployed far enough away that visitation isn't possible. The idea is that staying in touch with the service member's family helps the children to feel connected to that parent.

Distant parents, including those who are deployed overseas, can also try to keep in touch with their kids through some of the methods discussed in Chapter 2, like Skype, webcams, instant messaging, and email.

Visitation When a Parent Is Overseas

Older children may be able to visit a military parent who is stationed overseas in a noncombat area. It's like arranging a visit with a civilian parent who lives across the country or in another country—parents still have to arrange for travel, plan the visitation schedule, and decide how expenses of traveling will be shared.

Most such visits work out fine. However, what if a service member keeps a child after the agreed-upon visit ends? The distance can give the service member an advantage here, because the civilian parent may have a hard time finding out what's going on and how to fix it. Keeping a child longer than allowed by a court-ordered parenting plan is kidnapping, though, and the courts and the military both understand that it's illegal. If military authorities know that a service member has violated a child custody order, they must turn the service member over to the United States State Department or the police, and return the child to the United States.

If the other parent retains your child in violation of a court order, notify your local police and take the other steps described in Chapter 10. Also contact the other parent's commanding officer or authorities of the appropriate branch of the service to get the military involved in safely returning your child.

Because of the distance and the potential for problems, especially if your divorce is high-conflict, be sure your visitation plan is clear, specific, and detailed. Include itineraries, details of travel plans, and especially specific dates for the child's travel. Having this information won't necessarily prevent kidnapping, of course, but it might save you some time if you need to prove to the commanding officer that the other parent is violating your parenting plan, and give you a place to start looking for your child.

Child Support

Just like every other parent, service members must support their minor children. But unlike other employers, the Department of Defense punishes service members for failure to pay support, ranging all the way from a reprimand to discharge from military service. Because of this, most likely, the percentage of service members who are current on child support payments is much higher than the rate among civilians, whose compliance is abysmal.

Where to Start

To calculate a reasonable amount of child support, start with your state's support guidelines. (Chapter 3 explains how.) If you and the other parent can't agree on the support amount and a court hasn't yet weighed in, you can consult military guidelines. Each branch of the military has its own guidelines for appropriate interim family support when the state hasn't yet established a support order—generally, the amounts are less than what state guidelines provide. It's difficult to find information about the military's child support guidelines—if you need to establish interim support, check with your state's child support enforcement agency (see the appendix for a list) or seek help from a military Legal Assistance Office (see "Locating a Service Member," below).

Calculating a Service Member's Income

Because military paychecks are unlike any other paychecks, it can be a real challenge to determine what a service member's actual pay is. This is unfortunate given that a parent's income is always the basis for calculating child support. To get started with your state's child support guidelines, you'll need to know the service member's income as well as the amount of any payments the service member is making for the children's health insurance or for work-related day care.

Start with the service member's base salary. There's also a housing allowance, calculated using location, family commitments, and the service member's pay grade. There are also pay differentials for hazardous assignments and other variations in responsibilities. It's possible that the service member is receiving "in-kind" compensation in the form of housing, meals, and other nonmonetary compensation.

In trying to determine the other parent's income, don't use a tax return, because some of the income that service members receive is tax-free, and you'll be working with an amount that's too low. Instead, use the Leave and Earnings Statement (LES), which is similar to a pay stub but more comprehensive. The LES will show you the service member parent's basic pay and housing and other allowances, as well as information about how many dependents the service member is claiming and how much accrued leave is available.

The IRS doesn't tax military housing and food allowances, but most states' child support guidelines include all income, whether it's taxable or not. In recent years, with many more service members on active duty, state courts have begun to weigh in on this issue. They appear to universally agree that even though allowances and in-kind compensation are nontaxable, they should be counted as income for purposes of calculating support. In-kind compensation can include on-base housing—so if a service member lives on the base, the value of the housing can also be included.

As always when you're dealing with the U.S. military, you may not have an easy time getting access to the information you need. In fact, you may be required to submit a Freedom of Information Act request if your spouse won't cooperate and provide the LES. You'll probably need an attorney's help for this, but you also could seek assistance from a child support enforcement agency. (See the appendix.)

Enforcing Child Support Orders

In today's automated world, deployment shouldn't affect child support payments, which can be automatically deducted from the service member's pay and sent to the recipient parent, even when the service member is far afield.

The Defense Finance and Accounting Service (DFAS) provides payroll for all military employees (except the Coast Guard, which falls under the Department of Homeland Security). DFAS is responsible for withholding income to pay child support orders. If you have an income withholding order for a service member, send it to the DFAS office in Cleveland, Ohio:

> DFAS Cleveland
> DFAS-HGA/CL
> P.O. Box 998002
> Cleveland, OH 44199-8002

> You can also fax the order to:
> DFAS Fax: 877-622-5930
> The DFAS Income Withholding toll-free Customer Service Number is
> 888-332-7411.

If, however, the service member stops paying, a civilian spouse could find the SCRA in the way. It lets a service member delay child support hearings as well as custody matters. (See "Delaying Court Decisions: The Servicemembers Civil Relief Act," above.) If you have a deadbeat service member on your hands, you can use many of the strategies listed in Chapter 10 to try to enforce the order, including an income withholding order (IWO), also called a wage garnishment. You might also try going directly to the military to ask for enforcement. There's a process called "involuntary allotment" that allows the military to withhold more income than the usual percentage allowed under federal law (see Chapter 9 for more about that) when there is an arrearage of at least two months' support.

The DFAS issued a guide in 2010 designed to help child support enforcement agencies work cooperatively with the DFAS and Department of Defense to establish and enforce child support orders. It's a very clearly written, informative document that you can find at www.dfas. mil/garnishment.html. If you're working with your local child support enforcement agency or an attorney, make sure they've seen it—and you may find it useful to orient yourself to the world of military child support.

Special Issues for Reservists

A sudden switch from reservist to active-duty service member can have a huge impact on the ability to pay child support.

Support Orders: Planning for Mobilization

When a support-paying parent is in the military reserves, it's important to plan for a possible call-up. Most reservists have regular civilian jobs, and in most cases when the reservist is called to duty, the civilian pay ends for the duration of the duty. This means that if you're the parent receiving child support through an income withholding order and you don't plan ahead, you might end up with a well that has suddenly gone dry. Make sure that your court order for child support says that any wages that the other parent receives are subject to garnishment, not just wages from the civilian job. Then, if the other parent is mobilized, you can transfer the garnishment to the military pay.

Dealing With Reduced Income

It's also possible that a reservist's total income will take a hit after mobilization. A court wouldn't necessarily consider this a change of circumstance that would automatically justify a reduction in support, however, because it's so likely that the service member will go back to full salary upon returning to the civilian job, and the change might not be in the child's interest. Still, depending on how long the mobilization is likely to be and how great the disparity between civilian and military pay, the paying parent may seek—and may get—a court order reducing support for the duration of the mobilization.

If you're a reservist facing a significant income reduction, go to the other parent first and ask for a temporary reduction in support payments. If you get agreement, write it down, ask the other parent to sign it, and submit it to the court to have it made into an order. Otherwise, you'll have to ask the court for a reduction, in which case you'll undoubtedly need to hire an attorney who can help to get the hearing expedited or make arrangements for you to participate from wherever you're going.

Whatever you do, don't just miss payments or pay less than the amount required by court order. Under federal law, each missed child support payment is immediately "vested," meaning you can't get rid of the debt, even if you file for bankruptcy. Having a court modify support later won't do anything about the earlier missed payments, either. Go to court now and get the change taken care of before your deployment.

Medical Benefits for Children

After a divorce, children of a service member continue to qualify for TRICARE, the medical benefits program available to all active duty service members, retirees, and service members' families. To qualify, each eligible person, including each child, must have on file complete and correct information with the Defense Enrollment Eligibility Reporting System (DEERS). There are a number of different types of TRICARE plans, but basic coverage is free, with no co-payments and no costs for prescriptions—to a service member and the service member's children.

According to the TRICARE website (www.tricare.mil), most TRICARE plans are considered "qualifying coverage" under the Patient Protection and Affordable Care Act, which means that TRICARE beneficiaries won't have to pay a financial penalty that applies to people without qualifying coverage. However, participants who are eligible for care only at military hospitals and clinics probably do not have minimum essential coverage and must supplement their coverage. Nothing in the legislation changes any fees or other aspect of TRICARE. The law's provisions that require insurers to provide medical coverage to children of covered parents can be met by TRICARE's new Young Adult plans.

Other Benefits

There are a variety of other benefits that service members can receive. Some of these aren't directly relevant to child support payments, but could provide other important financial security to a service member's children.

Survivor Benefit Plan

The Survivor Benefit Plan (SBP) is an annuity through which retired service members can leave a death benefit to specified survivors, including a child or children. Starting when the service member retires, the service member pays premiums and retains control over both the amount of the benefit and the beneficiaries. When the service member dies, the beneficiary receives a lifetime annuity. The amount currently is 55% of the retired pay the service member would have been entitled to if the date of death were considered the date of retirement.

The service member may designate a former spouse as a beneficiary, so if your spouse is in the military you may want to negotiate for having yourself, your kids, or both listed as your ex-spouse's beneficiary. This would be part of the overall negotiation of your divorce.

Life Insurance

If the support-paying parent is in the service, it's a good idea to confirm that there's life insurance coverage in place that would compensate for the loss of support if the military spouse died. Military service members are entitled to life insurance coverage under the Servicemembers Group Life Insurance (SGLI), but you will want to obtain a private insurance policy instead of relying on that coverage. The service member could change the beneficiary designation under the SGLI, so you can't be completely sure that your children will remain the beneficiaries. If you buy a private policy, you can keep control over who the beneficiaries are— and make sure the premiums are paid and the policy doesn't lapse. If you run into problems purchasing a policy on your ex's life, an alternative is to include a provision in your settlement agreement stating that the other parent will maintain life insurance in a certain amount with the children as beneficiaries.

Tax Issues

Military service members can qualify for head of household status and can transfer dependency exemptions just like civilian taxpayers. (See Chapter 3 for more about taxes and child support.)

Locating a Service Member

Have you lost track of your child's other parent who is in the service? It doesn't happen very often, but it's possible, and if you need to get or enforce an order for child support (or formally modify a custody order because the other parent has taken off), you'll face a challenge. Especially since September 11, it can be difficult to find military personnel.

If you know the other parent's Social Security number, you're one step ahead. Even without that, a copy of a military identification card will be very helpful. Without either one, you're going to have an uphill battle.

If you do have a Social Security number, you can try a number of ways to locate the other parent.

Military locators. Each branch of the service has a Worldwide Military Locator Service. You can find contact information and links for all of them at the National Archive at www.archives.gov/veterans/locate-service-members.html. There are also a number of sites that aren't affiliated with any government agency, like www.gisearch.com. An experienced attorney should be able to expedite your search.

Base commander. You can try contacting the base commander or person designated as the "base locator" at the last known military base, to ask for information about your spouse's new assignment.

Legal assistance office. The military has a group of lawyers called "legal assistance attorneys" (LAAs) whose job is to help service members (and their families) with nonmilitary legal issues. An LAA might be able to help you find out your spouse's current whereabouts. You can get help from any LAA office, whether or not it's in a different branch of the military from your spouse. To find a legal assistance office, try the Legal Assistance Locator at http://legalassistance.law.af.mil/content/locator.php.

Federal Parent Locator. If child support is involved, you might be able to make use of the Federal Parent Locator Service at www.acf.hhs. gov/programs/cse/fpls. There's more about this tool in Chapter 9.

Other internet sources. The "Globemaster U.S. Military Aviation Database" is a private website that contains links to all branches of the U.S. armed forces, and provides extensive information, including a locator for U.S. military personnel, at www.globemaster.de.

Serving Papers on Someone on a U.S. Military Base

If you need to deliver legal papers relating to custody or support, and the other parent is in the military, you'll have to follow some special procedures. Military bases are closed communities with careful scrutiny of anyone going in and out, but it's not impossible to serve someone who lives on a base. Certainly on a U.S. base, you should be able to serve the other parent following the instructions in Chapter 3.

Each branch of the military has its own rules about service of process, and most have people whose job description includes facilitating service. (In the Marines, for example, that person is called the "civil process officer.") Some branches of the service, including the Army, have a policy of assisting with serving military personnel on U.S. bases, and you should get support from the service member's superior officers. It's not that common, but depending on where the base is, you may even be able to send a deputy sheriff or process server onto the base to serve the papers.

Having said all this, though, if you're not in a position to serve a cooperative spouse by mail as described in Chapter 3, it's probably best for you to have an attorney help you with service. A local attorney with expertise in military matters will most likely know how things operate at the base, and you'll save time and money by taking advantage of this expertise. In some states, you may also be able to ask your attorney to request permission from a judge to serve an uncooperative spouse by registered mail.

Domestic Violence and Other Abuse

Chapter 10 has information about child abuse and domestic violence that should be of use to both civilian and military spouses. But the military deals with issues of family violence differently than the civilian authorities do. When the abuser is a service member, military policies and procedures take precedence over civilian rules. If you're a service member being abused by a civilian, you're probably going to have to use civilian methods to deal with the abuse. However, you might find that a base commander will bar a civilian abuser from the base for your protection.

The Department of Defense has two family abuse-related programs: the Family Advocacy Program, which investigates, and the Military Justice system, which deals with consequences. All military personnel must report any suspicion of family violence to the Family Advocacy Program, which will assign an investigator. The investigator's commanding officer decides, after receiving the investigator's report, whether the charges are substantiated and then whether the offender should be offered counseling or be subject to discipline under the Military Code of Justice. (In case you've read or heard that FAP counseling is not confidential, that rule has been changed. You can now receive assistance from the FAP without the report having to be passed along to the service member's commanding officer.)

Base commanders have the authority to issue Military Protective Orders that require a service member to stay away from the person being abused, whether it's a spouse or a child. A Military Protective Order is valid only on a military base; civilian authorities won't enforce them.

If you want an abuser kept away from a civilian workplace, an off-base school, or other places off base where you feel unsafe, you need to get a restraining order from a civilian court. (See Chapter 10.)

Where military authorities find a service member guilty of abuse, penalties can be severe, up to and including discharge from the service. Many spouses married to service members are reluctant to report abuse because they fear that an abusive spouse who is discharged won't be able to help support the children. But there is something called "transitional compensation" that provides some protection. Transitional compensation can be paid when a service member is separated from military service under a court-martial sentence for abuse of a family member who was living in the home or married to the service member when the relevant abuse happened. In addition:

- The service member must have served at least 30 days on active duty.
- The service member must have been sentenced to a forfeiture of all pay and allowances or administratively separated from military service for offenses that include a dependent-abuse offense. (In other words, the dependent-abuse offense doesn't have to be the only reason for the separation, but it has to be listed as one reason.)

The amount of the transitional compensation changes every year and can be found at the Department of Veterans Affairs website at www. benefits.va.gov/compensation. Transitional compensation lasts at least 12 months and can last up to 36 months, depending on how long the service member was obligated to stay in the military—and it ends if the abused spouse remarries or moves back in with the former service member during the benefit period. The abused spouse may also be eligible for continuing medical care and exchange and commissary privileges.

A civilian spouse can also receive the equivalent of retirement payments directly from the military if the service member was denied retirement as a result of spousal or child abuse. The spouse can ask a divorce court for an order, under the Uniformed Services Former Spouse Protection Act, for payment of the amount the service member would have received if his or her military career had continued. The military will honor the payments. If you're a civilian spouse who wants to take advantage of this rule, the Family Advocacy Program can help you.

RESOURCE

The Department of Defense provides a website at www.militaryonesource.mil that offers extremely detailed and well-organized information, resources, and services to military families in all branches.

The Armed Forces Legal Assistance Office website, http://legalassistance.law. af.mil/index.php. Be cautious in relying on this source; not everything is accurate or complete. However, there's some good basic information for divorcing service members and their families.

The American Bar Association's Family Law Section's Military Committee provides information and resources at www.americanbar.org/groups/family-law. org.html. Click "committees" then "Legal Assistance of Military Personnel" to find the committee's home page.

The website of Nevada attorney Marshal Willick, www.willicklawgroup.com, contains links to many of his publications, including "Division of Military Retirement Benefits in Divorce."

The Military Divorce Handbook: A Practical Guide to Representing Military Personnel and Their Families, by Mark E. Sullivan, is a comprehensive resource. Sullivan has also authored articles, pamphlets, and information sheets on the subject. An Internet search for "military divorce" will turn up many of his shorter, more accessible works.

See *Nolo's Essential Guide to Divorce*, by Emily Doskow (Nolo), for more detail about where to file papers when one parent is in the military, as well as property and alimony issues.

If you're looking for books for your kids explaining deployment and military service in age-appropriate ways, check out the resource guide at www.militaryonesource.mil. Go to the main site and search "books and resources for children about deployment." ●

The Law: How to Work With a Lawyer and Do Your Own Legal Research

Whether you're mediating, using a collaborative process, or heading for trial, you must decide whether you're going to hire a lawyer to help you with some or all of your divorce. It's a big decision. Representing yourself is a challenge, but hiring a lawyer to do it for you can be a huge financial burden.

Should You Lawyer Up?

In nearly three-quarters of all divorce cases, at least one of the parties is self-represented. Many, but not all, of those cases are uncontested.

The court calls people without lawyers "In Pro Per" or "Pro Se" parties, both of which are Latin phrases for representing yourself in court without a lawyer. (Some courts have dropped the Latin and just call people without attorneys "self-represented litigants.") They are intrepid souls, launching themselves into a complex system that will sometimes seem like a trip down the rabbit hole—especially if there's a dispute that requires court hearings and submitting written arguments, called "briefs." If you're considering joining their ranks, take some time to consider what's involved.

Uncontested Divorces

If your case isn't contested—meaning you and your spouse agree on property, custody, and support, and are simply trying to get the paperwork through the system—then representing yourself is a completely reasonable option. If you're comfortable with paperwork and with using a computer and are able to follow a detailed list of tasks, you will have no problem completing your own uncontested divorce.

Contested Divorces

It's tougher to go it alone if you and your spouse are at odds about custody or support. But it is certainly not impossible to represent yourself in a contested family law case; many people do handle their own divorces even if they involve serious disputes over custody, visitation, or support. At a minimum, in order to represent yourself in a disputed custody or support case you must:

- learn which forms you must file to get your divorce started (information that's usually available on your local court's website or from the court clerk)
- be able to fill the forms out correctly and completely
- become familiar with the rules of your local court
- know the child support guidelines for your state (usually available through your court's website or another online source)
- learn the law of child custody in your state (possibly the most challenging part of what you'll need to know and learn)
- figure out how to interact with the court staff, and
- prepare yourself to argue your case in front of a judge.

Knowing how to use a computer and navigate the Internet will serve you well if you're going the do-it-yourself route.

What if your spouse hires a lawyer? When both spouses are representing themselves, the playing field might not be exactly level (one person may have more education or be more comfortable with paperwork and details), but at least neither spouse has professional training or relationships with the local judges. On the other hand, if one spouse hires a lawyer, then the other is at a distinct disadvantage.

If your case isn't terribly complicated, you may still want to proceed on your own. For example, if you're arguing about the percentage of time each of you will spend with the kids, and the question boils down to whether it's better to have them in after-school care at their school or at a recreation center near their other parent's house, you can probably continue to represent yourself and make that argument on your own. Other issues might be better presented by a lawyer. For example:

- If you or your spouse wants to move far enough away that your parenting schedule would be disrupted, lots of legal rules come into play, and it might be much more difficult for a nonlawyer to make a successful argument. (Chapter 8 has more about relocation cases.)

- If there's a conflict about your children's best interest that involves their emotional or mental health and might require expert testimony, represent yourself only if you're really confident in your own ability to choose and work with an expert witness whose job is to evaluate the kids and testify about their best interests.

You and the Courthouse

If you're representing yourself, you'll probably get to know your local courthouse very well, whether it's the court clerk's office or the courtroom. You'll get especially cozy with the court clerks—you'll deal with them much more than you will with a judge. The clerks work in the front office of the court. When you submit paperwork, schedule a hearing, or need a blank form that isn't available on the Internet, the court clerk will be the person helping you. Court clerks aren't allowed to give legal advice, so although you can ask them which forms you need and they will check to be sure everything is properly signed and you've submitted the right fees, they will not help you with what boxes to check or tell you about important deadlines.

The judge will also have a courtroom clerk, who may help with some scheduling issues and some of the paperwork, especially if you end up in a trial.

Many courts now have self-help programs where court staffers will go a little further in giving you some advice about your paperwork and how best to proceed. In some places, these services are only available to help with domestic violence restraining orders, but in many others there is a broader range of help available. To find out whether your local court helps self-represented parties, ask the clerk or look on the court's website.

You won't see the judge very often. You might see the inside of the courtroom for a hearing or a settlement conference, but you'll deal with all of your paperwork at the clerk's office.

- If either you or the other parent is going to argue that the other person is doing things that are bad for the kids—for example, abusing substances or neglecting the children—then a lawyer will almost always do better at presenting this type of evidence.

If you decide to represent yourself, find out what help is available in your local court, and consider using a lawyer as a coach or using unbundled legal services. (See "Unbundled Representation," below.) And get a copy of *Represent Yourself in Court: How to Prepare & Try a Winning Case*, by Paul Bergman and Sara Berman (Nolo), which covers all the ins and outs of litigation and has a chapter specifically about family law cases.

Working With a Lawyer

In most family law cases that involve a lawyer, the lawyer takes charge of the entire case and works with the client and the other attorney (or unrepresented party) to resolve the case or go to trial. But that's not the only way to work with an attorney—you can also find a lawyer who will coach you while you represent yourself, or handle discrete parts of your case while you take care of the rest.

What Services Do You Need?

Consider what you want an attorney to do for you. There are a number of different options.

Full Representation

Most lawyers are used to having clients come in and turn over all of the work of a divorce case. The client must always be consulted about decisions like whether to accept a proposal from the other side, but the lawyer usually decides strategy, interacts with the other attorney, and prepares all the paperwork. This is the most expensive way to work with a lawyer, and for many people it's the most comfortable. Many lawyers only accept clients who are looking for this type of representation, feeling that they can't do a good job unless they have all the information and retain control over the case.

Unbundled Representation

Because of the proliferation of self-represented parties in family law cases, lawyers have become somewhat more flexible about representation. These days, not every lawyer insists on taking charge of your entire case from beginning to end. Instead, some are willing to help you with specific, limited elements of your case while you do the rest of the work. This is called "unbundled representation," "unbundled services," or "limited representation."

What does this look like? As an example, you could file the papers to get your divorce started yourself and to ask for temporary child support and schedule a hearing. Then you could hire a lawyer just to come to the hearing and represent you in front of the judge. Or you could ask a lawyer to prepare the paperwork and coach you on how to present your argument in court, and then go to court yourself.

Other things that a lawyer can do for you:

- Review forms and documents that you've drafted
- Draft forms and documents for you
- Explain legal concepts and court rules
- Help you evaluate property rights
- Assess the strength of your legal position and help you strategize
- Coach you before mediation sessions, and
- Provide referrals to therapists, custody evaluators, and other experts.

The most important part of your relationship with a lawyer who is providing unbundled services is having a contract that clearly states the parameters of the lawyer's work. Because lawyers are anxious about working on cases that they don't have total control over, you'll probably find the lawyer eager to complete such a contract, but just in case it's not forthcoming, make sure you get an agreement in place before you begin working together. The last thing you want is for the lawyer to do a lot more—and bill a lot more—than you agreed to.

Divorce Coaching

If you're representing yourself for all purposes but you want the backup of having a lawyer review your paperwork and advise you on strategy, you can ask an attorney to be your divorce coach. Coaching is a form of unbundled services. A divorce coach won't participate in your case in any formal kind of way (like appearing for one motion as described below), but will be behind the scenes answering your questions, reviewing the paperwork you've prepared, and helping you stay on track.

A Combination

Some people feel fine about representing themselves in negotiations with the other parent and are comfortable preparing paperwork that's agreed upon, but aren't as comfortable with the idea of going to court, submitting paperwork in a contested situation, and speaking in front of the judge. It's fine to start out representing yourself but hire an attorney when it gets to the point that you don't think you can handle things alone. It's also fine to continue representing yourself for most purposes, but to seek a lawyer's help with preparing the paperwork, attending a court hearing, or both.

Looking for a Lawyer

Whether you're looking for a lawyer to represent you in all aspects of your case or someone to coach you or provide limited representation, you may find yourself at a loss when it's time to find and hire a lawyer. It's an important process, because you'll be working closely with the lawyer, and you need to feel comfortable and have confidence in the lawyer's skills. Don't pick a lawyer just because your best friend recommends the person or you like the look of the lawyer's website. Do your homework, and you won't have to make a change later or end up dissatisfied.

Your first decision is what kind of lawyer you want. Some lawyers have a reputation for being very aggressive, while others are known for settling every case and never going to trial. What type of lawyer you want depends on what your expectations are about your case. Is it already clear to you that your spouse is going to take a no-holds-barred approach? If so, an aggressive attorney might be best. But the best attorneys are the ones who start with an expectation that everyone's going to be reasonable and things will get resolved—and then move on to being more aggressive if they see that's not going to happen. It's much more important to find a lawyer who is experienced, knowledgeable, and respectful of the way you want to handle the divorce.

Getting Recommendations

The starting point of your lawyer search should be recommendations from people who are personally acquainted with the lawyers they're referring you to.

- If you've ever hired a lawyer you liked, ask your former lawyer for a referral to a divorce lawyer or for help checking out the reputation of lawyers whose names you get from others.
- A marriage counselor or individual therapist, if you're seeing one, is very likely to know attorneys.
- Ask family members, friends, and acquaintances, especially if they've used divorce lawyers (their recommendations aren't as useful if the lawyers they're familiar with practice criminal defense). If the same name pops up more than once, that's worth something, but it shouldn't necessarily be the end of your inquiry.

If you can't find a personal referral, try professional associations of family law attorneys. The American Academy of Matrimonial Lawyers (AAML) is a national organization with stringent admission standards. It shouldn't be a deal-breaker if the lawyer isn't a member, but membership is a good indication that the lawyer is reputable and competent. The AAML online directory (www.aaml.org) lists members.

Your state and local bar association may refer you to a lawyer, but these referrals are a mixed bag. The downside is that some of the lawyers on the referral panels are inexperienced or in need of referrals because they're not successful at bringing in clients in other ways. But this is not always the case. Some lawyers consider it a service to the local bar to include themselves in the local directory, and a big benefit is that the bar association makes sure that the lawyers are licensed to practice law and have professional liability (malpractice) insurance.

Many divorce websites list attorneys, but they may not provide a lot of information. A directory with in-depth profiles can be especially useful if you're looking for a lawyer who will provide unbundled services. The detailed profiles in Nolo's lawyer directory at www.nolo.com include the lawyer's position on helping people who are representing themselves, so it might be a good place to start. If you have other referrals, simply call the attorneys and ask whether they're willing to work with you that way. Some may not have done it before but might be game to try.

No matter how you search for lawyers, once you've got a list of names, be sure to check with your state's regulating agency (usually the state bar) to make sure the lawyer hasn't been disciplined and to confirm education and experience—this information is usually public record. It's also a good idea to search online for information about any lawyer you're considering hiring.

Interviewing Lawyers

You are going to be spending the next year or more with your lawyer—and most likely paying the lawyer a significant amount of money—so don't try to choose one without an in-person meeting. Especially if you're anticipating a lot of conflict in your divorce, it's really important that you trust and feel comfortable with your attorney. So once you have a few recommendations, set up appointments with the lawyers who seem the most likely to be a good fit.

Don't be surprised if an attorney you contact declines to consult with you—it may be because of a conflict of interest, in most cases because your spouse has already consulted that lawyer. You may or may not learn the reason, because the lawyer shouldn't tell you that your spouse has been there (confidentiality rules prevent it). Instead, you'll just be told that the lawyer's not available. The same would be true if your spouse contacted a lawyer you had already spoken to, and to whom you gave confidential information about your marriage or divorce.

Some lawyers offer no-cost initial consultations so that you and the lawyer both have a chance to decide whether or not to work together. Others charge for the consultation, especially if they are giving you strategic advice about your case. Be prepared to pay. You may have an idea of what you want to ask the attorney, and here's a list of suggested questions to add to yours, to help you figure out what kind of lawyer you're talking to. Before you go, check the attorney's website or the state bar website for answers to some of the basic questions about education and length of time in practice.

Questions to Ask a Lawyer You May Hire

- How long have you done family law?
- How many family law cases have you completed?
- Do you do other kinds of cases? What kinds?
- Who else in your office would be working on my case? Under what circumstances would someone other than you work on my case? What will the charges be?
- Can I expect responses to phone calls and emails within 24 hours by you or someone on your staff?
- How many divorce cases have you brought to trial?
- How often do your divorce cases go to mediation?
- Do you encourage mediation?
- Are you a certified specialist in family law? (Check your state bar's website first to find out whether your state grants certification.)
- Have you published any articles about family law?
- Are you familiar with the judges and the courts in the county where my divorce will be filed?
- Do you think kids should ever testify in a divorce trial? (If you want to protect your kids from testifying—or you think it's going to be necessary—ask up front. You certainly don't want to argue about it when you're close to trial.)

> ## Questions to Ask a Lawyer You May Hire (cont'd)
>
> - Are there local attorneys with whom you have particularly good or particularly bad relationships? (This can give you a sense of the lawyer's experience, and also of whether they themselves are difficult to work with. If they tell you that there are six other lawyers who are simply impossible, you might want to consider the common denominator.)
> - Do you know my spouse's lawyer? Have you worked on the other side of cases with this lawyer before? Would you say you have a good relationship?
> - What do you think your reputation is among other family law lawyers?
> - What do you think is the likely outcome of my custody dispute?
> - What is your opinion about arbitration? Have you taken divorce cases to arbitration?
> - Can you estimate how much I'm going to pay in attorneys' fees? What about expenses?
> - Will you accept my input on strategic decisions like how much support to ask for or when to use an expert witness?
> - What else should I know about you or your practice?

The most important piece of advice is this: Don't ignore your gut feelings about the lawyers you interview. If you think the lawyer isn't a good fit, you're probably right. Keep looking. The cost of switching to a different lawyer midstream when you find out you were right about it not being a good working relationship is far greater than the cost of having a few more consultations with potential lawyers.

Paying a Lawyer

How much you'll pay your lawyer depends entirely on how far you go toward a trial. If your lawyer simply helps you through a mediation by coaching you and reviewing a draft settlement agreement, you'll pay a few thousand dollars at most. On the other hand, if you go all the way to a contested trial, you'll pay many tens of thousands. In between, the cost will vary depending on how much your lawyer has to do.

No matter what, though, you and your lawyer will enter into a written contract defining the terms of your relationship.

The Retainer

Nearly every divorce lawyer working on a contested case will ask you to pay a "retainer," or deposit, when you hire them. (A lawyer who is coaching you through mediation or self-representation might not, and a lawyer working on an unbundled basis also might work on a pay-as-you-go hourly basis.) The retainer represents your first payment toward the fees that you will owe as the case goes along.

Divorce lawyers charge by the hour, and the retainer will pay for a certain number of hours. The amount of the retainer depends on the lawyer's hourly rate and what is usual in your area. If the lawyer thinks you might be able to collect some fees from your spouse during the divorce, especially at an early stage, the retainer might be lower. If you are anticipating litigation, the lawyer will expect to put in a significant number of hours. Many lawyers ask for $10,000 to $15,000 up front. If the lawyer charges $250 per hour, $10,000 will last only 40 hours, a relatively short time given the legal work the lawyer will do. And $250 is an average. If you live in a metropolitan area and your lawyer is a specialist, you could pay up to twice that. Most lawyers accept credit cards for the retainer and ongoing billing.

The retainer goes into a special account that's monitored by your state's bar association or other entity that regulates lawyers, called a trust account. It's still your money until it's earned, and the lawyer can't withdraw any of it until fees are earned and billed to you. You should get a bill every month itemizing the time that the lawyer has spent, listing expenses, and giving an accounting of how much the lawyer took for fees and how much of your retainer is left in the trust account. You are always entitled to know how much is in your account. When the money gets low, the lawyer will probably ask you for more.

The Fee Agreement

The lawyer should give you a written fee agreement that spells out the terms of your relationship before you write your first check for the retainer. Most states have rules requiring lawyers to enter written agreements in any case in which fees are expected to be over a certain amount, often $500 or $1,000, but it's a good idea to have one in every case. It's especially important if you're using a lawyer only for parts of your case; the agreement should be very specific about what the lawyer's responsibilities are. If the lawyer doesn't offer a written agreement, ask for it. The agreement should cover at least these issues:

Hourly rate or flat fee. The contract should state the lawyer's hourly fee and the rates of anyone else who might work on your case. You may, for example, be asked to pay for the time of a paralegal who works for the lawyer, or for an associate (less experienced) lawyer at a much lower hourly rate than that of the lawyer. Some lawyers charge a higher hourly rate for time actually spent in the courtroom during trial.

Some attorneys offer flat-fee services. This isn't very likely in a contested custody or support case, which will almost certainly be on an hourly basis. But a lawyer might agree to complete the paperwork for an uncontested divorce for a flat fee. Again, make sure the fee agreement is very specific about what the lawyer will do for the amount charged.

Billing practices. Make sure it's clear how often the lawyer will bill you, how quickly you'll be expected to pay, and what your bills will look like—ask to see a sample bill to see whether the details look adequate to you. "Legal services" isn't very informative—you want to know exactly what the lawyer did.

Expenses. In addition to the hourly charges, you will have to pay for filing fees for your paperwork, and you may have to pay for expenses such as copying or postage. Make sure the agreement says what you'll be responsible for, and don't hesitate to suggest a limit—for example, the agreement can say that the lawyer will check with you before incurring expenses that exceed a certain amount, like $250.

Experts. Especially in a contested custody case, it's possible that the lawyer will want to hire other professionals to work on your case—most commonly a custody evaluator. (There's more about evaluations in Chapter 7.) Make sure that the agreement says the lawyer must get your permission to hire experts, at least if they're going to be paid over a certain amount.

Unearned fees. Don't sign a fee agreement that says that your retainer is nonrefundable. If there is money in the trust account when your case is over, you should get it back. In fact, a nonrefundable retainer is likely to violate ethics rules in most states, so think twice about the lawyer, too.

Ending the agreement. The fee agreement should say that you can end your relationship with the lawyer whenever you want to, and that the lawyer can also end the lawyer-client relationship, but not in a way that would affect you negatively. That is what's meant by saying that the lawyer can't withdraw at a time that would "prejudice" your interests.

Whatever lawyer you choose will have a standard fee agreement that may have other provisions as well; the ones listed here and in the sample contract below are just the basics. Make sure you read over the contract very carefully before you sign it, ask the lawyer about anything you don't understand, and have a trusted friend review it as well to catch anything that you didn't see.

Sample Attorney-Client Agreement

Attorney-Client Agreement

This agreement is made between Allison Peters, Attorney, and Matthew Milton, Client. Attorney and Client agree that Attorney will provide legal services to Client according to the following terms.

1. **Engagement.** Attorney will represent Client in connection with dissolution of his marriage to Susan Milton and custody dispute related to the minor child Mark Milton. No other legal matters are covered by this agreement. This agreement also does not cover appellate work, for which a new fee agreement will be required.

   Attorney will begin working on Client's case when Client has returned a signed copy of this agreement to Attorney, along with the deposit described in Paragraph 7, below.

2. **Attorney's Obligations.** Attorney agrees to provide competent legal services in the promotion of Client's interests and the protection of Client's rights, to make every reasonable effort on Client's behalf, and to work toward achieving a favorable outcome. Attorney will keep Client informed of progress and respond promptly to inquiries. Attorney makes no promises about the ultimate outcome or resolution of the case, but will offer informed opinions and advice about possible outcomes and legal conclusions.

3. **Client's Obligations.** Client agrees to provide all relevant information and documents that Attorney requests, and will be forthcoming and truthful with Attorney at all times. Client will pay fees and reimburse costs expended in accordance with this agreement. Client will keep Attorney informed of Client's current contact information at all times.

4. **Information.** Client authorizes Attorney to gather whatever information is needed to be effective in providing the services described above and to negotiate on Client's behalf.

5. **Costs.** All expenses, including filing fees, service of process, depositions, appraisals, witness fees, court reporter fees, transcripts, telephone, postage, photocopying, messenger service, travel, and similar expenses, as well as all legal costs and fees charged by investigators, accountants,

custody evaluators, and other experts consulted for their professional advice necessary to prepare and present Client's claims are to be advanced by and paid for by Client. No professionals will be consulted or retained without Client's prior consent.

6. **Termination of Attorney-Client Relationship.** Attorney may withdraw at any time upon giving Client reasonable notice, if such withdrawal would not prejudice Client's case. Client may discharge Attorney at any time upon written notice to Attorney.

7. **Attorneys' Fees.** In consideration for services rendered and to be rendered by the Attorney on behalf of Client, Client agrees to pay any and all costs incurred and an hourly rate for services of Attorney and Attorney's staff as listed below:

Attorney and other partners	$300/hr
Associates	$225/hr
Paralegals	$75/hr
Law clerks	$100/hr

Attorney will bill Client in increments of tenths of an hour and will submit billing to Client at least once per month. Bills are due when presented.

Client will pay an initial deposit of $7,500, which will be held in Attorney's trust account. Hourly charges will be charged against the deposit, and Client authorizes Attorney to transfer funds from the trust account to Attorney's business account as charges are incurred and billed. When the deposit is reduced to $2,500 or less, Attorney may demand further deposits of no more than $5,000, which Client agrees to remit within ten days of demand.

At the conclusion of the case, any unused balance will be refunded to Client.

If Client fails to pay fees or to replenish the trust account as described, Attorney may file a motion to withdraw from the case.

8. **Retention of File.** When Client's case is completed, Attorney will retain Client's file for at least five years. If Client does not retrieve the file after that, Attorney may destroy it without further notice to Client.

10/10/20xx	*Matthew Milton*
Date	Client
10/10/20xx	*Allison Peters*
Date	Attorney

What You Can Expect to Pay

The total cost of a divorce trial depends mainly on the length of the trial and your lawyer's hourly rate. Lawyer hours are, by far, the major expense in a trial.

Here's an estimate of the costs of a two-day trial with the most basic expert testimony. Let's assume the lawyer charges $250 per hour—probably a conservative estimate. Expert witnesses sometimes charge less for their out-of-court work but more for court testimony, so we'll use an average for each of the experts.

The Price of Fighting It Out			
Initial meeting and information gathering	10 hours @ 250/hr	=	$ 2,500
Discovery	50 hours @ 250/hr	=	12,500
Trial preparation	100 hours @ 250/hr	=	25,000
Pretrial motions	30 hours @ 250/hr	=	7,500
Court time	15 hours @ 250/hr	=	3,750
Expert fees			
Custody expert	40 hours @ 250/hr	=	10,000
Actuary	15 hours @ 200/hr	=	3,000
Vocational expert	20 hours @ 200/hr	=	4,000
Court reporter fees		=	2,500
Total			**$ 70,750**

Costs, such as copying or investigative fees, will add to this total—and can be high when you're preparing for a trial. The monetary total also doesn't account for the many hours of your time that you'll spend preparing with your attorney and sitting in court, missing work, and being away from your kids.

It's entirely possible that your trial could be less expensive than this, but even a half-day or one-day trial will cost you tens of thousands of dollars. A more complex one will easily take you into the six-figure realm. If you're the higher earner, you might end up on the hook for your spouse's attorneys' fees as well as your own if you lose and the judge thinks you have the ability to pay.

If You Have Problems With Your Lawyer

As a client, you are responsible for providing your lawyer with information the lawyer asks you for, staying in contact with the attorney, and being ready to make decisions as the case proceeds. You are also required to pay your bills in a timely way. In turn, you are entitled to expect the lawyer to respond promptly to your phone calls and emails, to provide you with whatever information you ask for about your case, and to provide competent services. If you find yourself unhappy with your lawyer despite the careful work you did to hire the right person, first try talking to the attorney about your complaints. (If you're not sure whether the lawyer's actions are appropriate or not, ask another attorney.) The most common complaint that clients have about attorneys is about a lack of communication. If this is your concern, let your attorney know that you expect an improvement in response time. This may be all it takes.

If the communication problem continues, or if you have other issues with your lawyer, you have the right to fire your attorney at any time. It's a good idea to find a new attorney before you end your relationship with your current one. That way, the new lawyer can handle the details of getting your file transferred. But if you haven't found a new lawyer yet, or if you intend to represent yourself going forward, just send the attorney a letter (ask for a return receipt) stating that you're terminating the relationship and asking for your file. In most states, you have the right to get your file back even if you owe the lawyer money, but that's not true everywhere.

If you think your lawyer has acted unethically, you can make a report to the state bar or other registration agency in your state. There's a list of the agencies that regulate lawyers in each state on the American Bar Association website. Go to www.americanbar.org/groups/professional_ responsibility.html; click on "Resources" and then on "Directory of State Disciplinary Agencies."

Getting the Other Parent to Pay Your Attorneys' Fees

Sometimes, courts will order one parent to pay some (and very occasionally, all) of the other parent's attorneys' fees. This could happen if:

- One parent is the only parent with income or earns a lot more than the other parent, and the other wouldn't be able to hire an attorney without a fee award.
- One parent forces the other one into litigation over issues that the judge thinks are frivolous or should have been resolved without going to court.
- One parent doesn't comply with court orders, so that the other parent has to come to court to try to enforce the orders.

If a judge does order one parent to pay the other's fees, it will almost always be just a portion of the fees. States have different rules about when judges may award attorneys' fees, so check your state's laws or ask an attorney if you think the other parent should pony up for some of your expenses.

Help With Self-Representation: Legal Document Preparers

Some states allow nonlawyers to help with document preparation for people who are representing themselves in court. This occupation used to be known as paralegal work, but people who do it now are usually called legal document preparers, or LDPs.

A legal document preparer isn't allowed to give individualized legal advice. (Only licensed lawyers can do that.) LDPs prepare forms for you, using the information you supply. An LDP will start by having you complete a questionnaire that asks for the information the preparer needs to fill out court forms for your county. The LDP will transfer the information onto the forms, and then either you or the LDP can file them with the court.

Legal Document Preparers charge from $175 to $750 to do all of the paperwork, depending on where you live, whether you have children, and whether you need a separate settlement agreement (which depends on how your state's forms are structured). They work only on uncontested cases, and some states limit what LDPs can do or prohibit them entirely.

To find a legal document preparer, first ask your divorced friends and acquaintances whether they used one, and what the experience was like. If you don't get a referral that way, check the Internet or the yellow pages by searching "legal document assistant," "paralegal," or "typing services."

There are also a number of Internet-based document preparation services, which may work for you if your state doesn't allow LDPs. Again, you can only use a service like this if your divorce is uncontested. You'll answer questions on the website of a service like www.divorcesource.com or www.legalzoom.com, and print the forms from your computer or receive them by mail within a few days, along with instructions. You'll need to file the forms with the court yourself and comply with your state's service requirements. The main differences among the sites are how quickly your paperwork is available to you, and how much you'll pay. Most online preparation services charge from about $139 to $300.

Knowledge Is Power: Learn the Law

One of the best ways to avoid a court fight is to know the law that applies to your situation. If you learn what the law says and so can predict what a judge is likely to do, you are much less likely to go into court with an argument that you can't win. You will also have more leverage if you can argue that the position your spouse is taking isn't supported by the law.

Knowing the law won't always tell you what a judge will decide. For example, if you're arguing about custody, you'll have to present the facts, make your arguments, and let the judge decide what's in your child's best interests. But knowing when a parent can win an argument about moving away, or how old a child has to be before the child can have a say in custody decisions, can make a difference in how you decide to proceed in your case.

You can always learn about the law by asking a lawyer, and if you have a lawyer representing you this is the best way to go. Even if you don't have a lawyer handling your case, it might be well worth it to have a consultation or two with a lawyer who can research legal issues or explain the law to you. (See "What Services Do You Need?" above, for more about working with a lawyer in this way.)

You can also do your own legal research. The state-by-state tables in the appendix will help you find the law on subjects that come up frequently:

- when and whether a parent can relocate with the children
- modifying custody or support after an order has been entered, and
- factors the courts consider in evaluating a child's best interests.

Quick Guide to Legal Research

If you're acting as your own lawyer, you'll need to do your own legal research. For example, you may need to look up when your state allows deviations from guideline child support, or read some cases where parents asked the court for permission to move away. Legal research is probably different from other kinds of research you may have done, but once you know a few simple rules and procedures, you should be able to find what you need.

What to Look For

There are four types of resources that you might seek out to educate yourself or to support you as you represent yourself in your custody or support case:

- state statutes, which set out the laws for your state
- court decisions (cases), which are the written opinions of appeals courts, applying current legal rules from statutes and previous court decisions to individual disputes
- background resources, which give you an overview of a topic and the legal issues that are important, and
- practice guides to help you with preparing paperwork.

Statutes and Regulations

Statutes are the basic laws of your state, made by the state legislature and covering everything from criminal laws to education law to family law. Statutes are also called laws or codes.

Many states divide their statutes into sections, sometimes called "codes"—for example, the "Family Code" or "Domestic Relations Code" probably contains the divorce laws for your state. If there's no separate code for family law, the laws are probably in the Civil Code. Look in the index to find the specific sections that cover the topic you want to learn about, whether it's divorce generally, or custody, or the best interests standards in your state. The codes are numbered, and once you find the general area you should be able to use the table of contents to find the law you need. Ask a law librarian for help if you're not finding what you need. After you've found a law that you need, always look in the back of the book to see whether there's a paperback addition ("pocket part") that shows changes in the law since the book was printed.

Some laws can be difficult to read and understand, and that's where the court decisions described below can come in handy. If you look at an "annotated" copy of your state statutes (a law librarian can show you where the annotated codes are), you'll find supplemental material like descriptions of cases that interpret the laws, which can be helpful if you want to find cases with facts similar to yours. Case annotations are brief (one paragraph) descriptions of decisions made by judges about the laws you're concerned with. Cases that mention the statutory section you're looking at will be in the annotations following the law. After you've reviewed the law itself, you can look through the annotations to see whether there are any cases that might help you understand what the law means.

Court Decisions

Every day, new court decisions come out when judges rule in individual cases. Those decisions are then collected and published in books and online. These are usually cases that have been appealed after a trial. If there's a case you want to look at because you've learned about it in the statutory annotations (see above) or in another source, you can use the case's "citation," which tells you what book the case is published in. It's a fairly simple task once you know the trick.

Here's an example: the case of *In re Marriage of Brown v. Yana*. It's a California case in which one parent wants to move away and the other parent objects. There are two different citations for the case: 37 Cal.4th 947 and 127 P.3d 28. In each citation, the first number refers to the volume of the set, the second letter/number combination refers to the set of books the volume is in, and the third number refers to the page where the case begins.

"Cal.4th" means the California Reports, 4th Series. Once you've found the series, find Volume 37 and turn to page 947. The second citation is to the Pacific Reporter, 3rd Series. (This set of books includes decisions from courts in several West Coast states; there's also a Southern Reporter that covers Florida and other southern states, and other regional sets of books.) Once you've found the series, find Volume 127 and turn to page 28.

Not all law libraries have the state reporters—some only have the regional ones. But whichever citation you use, you'll get exactly the same case.

In re Marriage of Brown v. Yana

37	Cal.4th	947
↑	↑	↑
volume of the set	set of books	page where the case begins
↓	↓	↓
127	P.3d	28

Background Resources

You've already gotten one background resource: this book. You may also want to check out other books and websites on divorce for general information. If you're looking for books on divorce and the law, go to the law library and search that database for family law resources, or ask the law librarian to guide you to the right section of the library.

A legal encyclopedia may be another good resource if you are really dedicated to doing your own legal research, but encyclopedias aren't for the fainthearted—they can be challenging to use. The two major encyclopedias, covering laws across the whole country, are the *American Law Reports* (ALR) and *American Jurisprudence* (Am.Jur.). You can search the index of either set by subject—for example, custody or visitation—and then review brief summaries of cases on that subject. If you find court decisions from your state that look like they might address a situation like yours, you can look them up as explained above.

Practice Guides

A practice guide or practice manual is designed to help lawyers learn about their practice areas. Most have forms and instructions, and you are very likely to find sample pleadings and other forms. They are designed for lawyers, so some of them may be written in a style that's not very accessible, but you may find others perfectly readable and very useful for your purposes.

Some practice guides are directed at a national audience, and you'll also find guides that are specific to your state, which might be more helpful to you in representing yourself. The law librarian can show you where they are, and might be willing to explain how to use them and what you might find in them. You can also check the websites of some of the legal publishers, like LexisNexis, Matthew Bender, and ThomsonWest, and see what they have to offer for your state. Practice guides are extremely expensive, though, so you'll probably be better off using them in the library.

RESOURCE

If you want to learn more. *Legal Research: How to Find & Understand the Law*, by Stephen Elias and the Editors of Nolo (Nolo), explains in detail how to find legal information and resources and how to use the law library and the Internet to find what you need.

Where to Look

A great deal of information is available online, and you can also use your local law library.

Online

You can find a lot of state laws on the Internet by simply entering your state's name and the word "statute" or "family code." You can find a specific code section that way, or just locate the family code and then search the table of contents for the topic you're interested in. You can also find cases that way, often just by putting in the name of the case. For example, entering "Brown v. Yana" into a search engine will get you the same opinion you would find in the law books if you had the citation.

Many legal websites like www.nolo.com, www.alllaw.com, www.divorcenet.com, and www.justia.com can also be helpful resources, with free legal information as well as links to state laws.

To get your state's laws, you can also go to www.totaldivorce.com, where the divorce laws are separated out from other state laws and presented in an easy-to-review format.

The Law Library

No matter where you live, there should be a law library fairly nearby. Nearly every county has a public one; often it will be at the same courthouse where you file your paperwork and go to court. A public law school or a government building like the state capitol are other likely locations. Ask the court clerk where you would find the nearest law library that's open to the public. Some local public libraries also have certain law books.

Divorce laws are very different in different states, but you will definitely find all of the following in the law library:

- the text of your state's laws on divorce and family issues (statutes and regulations)
- published court decisions (cases) that interpret the statutes, and
- legal articles, books, and practice guides on specific topics that explain the law in depth.

The law librarian can be a big help to you when you're doing your own research. The librarian can't give you legal advice or explain what you find in the law books, but will point you to the right area of the library, help you find specific books, and maybe orient you to the indexing system of a particular set of books. ●

50-State Charts

Residency Requirements

Before you can file for divorce in the state where you live, you must have lived there for a certain period of time. A few states don't require a specific period of residence, but most have a residency requirement ranging from six weeks to one year. (If you or your spouse is in the military, residency requirements don't apply, and most of the time you may file in the state where the military spouse is stationed.) The requirements for each state are listed below.

Alabama	6 months
Alaska	Must be a resident at the time of filing
Arizona	90 days
Arkansas	60 days
California	6 months
Colorado	91 days
Connecticut	No requirement for filing[1]
Delaware	6 months
District of Columbia	6 months
Florida	6 months
Georgia	6 months
Hawaii	3 months
Idaho	6 weeks
Illinois	90 days
Indiana	6 months
Iowa	1 year[2]
Kansas	60 days
Kentucky	180 days
Louisiana	6 months
Maine	6 months

[1] Must establish residency for 12 months before final judgment can be entered, unless one party lived in Connecticut at marriage and returned with intention to stay, or the cause for dissolution arose after either party moved to Connecticut.

[2] No durational residency requirement if respondent is in Iowa, but there is a one-year residency requirement if only petitioner is in Iowa.

Residency Requirements (cont'd)	
Maryland	1 year (or if cause of divorce occurred in state, must be a resident at the time of filing)
Massachusetts	1 year (or if cause of divorce occurred in state, must be a resident at the time of filing)
Michigan	180 days
Minnesota	180 days
Mississippi	6 months
Missouri	90 days
Montana	90 days
Nebraska	1 year (none if either spouse is continuously a resident from date of marriage to date of filing)
Nevada	6 weeks
New Hampshire	1 year[3]
New Jersey	1 year
New Mexico	6 months
New York	1 year
North Carolina	6 months
North Dakota	6 months
Ohio	6 months
Oklahoma	6 months
Oregon	6 months
Pennsylvania	6 months
Rhode Island	1 year
South Carolina	1 year (unless both spouses are residents, then 3 months)
South Dakota	Person filing must be a resident or service member stationed there at the time of filing
Tennessee	6 months

[3] The filing spouse must be a resident of New Hampshire for one year before filing for divorce. This requirement is waived where both spouses reside in the state when the action is commenced, or where the filing spouse resides in the state when he or she files for divorce and personally serves the other spouse with divorce papers within the state.

Residency Requirements (cont'd)	
Texas	6 months
Utah	3 months
Vermont	6 months
Virginia	6 months
Washington	The filing spouse must be a resident of the state or a member of the armed forces stationed in the state
West Virginia	1 year (no time requirement if marriage was in West Virginia and one of the parties is a resident at the time of commencement of the divorce action)
Wisconsin	6 months
Wyoming	60 days

Grounds for Divorce				
State	**Fault**	**No-fault (other than separation)**	**Separation**	**Length of separation**
Alabama	✓	✓	✓	2 years
Alaska	✓	✓		
Arizona		✓		
Arkansas	✓		✓	18 months
California		✓		
Colorado		✓		
Connecticut	✓	✓	✓	18 months
Delaware	✓	✓	✓	6 months
District of Columbia			✓	6 months if both parties agree; otherwise 1 year
Florida		✓		
Georgia	✓	✓		
Hawaii		✓	✓	2 years under a decree of separate maintenance, or after a decree of separation from bed and board has expired
Idaho	✓	✓	✓	5 years
Illinois	✓	✓	✓	2 years (6 months if both parties agree)
Indiana	✓	✓		
Iowa		✓		
Kansas	✓	✓		
Kentucky		✓		
Louisiana	✓		✓	1 year or 180 days if there are no minor children
Maine	✓	✓		
Maryland	✓		✓	12 months
Massachusetts	✓	✓		
Michigan		✓		
Minnesota		✓		
Mississippi	✓	✓		

State	Fault	No-fault (other than separation)	Separation	Length of separation
Missouri	✓	✓	✓	12 months if both parties agree; otherwise 2 years
Montana		✓	✓	180 days
Nebraska		✓		
Nevada		✓[1]	✓	1 year
New Hampshire	✓	✓		
New Jersey	✓	✓	✓	18 months (6 months if there are irreconcilable differences)
New Mexico	✓	✓		
New York	✓	✓	✓	1 year (must have a written separation agreement)
North Carolina			✓	1 year
North Dakota	✓	✓		
Ohio	✓	✓[2]	✓	1 year
Oklahoma	✓	✓		
Oregon		✓		
Pennsylvania	✓	✓	✓	2 years
Rhode Island	✓	✓	✓	3 years
South Carolina			✓	1 year
South Dakota	✓	✓		
Tennessee	✓	✓	✓	2 years
Texas	✓	✓	✓	3 years
Utah	✓	✓	✓	3 years
Vermont	✓		✓	6 months

[1] Divorce may be granted on the basis of "incurable insanity;" otherwise, divorce is no-fault.

[2] No-fault divorce will be denied if one party contests ground of incompatibility.

Grounds for Divorce (cont'd)				
State	**Fault**	**No-fault (other than separation)**	**Separation**	**Length of separation**
Virginia	✓		✓[3]	1 year
Washington		✓		
West Virginia	✓	✓	✓	1 year
Wisconsin		✓	✓	12 months
Wyoming		✓[4]		

[3] May be reduced to six months if there are no minor children.

[4] Divorce may be granted on the basis of "incurable insanity;" otherwise, divorce is no-fault.

State Child Support Calculators

State	Support Information/Calculators
Alabama	www.alacourt.gov/childsupportobligations.aspx
Alaska	https://webapp.state.ak.us/cssd
Arizona	www.azcourts.gov/familylaw/childsupportcalculator.aspx
Arkansas	https://www.ark.org/dfa_ocsee/app/welcome.html
California	www.childsup.ca.gov (click link to "Calculate Child Support")
Colorado	www.courts.state.co.us/Forms/SubCategory.cfm?Category=Divorce (link to Custody & Child Support electronic and manual worksheets)
Connecticut	http://www.jud.ct.gov/Publications/ ChildSupport/2005CSguidelines.pdf (worksheet on pp. 26-27)
Delaware	http://courts.delaware.gov/SupportCalculator
Dist. of Col.	http://csgc.oag.dc.gov/application/main/intro.aspx
Florida	http://dor.myflorida.com/dor/childsupport/guidelines.html
Georgia	http://www.georgiacourts.gov/csc
Hawaii	www.hawaii.gov/jud/childpp.htm
Idaho	No official calculator, try http://www.alllaw.com/calculators/ childsupport/idaho. Some information is located at www.isc.idaho. gov/family-court/fc-home
Illinois	www.childsupportillinois.com/general/calculating.html
Indiana	www.in.gov/judiciary/2625.htm
Iowa	https://secureapp.dhs.state.ia.us/estimator
Kansas	http://www.kscourts.org/rules-procedures-forms/child-support-guidelines/current_guidelines.asp (PDF worksheet and schedules are included in guidelines, which are complex)
Kentucky	https://csws.chfs.ky.gov/csws/General/EstimateDisclaimer.aspx
Louisiana	www.dss.state.la.us/assets/docs/searchable/OFS/overview/SES/ SES_OBL_A_330.pdf
Maine	www.courts.state.me.us/maine_courts/family/divorce/child_ support.html
Maryland	www.dhr.state.md.us/CSOCGuide/App/disclaimer.do
Massachusetts	https://wfb.dor.state.ma.us/DORCommon/Worksheets/CSE/ Guidelines.aspx

State Child Support Calculators (cont'd)	
State	**Support Information/Calculators**
Michigan	No official calculator. Try www.alllaw.com/calculators/childsupport/michigan and see http://courts.mi.gov/administration/scao/officesprograms/foc/pages/child-support-formula.aspx
Minnesota	http://childsupportcalculator.dhs.state.mn.us
Mississippi	No official calculator. Try http://www.alllaw.com/calculators/childsupport/mississippi and see http://www.mdhs.state.ms.us/field-operations/programs/child-support/determine-child-support-obligations
Missouri	www.courts.mo.gov (click "Court Forms" to find child support forms), including http://www.courts.mo.gov/file.jsp?id=29741 (worksheet on p. 11)
Montana	http://dphhs.mt.gov/CSED/publicationsandFAQs/guidelinespacket.aspx (links to guidelines and worksheets)
Nebraska	No official calculator. Try http://www.alllaw.com/calculators/childsupport/nebraska and see guidelines at https://supremecourt.nebraska.gov/supreme-court-rules/ch4/art2
Nevada	No official calculator. Try www.alllaw.com/calculators/Childsupport/Nevada
New Hampshire	www4.egov.nh.gov/DHHS_calculator/calc_form.asp
New Jersey	www.judiciary.state.nj.us/csguide/index.htm (Appendixes IXB and IXC)
New Mexico	https://elink.hsd.state.nm.us/eCSE/pubCalculator.aspx
New York	See worksheets at www.childsupport.ny.gov/dcse/pdfs/cssa_2013.pdf (worksheet on p. 22) and https://www.nycourts.gov/divorce/forms_instructions/ud-8.pdf
North Carolina	https://nddhacts01.dhhs.state.nc.us/home.jsp?TargetScreen=WorkSheet.jsp
North Dakota	www.nd.gov/dhs/services/childsupport/progserv/guidelines/guidelines.html
Ohio	Worksheets at http://codes.ohio.gov/orc/3119.022 http://codes.ohio.gov/orc/3119.023
Oklahoma	www.okdhs.org/onlineservices/cscalc
Oregon	https://justice.oregon.gov/guidelines

State Child Support Calculators (cont'd)	
State	**Support Information/Calculators**
Pennsylvania	https://www.humanservices.state.pa.us/csws (click "Estimate My Child Support Amount")
Rhode Island	http://www.cse.ri.gov/documents/GuidelineWorksheet_2013.pdf www.cse.ri.gov/services/establishment_childsup.php
South Carolina	www.state.sc.us/dss/csed/calculator.htm
South Dakota	http://apps.sd.gov/ss17pc02cal/calculator1.aspx
Tennessee	http://www.tn.gov/humanserv/is/isdownloads.shtml
Texas	https://www.texasattorneygeneral.gov/cs/calculator
Utah	http://orscsc.dhs.utah.gov
Vermont	http://dcf.vermont.gov/ocs/parents/guidelines_calculator (downloadable free software)
Virginia	www.courts.state.va.us/forms/district/dc637.pdf
Washington	www.courts.wa.gov/forms/documents/CSWorksheet.pdf https://fortress.wa.gov/dshs/dcs/SSGen/Home
West Virginia	www.legis.state.wv.us/wvcode/code.cfm?chap=48&art=13 (scroll down for worksheets)
Wisconsin	http://dcf.wisconsin.gov/bcs/order/guidelines_tools.htm
Wyoming	http://www.courts.state.wy.us/Documents/Forms/ProSe/ECVSP/201407/ECVSP13.pdf http://www.laramiecounty.com/_departments/_district_court/calculator.aspx

Court and Court-Related Websites

State	Websites	What you'll find
Alabama	http://eforms.alacourt.gov/ Child Support Forms/Forms/ AllItems.aspx and http://www. alabamalegalhelp.org/resource/ do-it-yourself-instructions-and-forms	Child support and divorce forms and information
Alaska	www.courts.alaska.gov/ shcforms.htm	Family law self-help center; extensive family law forms and instructions
Arizona	www.azcourts.gov/familylaw/ Home.aspx	Links to forms and other resources
Arkansas	https://courts.arkansas.gov/ forms-and-publications	Selected domestic relations forms
	www.arlegalservices.org	Arkansas Legal Aid's website with family law forms and instructions
California	http://www.courts.ca.gov/ selfhelp.htm?genpubtab	Extensive family law resources
Colorado	www.courts.state.co.us/Forms/ Index.cfm	Extensive family law resources
Connecticut	www.jud.ct.gov/webforms	Family law forms and do-it-yourself divorce guide available for download
	www.jud.ct.gov/lawlib/law/ divorce.htm	Divorce guides and resources
Delaware	http://courts.delaware.gov/ Family/index.stm	Information about family law and divorce law; link to forms online
District of Columbia	www.dccourts.gov/dccourts/ superior/family/index.jsp	Information about family courts; link to forms and instructions online
Florida	www.flcourts.org/gen_public/ family/self_help/map.shtml	Information about local self-help centers; divorce forms and other resources
	www.clerk-17th-flcourts. org/Clerkwebsite/BCCOC2/ SelfService.aspx	Broward County's pilot program for interactive divorce forms online

Court and Court-Related Websites (cont'd)		
State	Websites	What you'll find
Georgia	http://www.georgialegalaid.org/ issues/family-law-and-domestic- violence	State legal aid site with links to divorce and child custody information and forms
Hawaii	www.courts.state.hi.us	Link for Self-Help–>Court Forms leads to information and resources, including forms
Idaho	www.courtselfhelp.idaho.gov	Court assistance office's home page lists local offices that can assist you with self-help or low-cost legal services; links to forms and instructions for family law cases online
Illinois	http://www.law.siu.edu/ selfhelp/info/divorce/packets. html	Southern Illinois University School of Law provides instructions and forms for filing for divorce
	www.state.il.us/court/links/ circuit.asp	Locations of your local court; some local sites provide forms
	http://www.illinoislegalaid.org/ index.cfm?fuseaction=home. formLibrary	Family law forms from Illinois Legal Aid
Indiana	www.in.gov/judiciary/selfservice	Links to self-help legal center, child support calculators; general information about self-representation
Iowa	http://www.iowacourts.gov/ For_the_Public/Representing_ Yourself_in_Court/ DivorceFamily_Law/ (link to "Forms" in side menu)	Divorce information and forms
Kansas	www.kansasjudicialcouncil.org/ DivorceForms.shtml http://www.kansaslegalservices. org/node/1237/all-about-kansas-divorce	Family law information and forms

Court and Court-Related Websites (cont'd)

State	Websites	What you'll find
Kentucky	http://courts.ky.gov/ stateprograms/ divorceeducation/cpd.htm	Divorce information and court locations and rules; not much in the way of forms
	http://kyjustice.org/topics http://kyjustice.org/ divorceforms	Family law information and forms from Legal Aid Network of Kentucky
Louisiana	http://files.lsba.org/ documents/PublicResources/ LSBADivorceBrochure.pdf	Louisiana state bar association's pamphlet with general information on Louisiana divorce
	http://louisianalawhelp.org/ issues/family-children	Family law information and forms
Maine	http://www.helpmelaw.org/ library/3081	Family law information and forms
	http://courts.maine.gov/fees_ forms/forms/index.shtml#fm	
Maryland	www.mdcourts.gov/family/ formsindex.html	Court forms and links to self-help information
Massachusetts	http://www.mass.gov/courts/ selfhelp/family	General court information and family law self-help center, including forms
Michigan	www.courts.michigan.gov/scao/ selfhelp/intro/family/domrel.htm	Family law information and forms
	http://michiganlegalhelp.org/ self-help-tools/family	
Minnesota	www.courts.state.mn.us/forms	Browse through "Court Forms Categories" section to find relevant forms and information
Mississippi	http://www.mslegalservices. org/issues/family-and-juvenile	Family law information and forms
	http://www.mslegalservices.org/ online-legal-forms	
Missouri	www.courts.mo.gov	Click link for "court forms" to find family law forms
	http://www.selfrepresent. mo.gov/page.jsp?id=5240	Family law information and forms

Court and Court-Related Websites (cont'd)		
State	Websites	What you'll find
Montana	http://www.courts.mt.gov/library/topic/default.mcpx	Extensive information and forms
Nebraska	https://supremecourt.nebraska.gov/self-help/welcome	Family law information and forms
Nevada	http://nvcourts.gov/Law_Library/Resources/Forms/Resources_by_Subject	Family law information and forms
New Hampshire	http://www.courts.state.nh.us/fdpp/forms/allforms.htm http://www.courts.state.nh.us/fdpp/divorce_parenting.htm	Family law information and forms
New Jersey	www.judiciary.state.nj.us/family	Information about family court; some forms; links to general information about family law
New Mexico	www.nmcourts.com/cgi/prose_lib	Forms for uncontested divorce and domestic violence filings
	http://www.lawhelpnewmexico.org/?q=familylaw	Family law information provided by New Mexico Legal Aid
New York	http://www.nycourts.gov/law	Extensive court forms, family law information, and information about self-representation
North Carolina	www.nccourts.org/Citizens/GoToCourt/Default.asp	Information about self-representation; click links under "civil" heading for family law forms and information
	http://www.lawhelpnc.org/issues/family-and-juvenile	Family law information and forms
North Dakota	www.ndcourts.gov/court/forms/divorce/forms.htm http://www.ndcourts.gov/ndlshc/FamilyLaw/FamilyLaw.aspx	Forms for child support and simple, uncontested divorce; links to rules of court and policy on self-represented parties

Court and Court-Related Websites (cont'd)		
State	**Websites**	**What you'll find**
Ohio	http://www.ohiolegalservices. org/public/legal_problem/ family-law/legal-separation- divorce-and-dissolution/ selfhelpct_view	Self help forms and information on child support, divorce, and divorce mediation
	www.sconet.state.oh.us/web_ sites/courts	Links to specific court websites, which have local family law forms for county courts
Oklahoma	http://oklaw.org/issues/family http://www.oscn.net/static/ forms/childsupport.asp	Family law information and forms
Oregon	http://courts.oregon. gov/OJD/OSCA/cpsd/ courtimprovement/familylaw/ index.page	Extensive collection of family law information and forms
Pennsylvania	http://www.pacourts.us/courts/ courts-of-common-pleas/ individual-county-courts http://www.pacourts.us/learn/ representing-yourself/divorce- proceedings	Scroll down to find link to your county's website; counties differ as to the extent of information and forms
	https://www.humanservices. state.pa.us/csws	Forms and information for divorce and child support
Rhode Island	https://www.courts.ri.gov/ Courts/FamilyCourt/Pages/ default.aspx	Family law court information and forms
South Carolina	http://www.judicial.state.sc.us/ forms/searchType.cfm http://www.judicial.state.sc.us/ selfHelp	Family law forms and information
South Dakota	http://www.ujs.sd.gov/Forms/ divorce.aspx http://dss.sd.gov/formsandpubs	Divorce and child support forms and information

Court and Court-Related Websites (cont'd)		
State	**Websites**	**What you'll find**
Tennessee	www.tsc.state.tn.us/help-center/court-approved-divorce-forms	Court-approved divorce forms
	www.tsc.state.tn.us/programs/parenting-plan	Forms and instructions specific to parenting plans
Texas	www.tyla.org/tyla/index.cfm/resources/general-public/family-law	Lengthy handbook about representing yourself in uncontested family law cases, with sample forms, from Texas Young Lawyers' Association
	http://texaslawhelp.org/issues/family-law-and-domestic-violence	Family law information and forms
Utah	www.utcourts.gov/resources/forms	Divorce information and forms; link to online interactive program that helps you fill out divorce forms
Vermont	www.vermontjudiciary.org/gtc/family/marriagerelated.aspx	Extensive forms and family law pamphlets
Virginia	www.courts.state.va.us/forms/district/jdr.html	Family court forms
	http://www.valegalaid.org/issues/family-and-domestic-and-sexual-violence	Family law information and forms
	www.fairfaxcounty.gov/courts/circuit/divorce.htm	A pro se divorce package provided by the Fairfax County Circuit Court
Washington	www.courts.wa.gov/forms
http://www.washingtonlawhelp.org/issues/family-law	Family law information and forms
West Virginia	http://www.courtswv.gov/lower-courts/family-forms/index-family-forms.html	Family law information and forms
Wisconsin	www.wicourts.gov/forms1/circuit/index.htm	Family law self-help site offers instructions, forms, and interactive program for completing forms; click on the "Family" link
Wyoming	www.courts.state.wy.us/DandCS.aspx	Family law information and forms

State Custody Best Interest Statutes		
State	**Statute**	**Notes**
Alabama	Ala. Code § 30-3-169.3	
Alaska	Alaska Stat. § 25.24.150	
Arizona	Ariz. Rev. Stat. Ann. § 25-403	
Arkansas	Ark. Code Ann. § 9-13-101	
California	Cal. Fam. Code §§ 3011, 3040	Wide latitude
Colorado	Colo. Rev. Stat. Ann. § 14-10-124	
Connecticut	Conn. Gen. Stat. Ann. §§ 46b-56	
Delaware	Del. Code. Ann. Tit. 13, § 722	
District of Columbia	D.C. Code Ann. § 16-914	
Florida	Fla. Stat. Ann. § 61.13(3)	
Georgia	Ga. Code Ann. § 19-9-3	
Hawaii	Haw. Rev. Stat. § 571-46	
Idaho	Idaho Code § 32-717	
Illinois	750 Ill. Comp. Stat. § 5/602	
Indiana	Ind. Code Ann. § 31-17-2-8	
Iowa	Iowa Code § 598.41	
Kansas	Kan. Stat. Ann. § 23-3202	
Kentucky	Ky. Rev. Stat. Ann. § 403.270	
Louisiana	La. Rev. Stat. Ann. Art. 134	
Maine	Me. Rev. Stat. Ann. Tit. 19-A, § 1653(3)	
Maryland	No statute	*Best v. Best*; 93 Md.App. 644, 613 A.2d 1043; Md.App., 1992.
Massachusetts	Mass. Gen. Laws ch. 208 § 31	No specific factors listed; court has latitude
Michigan	Mich. Comp. Laws § 722.23	
Minnesota	Minn. Stat. Ann. § 518.17	False allegation of child abuse is factor; parenting classes required in custody cases
Mississippi	Miss. Code. Ann § 93-5-24	*Hutchison v. Hutchison* 58 So.3d 46; Miss.App., 2011.

State Custody Best Interest Statutes (cont'd)		
State	Statute	Notes
Missouri	Mo. Rev. Stat. § 452.375	
Montana	Mont. Code Ann. § 40-4-234	
Nebraska	Neb. Rev. Stat. § 43-2923	
Nevada	Nev. Rev. Stat. Ann. § 125.480	
New Hampshire	N.H. Rev. Stat. § 461-A:6	
New Jersey	N.J. Stat. Ann. § 9:2-4	
New Mexico	N.M. Stat. Ann. § 40-4-9.1	
New York	N.Y. Domestic Relations Law § 240, subsection 1	
North Carolina	N.C. Gen. Stat. § 50-13.2 (a)	
North Dakota	N.D. Cent. Code § 14-09-06.2	
Ohio	Ohio Rev. Code Ann. § 3109.04(F)(1)	
Oklahoma	Okla. Stat. Ann. Tit. 43, § 112.5	
Oregon	Or. Rev. Stat. Ann. § 107.137	
Pennsylvania	23 Pa. Cons. Stat. Ann. § 5328	
Rhode Island	R.I. Gen. Laws Ann. § 15-5-16	No specific factors listed in statute. *Pettinato v. Pettinato*, 582 A.2d 909, 1990.
South Carolina	S.C. Code Ann. §§ 20-30-160, 63-15-30	No specific factors listed in statute; courts have wide latitude. *Gandy v. Gandy*, 297 S.C. 411, 377 S.E.2d 312, 1989.
South Dakota	S.D. Codified Laws § 25-4-45	No specific factors listed in statute; courts have broad discretion. *Hathaway v. Bergheim*, 2002 S.D. 78, 648 N.W.2d 349, 2002.
Tennessee	Tenn. Code Ann. § 36-6-404	
Texas	Tex. Family Code Ann. § 153.002	*Vazquez v. Vazquez*, 292 S.W.3d 80 Tex.App., 2007.
Utah	Utah Code Ann. § 30-3-34	
Vermont	Vt. Stat. Ann. Tit. 15, § 665	

State Custody Best Interest Statutes (cont'd)		
State	**Statute**	**Notes**
Virginia	Va. Code Ann. § 20-124.3	
Washington	Wash. Rev. Code Ann. § 26.09.184	
West Virginia	W.Va. Code § 48-9-102	
Wisconsin	Wis. Stat. § 767.41(5)	
Wyoming	Wyo. Stat. Ann. § 20-2-201	

State Custody Modification Statutes	
State	**Statute**
Alabama	Ala. Code § 30-3-169.3
Alaska	Alaska Stat. § 25.20.110
Arizona	Ariz. Rev. Stat. § 25-411
Arkansas	Ark. Code Ann. § 9-13-101
California	Cal. Fam. Code §§ 3047, 3087, 3088
Colorado	Colo. Rev. Stat. § 14-10-129
Connecticut	Conn. Gen. Stat. Ann. § 46b-56
Delaware	Del. Code Ann. Tit. 13 § 729
District of Columbia	D.C. Code Ann. § 16-914(f)(1)
Florida	Fla. Stat. Ann. §§ 61.13(2)(d) and (3)
Georgia	Ga. Code Ann. § 19-9-3(b)
Hawaii	Haw. Rev. Stat. § 571-46(a)(6)
Idaho	Idaho Code § 32-717
Illinois	750 Ill. Comp. Stat. § 5/610
Indiana	Ind. Code Ann. § 31-17-2-21
Iowa	Iowa Code Ann. § 598.21C
Kansas	Kan. Stat. Ann. §§ 23-3218, 23-3221
Kentucky	Ky. Rev. Stat. Ann. § 403.340
Louisiana	La. Fam. Code Ann. Art. 131
Maine	Me. Rev. Stat. Ann. tit. 19-A, § 1657
Maryland	Md. Code Ann. Family Law § 1-201 (granting jurisdiction); Md. Code Ann. Family Law § 8-103 (allowing change if in best interests)
Massachusetts	Mass. Gen. Laws ch. 208, § 28
Michigan	Mich. Comp. Laws § 722.27
Minnesota	Minn. Stat. Ann. §§ 518.18, 518.175
Mississippi	Miss. Code Ann. § 93-5-23
Missouri	Mo. Rev. Stat. § 452.410
Montana	Mont. Code Ann. § 40-4-219
Nebraska	Neb. Rev. Stat. § 42-364
Nevada	Nev. Rev. Stat. Ann. § 125.510
New Hampshire	N.H. Rev. Stat. § 461-A:11

State Custody Modification Statutes (cont'd)

State	Statute
New Jersey	N.J. Stat. Ann. § 2A:34-23
New Mexico	N.M. Stat. Ann. § 40-4-9.1
New York	New York Dom. Rel. Law § 240; Commentary 240:23
North Carolina	N.C. Gen. Stat. § 50-13.7
North Dakota	N.D. Cent. Code § 14-09-32
Ohio	Ohio Rev. Code Ann. § 3109.04(E)(1)(a)
Oklahoma	Okla. Stat. Ann. tit. 43, §§ 112, 112.5
Oregon	Or. Rev. Stat. Ann. § 107.431
Pennsylvania	23 Pa. Cons. Stat. Ann. § 5338
Rhode Island	R.I. Gen. Laws § 15-5-16
South Carolina	S.C. Code Ann. § 20-3-160
South Dakota	S.D. Codified Laws § 25-5-10.1
Tennessee	Tenn. Code Ann. § 36-6-405
Texas	Tex. Family Code Ann. § 156.101
Utah	Utah Code Ann. §§ 30-3-10.8; 30-3-10.4
Vermont	Vt. Stat. Ann., tit. 15, § 668
Virginia	Va. Code Ann. § 20-124.2
Washington	Wash. Rev. Code Ann. § 26.09.260
West Virginia	W.Va. Code §§ 48-9-401, 48-9-402
Wisconsin	Wis. Stat. § 767.451
Wyoming	Wyo. Stat. Ann. § 20-2-204

State Relocation Statutes			
State	**Statute**	**Burden of Proof**	**Notes and cases**
Alabama	Ala. Code §§ 30-3-160 to 30-3-169.10	Burden on relocating parent	
Alaska	Alaska Stat. § 25.24.150	None	
Arizona	Ariz. Rev. Stat. Ann. § 25-408	Burden on relocating parent	
Arkansas	Ark. Code Ann. § 9-13-101	Burden on party objecting	
California	Cal. Fam. Code §§ 3024, 3046 and case law	Burden on party objecting	*In re Marriage of Burgess*, 913 P.2d 473; *In re Marriage of LaMusga*, 88 P.3d 81
Colorado	Colo. Rev. Stat. § 14-10-129	Best interests	Relocation cases have priority in scheduling
Connecticut	Conn. Gen. Stat. Ann. § 46b-56d	Shifting burden	*Ireland v. Ireland*, 717 A.2d 676
Delaware	Del. Code Ann. tit 13, §§ 729, 730	Best interests	
District of Columbia	D.C. Code Ann. § 16-914(f)		
Florida	Fla. Stat. Ann. § 61.13001	Shifting burden: Relocating parent must show in best interest; objecting party may rebut	
Georgia	Ga. Code Ann. § 19-9-3, esp. sub. (f)	Burden on objecting party	
Hawaii	Haw. Rev. Stat. § 571-46		
Idaho	Idaho Code § 32-717		*Allbright v. Allbright*, 215 P.3d 472; *Roberts v. Roberts*, 64 P.3d 327

State Relocation Statutes (cont'd)			
State	**Statute**	**Burden of Proof**	**Notes and cases**
Illinois	750 Ill. Comp. Stat. § 5/609	Burden on relocating parent to prove 5 factors	*In re Marriage of Sale*, 808 N.E.2d 1125
Indiana	Ind. Code Ann. §§ 31-17-2.2-1 to 2-6	Shifting burden: relocating parent must show legitimate reason; objecting party may rebut	
Iowa	Iowa Code § 598.21D	Burden on relocating parent if move is more than 150 miles	
Kansas	K.S.A. § 23-3222		
Kentucky	Ky. Rev. Stat. Ann. § 403.340	Burden on relocating parent	
Louisiana	La. Rev. Stat. Ann. §§ 9:355.1 through 9:355.17	Burden on relocating parent	
Maine	Me. Rev. Stat. Ann. tit. 19, § 1653(14); tit. 19-A, § 1657	Burden on relocating parent	
Maryland	Md. Code, Family Law § 9-106		
Massachusetts	Mass. Gen. Laws ch. 208, § 30		
Michigan	Mich. Comp. Laws § 722.31		
Minnesota	Minn. Stat. Ann. § 518.18; § 518.175 subd. 3	Burden on relocating parent	
Mississippi	Miss. Code Ann. § 93-5-23	Burden on objecting party	*Spain v. Holland*, 483 So.2d 318 Miss., 1986
Missouri	Mo. Rev. Stat. § 452.377	Burden on relocating parent	
Montana	Mont. Code Ann. § 40-4-217	Best interests	

State Relocation Statutes (cont'd)			
State	**Statute**	**Burden of Proof**	**Notes and cases**
Nebraska	Neb. Rev. Stat. Ann. § 42-364		*McLaughlin v. McLaughlin*, 647 N.W.2d 577
Nevada	Nev. Rev. Stat. Ann. § 125C.200	Shifting burden: Relocating parent must show good faith and advantage; objecting parent must show not in best interests	
New Hampshire	N.H. Rev. Stat. Ann. § 461-A:12	Shifting burden: Relocating parent must show legitimate purpose and reasonable in light of purpose; objecting parent must show not in child's best interests	
New Jersey	N.J. Stat. Ann. § 9:2-2	Shifting burden: Relocating parent must show legitimate reason and move not inimical to child's interest	
New Mexico	N.M. Stat. Ann. § 40-4-9.1	Burden on relocating parent	
New York	N.Y. Dom. Relations Law § 240, commentary 240:25		*Tropea v. Tropea*, 665 N.E.2d 145
North Carolina	N.C. Gen. Stat. § 50-13.2(c)	Burden on objecting party	*Evans v. Evans*, 530 S.E.2d 576
North Dakota	N.D. Cent. Code § 14-09-07	Burden on relocating parent to show move is in best interests of child	
Ohio	Ohio Rev. Code Ann. §§ 3109.04(E)(1)(a) and (F)(1)(j)		

State Relocation Statutes (cont'd)			
State	**Statute**	**Burden of Proof**	**Notes and cases**
Oklahoma	Okla. Stat. Ann. tit. 43, § 112.3	Burden on objecting party	
Oregon	Or. Rev. Stat. Ann. § 107.159		
Pennsylvania	23 Pa. Cons. Stat. Ann. § 5337	Burden on relocating parent to show move is in best interests of child	
Rhode Island	R.I. Gen. Laws 1956 § 15-5-16(d)(1)		*Dupre v. Dupre,* 857 A.2d 242
South Carolina	S.C. Code Ann. § 20-3-160	Burden on relocating parent to show move is in best interests of child	*Latimer v. Farmer,* 602 S.E.2d 32
South Dakota	S.D. Codified Laws § 25-5-13	Burden on objecting party	
Tennessee	Tenn. Code Ann. § 36-6-108	No preference if equal parenting time; if unequal, okay to move unless objecting parent can show no reasonable purpose OR harm OR vindictive motive to frustrate visitation; then court will evaluate best interests	
Texas	Tex. Family Code § 156.101	Burden on relocating parent	
Utah	Utah Code Ann. § 30-3-37		
Vermont	Vt. Stat. Ann. tit. 15, § 668	Burden on relocating parent	*Hawkes v. Spence,* 178 Vt. 161, 878 A.2d 273 Vt., 2005
Virginia	Va Code Ann. § 20-124.5		
Washington	Wash. Rev. Code Ann. §§ 26.09.520; 26.09.520-560	Burden on objecting party	

State Relocation Statutes (cont'd)			
State	**Statute**	**Burden of Proof**	**Notes and cases**
West Virginia	W.Va. Code § 48-9-403	Burden on relocating parent if purpose is other than listed in statute; if purpose is listed in statute, presumption in favor of relocation	
Wisconsin	Wis. Stat. § 767.481	Burden on party objecting to relocation if sole custody; burden on party seeking relocation if joint custody	
Wyoming	Wyo. Stat. Ann. § 20-2-204	Burden on party objecting	

State Child Support Modification Statutes

State	Statute
Alabama	Alabama Rule of Judicial Administration 32
Alaska	Alaska Stat. § 25.24.170
Arizona	Ariz. Rev. Stat. § 25-503
Arkansas	Ark. Code Ann. § 9-14-107
California	Cal. Fam. Code § 4010
Colorado	Colo. Rev. Stat. §§ 14-10-122; 14-10-115
Connecticut	Conn. Gen. Stat. Ann. § 46b-86
Delaware	Del. Code Ann., tit. 13, § 513
District of Columbia	D.C. Code Ann. § 16-916.01(r)
Florida	Fla. Stat. Ann. § 61.30
Georgia	Ga. Code Ann. § 19-6-15(k)
Hawaii	Haw. Rev. Stat. § 571-51.5
Idaho	Idaho Code § 32-709
Illinois	750 Ill. Comp. Stat. § 5/510
Indiana	Ind. Code Ann. § 31-16-8-1
Iowa	Iowa Code § 598.21C
Kansas	Kan. Stat. Ann. § 60-1610
Kentucky	Ky. Rev. Stat. Ann. § 403.213
Louisiana	La. Fam Code Ann. § 9:311
Maine	Me. Rev. Stat. Ann. tit. 19, § 2009
Maryland	Md. Code Ann., Family Law § 12-104
Massachusetts	Mass. Gen. Laws ch. 119A, § 3B
Michigan	Mich. Comp. Laws § 552.455
Minnesota	Minn. Stat. Ann. § 518A.39
Mississippi	Miss. Code Ann. § 43-19-34
Missouri	Mo. Rev. Stat. § 452.370
Montana	Mont. Code Ann. § 40-4-208
Nebraska	Neb. Rev. Stat. § 42-364.16
Nevada	Nev. Rev. Stat. Ann. § 125B.145
New Hampshire	N.H. Rev. Stat. Ann. § 458-C:7
New Jersey	N.J. Stat. Ann. § 2A:34-23
New Mexico	N.M. Stat. Ann. § 40-4-11.4

State Child Support Modification Statutes (cont'd)

State	Statute
New York	N.Y. Dom. Rel. Law § 240-1(l)
North Carolina	N.C. Gen. Stat. § 50-13.7
North Dakota	N.D. Cent. Code § 14-09-08.8
Ohio	Ohio Rev. Code Ann. § 3119.66; R.C. § 3119.68
Oklahoma	Okla. Stat. Ann. tit. 43, § 118I
Oregon	Or. Rev. Stat. Ann. § 107.135
Pennsylvania	Pa. Cons. Stat. Ann. § 1910.19
Rhode Island	R.I. Gen. Laws § 15-5-16.2
South Carolina	S.C. Code Ann. §§ 63-17-310, 320; S.C. Code Ann. Regs. 114-4740
South Dakota	S.D. Codified Laws § 25-7A-22
Tennessee	Tenn. Code Ann. § 36-5-101
Texas	Tex. Family Code § 156.401
Utah	Utah Code Ann. § 30-3-5
Vermont	Vt. Stat. Ann. tit. 15, § 660
Virginia	Va. Code Ann. § 20-108.2
Washington	Wash. Rev. Code Ann. §§ 26.09.100, 26.09.175
West Virginia	W.Va. Code § 48-11-105
Wisconsin	Wis. Stat. § 767.59
Wyoming	Wyo. Stat. Ann. § 20-2-311

State Child Support Enforcement Agencies

State	Agency
Alabama	www.alacourt.gov/ChildSupportInfo.aspx
Alaska	www.csed.state.ak.us
Arizona	www.azdes.gov/dcss
Arkansas	www.dfa.arkansas.gov/offices/childsupport/Pages/default.aspx
California	www.childsup.ca.gov
Colorado	www.childsupport.state.co.us
Connecticut	www.ct.gov/dss/site/default.asp (click on "PROGRAMS & SERVICES," "Families With Children")
Delaware	www.dhss.delaware.gov/dhss/dcse
District of Columbia	http://cssd.dc.gov
Florida	http://dor.myflorida.com/dor/childsupport
Georgia	http://ocse.dhr.georgia.gov
Hawaii	http://ag.hawaii.gov/csea
Idaho	www.healthandwelfare.idaho.gov
Illinois	www.childsupportillinois.com
Indiana	www.in.gov/dcs/support.htm
Iowa	www.dhs.state.ia.us/consumers/child_support/childsupportindex.html
Kansas	www.dcf.ks.gov/Pages/Default.aspx
Kentucky	http://chfs.ky.gov/dis/cse.htm
Louisiana	http://dss.louisiana.gov/index.cfm?md=pagebuilder&tmp=home&pid=137
Maine	www.maine.gov/dhhs/ofi/dser/support-services/index.html
Maryland	www.dhr.state.md.us/blog/?page_ie=946
Massachusetts	www.mass.gov/dor/child-support
Michigan	www.michigan.gov/dhs (click "child support")
Minnesota	http://mn.gov/dhs (Select "Child Care and Child Support" from the "Partners and Providers" drop down menu)
Mississippi	www.mdhs.state.ms.us/child-support
Missouri	www.dss.mo.gov/pr_cs.htm

State Child Support Enforcement Agencies (cont'd)	
State	Agency
Montana	www.dphhs.mt.gov/csed/index.shtml
Nebraska	http://dhhs.ne.gov/children_family_services/CSE/Pages/CSEHome.aspx
Nevada	http://dwss.nv.gov (click link for "child support ")
New Hampshire	www.dhhs.state.nh.us/dcss/
New Jersey	www.njchildsupport.org
New Mexico	www.hsd.state.nm.us/csed/
New York	www.childsupport.ny.gov/dcse/home.html
North Carolina	www.ncdhhs.gov/dss/cse
North Dakota	www.nd.gov/dhs/services/childsupport/
Ohio	http://jfs.ohio.gov/OCS
Oklahoma	www.okdhs.org/programsandservices/ocss
Oregon	www.doj.state.or.us/dcs/index.shtml
Pennsylvania	www.humanservices.state.pa.us/csws
Rhode Island	www.cse.ri.gov
South Carolina	www.state.sc.us/dss/csed
South Dakota	http://dss.sd.gov/childsupport/
Tennessee	www.state.tn.us/humanserv/cs/cs_main.html
Texas	www.oag.state.tx.us/cs/
Utah	www.ors.state.ut.us
Vermont	www.dcf.vermont.gov/ocs
Virginia	www.dss.virginia.gov/family/dcse./iindex.cgi
Washington	www.dshs.wa.gov/dcs/
West Virginia	www.dhhr.wv.gov/bcse/Pages/Default.aspx
Wisconsin	http://dcf.wisconsin.gov/bcs
Wyoming	http://dfsweb.state.wy.us/child-support-enforcement/index.html

Index

△△ NOLO   *Save 15%* off your next order

Register your Nolo purchase, and we'll send you a **coupon for 15% off** your next Nolo.com order!

Nolo.com/customer-support/productregistration

On Nolo.com you'll also find:

Books & Software
Nolo publishes hundreds of great books and software programs for consumers and business owners. Order a copy, or download an ebook version instantly, at Nolo.com.

Online Legal Documents
You can quickly and easily make a will or living trust, form an LLC or corporation, apply for a trademark or provisional patent, or make hundreds of other forms—online.

Free Legal Information
Thousands of articles answer common questions about everyday legal issues including wills, bankruptcy, small business formation, divorce, patents, employment, and much more.

Plain-English Legal Dictionary
Stumped by jargon? Look it up in America's most up-to-date source for definitions of legal terms, free at nolo.com.

Lawyer Directory
Nolo's consumer-friendly lawyer directory provides in-depth profiles of lawyers all over America. You'll find all the information you need to choose the right lawyer.

NOCS3